THE REAL RUNABOUTS II

by Robert Speltz

Copyright 1978 by Robert Speltz

2nd Printing 1981
3rd Printing 1982
4th Printing 1984
5th Printing 1986
6th Printing 1988
7th Printing 1992

ISBN-0-89279-017-2

Printed by Graphic Publishing Co., Inc.
Lake Mills, Iowa 50450

DEDICATION

Stanley P. Speltz

I am dedicating this book to the memory of my dad, Stan Speltz who instilled in me a love of water, boats and related things. My dad taught me at the tender age of ten to enjoy boats and boating but to respect water and care for your boat regardless of what type or size it may have been.

Also I want to dedicate the book to my readers as well as everyone who has helped me with the preparation of it the last twelve months. Without so much help *THE REAL RUNABOUTS, Volume II,* would never have happened.

May God bless you all for everything you have done for me.

PREFACE

As in any hobby, not all women have an interest in antique boating. But for me the comforts of home and solid land can't hold a candle to the gentle, rocking motion of a beautifully restored, gleaming mahogany hull gliding through the water. And so when Bob asked me to write this foreword for his new book, *THE REAL RUNABOUTS, Volume II*, I was naturally flattered. Presenting the woman's role in antique boating as Bob suggested seemed to me at first to indicate a women's lib stance; but in addition to feelings of independence and accomplishment for women, working with wooden boats provides satisfactions even more fundamental—pleasure to the eye and pleasure from the aesthetic rewards only working with wood provides.

Women—wives, daughters, sisters, mothers and friends—are bringing their creativity, brain power, and elbow grease to the restoration of antique boats for many of the same reasons as men: the personal satisfaction of a job well done, joy in labor with beautiful materials, and on a broader spectrum for the pride of contributing even in a small way to the preservation of one of the most significant aspects of our heritage—building wooden boats.

As Bob is contributing by painstakingly researching and documenting the facts in his books, so countless women have provided the broken finger nails, the hours of sanding and polishing, the numberless days of physical and moral support. By doing so we were, and are, all playing a significant part in safeguarding a vital part of our history, capturing a moment before it is swept past by changing life-styles, capturing the outlook of an era when lives were enriched by the limits and strengths of the materials and energies they had to work with: wood instead of plastic, muscle instead of electricity, hand tools guided by knowledge of the craftsman instead of power machinery.

In all Bob has undertaken a herculean task but one which must be done immediately. The skills associated with fine wooden boat building should be passed from person to person as ought all artisan skills, but failing that, they are best preserved in print. Those who have worked building these boats have vast knowledge they are eager to share as they too want to see their techniques documented. Bob has given much time and effort in undertaking the massive amount of research necessary. Happily for all of us he has not allowed his physical handicap to deter him from his goal of recording this information.

THE REAL RUNABOUTS, Volume II is not merely an updating of his first book, *THE REAL RUNABOUTS, Volume I*; instead, it begins where that left off with new information and insight. It lists additional builders, more sources of hard to find items needed for completing restorations, and many more restoration centers in the United States and Canada.

Bob's book is a delightful diversion as well as a compendium of information it is important to capture at this time, and as a woman I applaud his accomplishment and recommend it highly for both your pleasure and instruction. In this new book, as in its predecessor, Bob has given us a reference of infinite value for the present and for future generations.

Jean Nelson[*]

---

[*]Jean Nelson and her husband, Ray, publish *ANTIQUE BOATING* magazine and were co-founders, along with other antique boat fans, of the Antique & Classic Boat Society, Inc. in 1974.

CONTENTS

INTRODUCTION *viii*

I. MORE MAJOR SPEEDBOAT BUILDERS
Lyman—Boats of the finest clinker construction   1
Higgins—Pioneers in plywood runabouts   12
Dodge—The world's lowest priced fine motor boats   22
Ventnor—Fine racing and pleasure boats since 1902   37
Correct Craft—For greater performance at lower prices buy Correct Craft   49
Truscott—Builders of fine boats since 1885   58
Sea Lyon—The aristocrat of the fleet   61

II. MORE REGIONAL BUILDERS
Mariner of Michigan—Queen of the sea   66
Fairliner—Built with custom-care for peak performance   69
Mercury of California—The finest name in solid mahogany planked boats   71
Dart—Pioneer in its class   79
Ensign—For discriminating sportsmen   85
Globe Mastercraft—Action a-plenty by Globe   86
Eckfield Boat Co.—The sensation of the season   89
Meteor—Greatest value in the history of motor boating   91
Falls Flyer—Uniqueness in motor boats   92

III. MORE CUSTOM BUILDERS
Robinson—Seagull . . . Often seen—rarely passed   96
Philbrick Boat Co.—Custom and stock runabouts since 1934   100
Gage-Hacker—For boating at its finest   101
Leather runabouts of England   104
Ancarrow Marine—Speed and performance speak for themselves   105
Commuter Cruisers—The ultimate real runabouts   109

IV. MORE EUROPEAN & CANADIAN BUILDERS
Taroni of Italy—Master of the ocean all over the world   115
Duke Boats of Canada—Builders of fine launches   116
Boesch Boats—Horizon Gliding   120
Brooke of England—Built like ships—drive like cars   123
Minett-Shields of Canada—For those not satisfied with normal standards   128

V. MATERIAL APPLYING TO VOLUME I   130

VI. TECHNICAL SECTION   179
Technical material on old inboard engines   183
Expanded listings of restoration shops, dealers and old parts sources   186
Collectors' guide to modern Century inboards   201
A wooden boat refinishing guide   222
Clubs, magazines and books   224

BIBLIOGRAPHY   227

CONCLUSION   229

ACKNOWLEDGEMENTS   230

3 antique Chris-Craft runabouts at rest near Desbarates, Canada. (Photo by Edward H. Bennett, Jr., Chicago, Illinois.)

INTRODUCTION

Many exciting things have happened to me since I wrote my first book, THE REAL RUNABOUTS, Volume I a year and a half ago. There has been a marked increase in interest shown in antique boating in general; new chapters have been formed of both the Chris-Craft Antique Boat Club as well as the Antique & Classic Boat Society. I will mention more about that later in this book.

The idea to write a second book following along the lines of Volume I came to me in the fall of 1977 after Volume I was released and selling well. A mass of material has come to me from other fans like yourself and I have also been able through more searching to come up with many great old photos, ads, etc. Therefore, I embarked on this second book to share with you, my faithful readers, more material that I hope you will find most interesting. Volume II will follow the same general sequence as Volume I, starting with other major speedboat builders. We shall first review the Lyman Boat Company of Sandusky, Ohio, most famous for their great, old lapstrake hull utility models. We then shall move on to Higgins Industries of New Orleans, Louisiana who may have done more for the development of lower priced plywood planked inboards than any one firm following the end of World War II. Another firm which many collectors really love is Dodge Boats; this company first built in Detroit in the 1920's and later at Newport News, Virginia up to about 1937 or so. Dodge boats today are some of the most prized speedboats around and were among the finest ever built. Ventnor, though mostly building inboard racing boats, also "turned a few eye brows" after World War II with some of the most radically designed pleasure boats ever built. We shall cover Ventnor quite closely too. Correct Craft Boat Company of Florida, a firm still very much in the inboard business, built some fine-looking high performance speedboats in its day. The name "Correct Craft" and "Cypress Gardens" were synonymous back in the 1940's and 1950's when their blue and white inboards pulled groups of skiers every day for excited tourists in the famous Florida vacation spot. Truscott Boat Company from St. Joseph, Michigan built some good-looking inboards for several years after World War II. Some of their top officials had worked for the Gar Wood Company and the Truscott runabouts bore a slight resemblence to the final boats offered by that builder. The final major firm we shall review will be Sea-Lyon; built in New York City, its inboard boats were sold factory-direct rather than through a dealer network. These boats were also very popular but few still are in use at this time.

We now shall move on to regional boat builders; firms who built and sold the bulk of their boats in their own three- or four-state area. The first firm we shall review will be Mariner of Algonac, Michigan. It started operations soon after Gar Wood Boats closed down, buying all that company's old jigs, forms, etc.; moving into an empty building, it started up its own production. Mariners were built into the mid-1960's and quite a few are still in use. A firm out in Washington state built a sleek little 17' "torpedo" inboard starting in 1947; Fairliner Boat Company built about 40 of these boats and only a half dozen or less are still in existence today. I am sure you will find them very unusual in their design and a boat that had few others, if any, built just like it. A very small firm that built only two models but yet played a role in the pleasure boat industry in the late 1940's was Ensign Boat Company of Holland, Michigan. Both of its boats were of the painted variety in a 14' and a 16' version. Some other regional firms we shall look at will include Dart Boats of Toledo, Ohio; Globe Mastercraft of Williams Bay, Wisconsin; and Eckfield Boats of Algonac, Michigan. Dart boats were very popular along the Great Lakes. Mastercraft built a cute little 14' 45 h.p. split-cockpit runabout; in fact, I was part owner of one of these boats that was built in 1950 which is in perfect running condition to this very day. The last two regional firms we shall review will be Meteor Boat Company in Piqua, Ohio; and Larson Boat Works who built Falls Flyers at Little Falls, Minnesota. All in all, I think you will find a good selection of smaller regional builders explored in Chapter Two.

Custom speedboats and commuter cruisers have always been popular with antique boat fans. Boats of this variety were built usually one at a time to a set of specific plans drawn up to the owner's own preference. Robinson Seagull cruisers, runabouts and commuters were about the epitome of the custom-built inboards. Chapter III shall review that firm as well as Philbrick Boat Company of California who this very day is building luxury twin-cockpit all-wood inboards. Bill Gage, owner of Gage Marine in Lake Geneva, Wisconsin, back from around 1961 until about 1967 built approximately 25 ultra-deluxe runabouts and utilities designed by the immortal naval architect John Hacker of Detroit, Michigan. I think you will enjoy the superb photos of the Gage-Hacker speedboats that accompany the review.

John Leather of England is currently, along with his son, working on plans for all-mahogany inboard runabouts which they will build in England and sell in this country. The utmost care will be given to the construction of each boat with up to 9 coats of hand-rubbed varnish applied to each hull. It will be interesting to see how the boats sell when they arrive here in this country. A firm who built luxury inboards, though not from mahogany but from plywood, was Ancarrow Marine; its super-luxury speedboats were the American answer to Riva and other luxury speedboats built abroad. Production by Ancarrow was very low and I am really quite sure very few of its boats are still in use; twin-powered Cadillac boats would be pretty costly to operate these days. . . . Finally, I included a section on Commuter cruisers themselves. A large number of builders turned out such craft, especially before the Depression. Most were a cross between a giant speedboat and an early cruiser. From the Commuter we would later see sleek, more streamlined cabin cruisers evolve. This section shows a wide variety of photos of various Commuters built by the leading builders of that era, including Chris-Craft, Hacker, Gar Wood and many others.

European-built runabouts proved very popular with readers of my first book. Because of that, and for other reasons I have procured an interesting assortment of material on five new firms not mentioned in *Volume I*. Probably the two most unique firms described would be Boesch Boats of Zurich, Switzerland and Brooke Boat Company of England. Boesch traces its "roots" back into the 1800's and built fine wooden inboards up into the late 1950's; it now builds fiberglass speedboats to the same high specifications used when building its wood craft. Brooke, on the other hand, built most of its nicest speedboats from about 1925 through 1940 or so. You are going to be surprised when you see photos of some of its very classic-looking runabouts.

Chapter Five, though short on text, is "chock-full" of photos all applying to firms covered in *Volume I*. In *Volume II* I have followed the same order of firms listed in *Volume I*; in other words, I started with Chris-Craft and ended with European builders. A special "thanks" to all who sent in photos, information, etc., for Chapter Five.

Chapter Six, the final chapter, deals with what I call "technical" material. I have obtained a wealth of information applying to prop sizes, serial number listings of old boats, etc., for starters. I am proud of my greatly expanded listing of restoration shops, as well as many new sources for old engine and boat parts, etc. There is no way I can list every shop offering refinishing, repairs, restorations, old parts, etc. If you know of some in your area that I do not have listed, would you please send me their names, addresses, etc. for listing in future issues? Since so many people have expressed true interest in what I would call "modern-classic" boats, I have thoroughly researched Century runabouts from 1955 through 1968 when the firm ceased to build wooden speedboats. I think everyone will enjoy this review and others could be done like it at a later date, if interest warrants it. The final portion of Chapter Six is what I call "A Wooden Boat Refinishing Guide". Mr. Tony Brown, excellent restoration expert from Lake Minnetonka, Minnesota has been kind enough to prepare an easy-to-follow review of a pastime very popular with many buffs.

Well, that's what you will find in this *Volume II*. I hope it meets with your satisfaction and I hope you enjoy the book very much. We are in for a fast-growing hobby and it appears that we will see much growth in the future if things keep going as they have so far. Now—on to Chapter One of *THE REAL RUNABOUTS, Volume II*.

PLEASE POST   **PLEASE POST**

ATTENTION!

presenting

The 3rd Annual Lake Minnetonka

NOTICE:
To The Public At Large

Once again we are proud to bring you a glimpse of a boating era gone by.

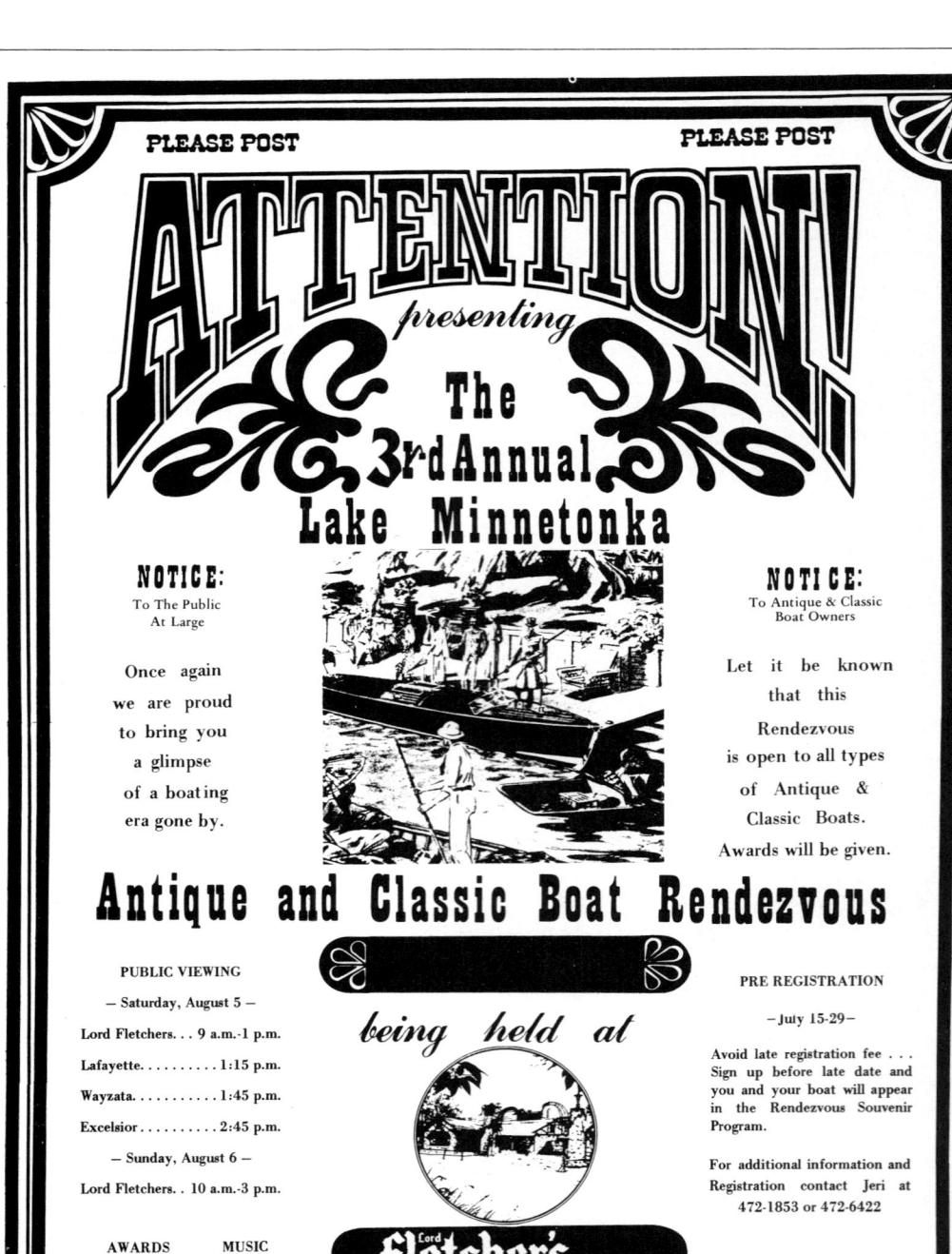

NOTICE:
To Antique & Classic Boat Owners

Let it be known that this Rendezvous is open to all types of Antique & Classic Boats. Awards will be given.

Antique and Classic Boat Rendezvous

being held at

Lord Fletcher's OF THE LAKE

PUBLIC VIEWING

— Saturday, August 5 —

Lord Fletchers . . . 9 a.m.-1 p.m.
Lafayette . . . . 1:15 p.m.
Wayzata . . . . 1:45 p.m.
Excelsior . . . . 2:45 p.m.

— Sunday, August 6 —

Lord Fletchers . . 10 a.m.-3 p.m.

AWARDS   MUSIC
FUN & FROLICS

PRE REGISTRATION

— July 15-29 —

Avoid late registration fee . . . Sign up before late date and you and your boat will appear in the Rendezvous Souvenir Program.

For additional information and Registration contact Jeri at 472-1853 or 472-6422

sponsored by

The Antique & Classic Boat Society, Inc.

LAND O' LAKES CHAPTER

Antique Boat Shows are bigger than ever!

CHAPTER I
MORE MAJOR SPEEDBOAT BUILDERS

LYMAN—BOATS OF THE FINEST CLINKER CONSTRUCTION

I have chosen as our first firm to review, Lyman Boat Works of Sandusky, Ohio. Some may feel this an unwise choice but I think you will see as we get into this report, the large role Bill Lyman played in the development of the inboard "utility" as we know it today. Most lapstrake or sea skiff hulls are painted white with varnished decks and wooden-framed windshields. Their style and design has changed little since they first were introduced about 1930 or so. Let's now take a look at Lyman Boat Works and see over the last 75 years how Lyman pioneered the idea of the utility type inboard in power boating circles nationwide.

Bernard E. Lyman, 1850-1934, founder of Lyman Boat Works, Sandusky, Ohio.

Born in 1850, Bernard Lyman came to this country just before the Civil War.[1] During his youth young Lyman learned the art of cabinet building, a job he loved very much. Since he enjoyed fishing in his spare time he set about building himself a nice clinker style rowboat. Soon his friends began asking to use the boat so often that he found himself strictly building boats and no longer turning out furniture. Thus we have the beginning of the Lyman Boat Works.

[1] Bob Meyers, "They Built a Reputation on Lapstrake Hulls", *MOTOR BOATING* (Jan. '50), 296.

The original shop opened by Mr. Lyman in Cleveland, Ohio was only twenty feet by twenty feet, but served the firm well in those early years. The bulk of the early Lyman boats built were smart little 13' rowboats that retailed for $24.50 each. Since there were numerous boat liveries around Cleveland Lyman had a steady market for rowboats, as livery operators kept replacing portions of their rental fleets each year.

Early sailing craft built at Lyman Boat Works in 1890's

By 1891 Lyman was building all types of craft. One example was a 65' cutter-rigged sail boat that sold for $3,300. Other large boats built at Lyman's would have to include a number of large inboard cabin cruisers—the grandest of all, a 75' model powered by a 100 h.p. Standard engine.[2]

View of Lyman shop and docks, about 1900

To begin with, Lyman boats were built totally by hand. No power tools were even invented yet, so the skill of Lyman and his employees was most important. A number of small double ended sailboats were also turned out

[2] "The Lyman Story", *MOTOR BOAT,* (May '51), 24.

at the Lyman plant about 1900 but from then on, power boats would be their full-time occupation.

Beautiful example of a 1904 Lyman gasoline pleasure launch

Wages were low, according to our modern standards, but the typical Lyman employee received $15.00 a week for 60 hours' work. Bill Lyman, son of the founder joined the firm prior to 1920 and earned just $3.00 a week acting as a handy man around the shop. 1914 saw the Lyman outboard boat well on its way to national acceptance. In fact, Lyman was one of the first boat builders to successfully market outboard-powered speedboats at such an early date.

World War I found the Lyman plant converted to military use for the construction of concrete war ships. Interestingly enough, no ships were ever launched from the location. . . . Evidently the world was not yet ready for the age of the concrete war ships![3]

In 1918 Lyman opened a new works in temporary quarters. He introduced to the boat-buying public a new 11' outboard that sped along at 18 m.p.h. with the all-new Lock Wood Ace outboard motor. The 11' hull proved to be so popular that a 13' and 15' outboard hull was added to the line. On through the 1920's the Lyman outboard hulls grew and grew in popularity. If it had not been for the Depression in 1932, Lyman Boat Works may have never gotten into the business of building inboard speedboats! It seems outboard boat sales really dropped off with the start of the stock market crash. Young Bill Lyman, now in charge of the Lyman operations, felt that there was an untapped market for larger inboard power boats for the upper class and wealthy of the country, Depression or not! Do you know, Bill was so right! One of his first actions upon taking over operations of the firm was to move everything to Sandusky, Ohio on Lake Erie where he rented a larger, more modern plant.

Here a real market existed for a deep, roomy power boat built to conquer the rough swells of the Great Lakes; a craft for fishing, cruising and hunting or anything else, in complete comfort and safety. As they became available, electric power tools were used by Lyman helping to raise production but still allowing for craftsmanship that Lyman owners had become accustomed to.

As other builders turned more toward the outboard

[3] "The Lyman Story", *MOTOR BOAT,* (May '51), 24.

boat in the early 1930's, Bill Lyman did just the opposite. He specialized in a new type of boat he called the "utility" runabout.[4] Rather than being a decked over speedboat the new Lymans were open except for short bow and stern decks. The rest of the boat consisted of an open cockpit with seating and storage space galore. Bill's

LYMAN
19-FOOT INBOARD RUNABOUT
Speed: 35 m. p. h.
Other sizes — 17-Ft. and 23½-Ft.
$795.00
and upwards.

Boats of finest Clinker Construction— dependable, seaworthy and fast!

Outboard Sea Skiffs, Runabouts and Tenders— $125.00 to $270.00

LYMAN BOAT WORKS
FOOT OF FIRST STREET   SANDUSKY, OHIO
Send for Catalog

1930 Lyman magazine ad

LYMAN!

17 Foot Runabout $995.00 Complete

LYMAN Clinker-Built boats for 1932 offer quality and lasting value at an economical price. Seaworthiness, perfect running trim, comfort and usefulness are characteristics of every LYMAN, whether inboard or outboard. Write for catalogs.
17', 19', and 23' inboard runabouts. A full line of fine outboard models and tenders, 8' to 15'.

LYMAN BOAT WORKS
FOOT OF FIRST ST.   SANDUSKY, OHIO

Extoling the virtues of the 1932 Lyman fleet!

first 17' "utility" was well accepted as was his idea of building a fast planing hull with no sacrifice in comfort or safety at any speed. A small 1930 ad shows a 19' Lyman inboard being offered for sale at $795 and up. By the year 1933 the following Lyman inboards were available:[5]

MODEL	LENGTH	H.P.
17' Service	17' 4"	Gray 49
17' Utility	17' 4"	Gray 49
19' Utility	19' 4"	Gray 93
23' Utility	23' 3"	Gray 93
23' Cabin	23' 3"	Gray 135

[4] Bob Meyers, "They Built a Reputation on Lapstrake Hulls", *MOTOR BOATING,* (Jan. '50), 297.
[5] *MOTOR BOATING,* (Jan. '33), 176.

As you can see, Lyman offered quite a selection of Sea Skiffs by 1933. The year 1934 found Lyman turning out even more inboards and a number of custom cabin cruisers as big as 47 feet. However, the mainstay of Lyman Boat Works would continue to be the ol' reliable lapstrake inboard speedboat.

In the years from 1933 through 1936 Lyman Boat Works built a number of outstanding yacht tenders. You will note in this section a series of three excellent factory photos covering two 23½' models, as well as one smaller 19' runabout. The smaller 19' runabout was equipped with what was called "the all-new Lyman all-weather top". It was designed to provide excellent vision as well as protection from both the hot sun and sudden showers that are common events on the Great Lakes all summer. Most of us today would agree the roofs added little to the beauty of the boat, but it did make for a true all-weather craft. The handsome 23½' hardtop model looks quite stylish as she lies at rest somewhere on the shores of Lake Erie.[6] She was built so that the driver's seat was in the open, much like the posh town cars of the period while the passenger compartment was enclosed with a hard top. Those who liked to ride in the stern seat could enjoy both the sun an an occasional spray, as this area was also left open. The other 23½' model was a basic open utility.

---

[6]"Lyman Inboards are Clinker-Built", *POWER BOATING*, (Feb. '34), 16.

1934 23½' utility streaking over Lake Erie

All new 1934 Lyman Runabout with "all-weather" top.

Custom 23½' Lyman Cabin-Runabout on Lake Erie in 1934

Nearly every Lyman ever built was painted the traditional white hull sides but a few were varnished and even a smaller group appeared as true runabouts—decked over much like a Chris-Craft or Hacker, etc. Few of these boats are still in existence, much less in use. I know of one and it is a striking boat to see. It seems the Europeans were much more active in varnishing all types of craft built in the lapstrake manner. It seems here in the states, the idea just was never that popular.

Some other Lyman yacht tenders also made the "big time" by being featured in the August, 1934 issue of *POWER BOATING* magazine. Four models were shown in sizes ranging from the small 15' rig up through a rare 20' all-varnished hull. Let's look at these four boats in more detail.

Rare, varnished Lyman runabout powered by a Scripps model 152 engine.

Special tiny 15' Lyman 1934 tender built for Keith Dunham of Chicago.

17' custom yacht tender also owned by Keith Dunham of Chicago. 1934 view.

Yet another 1934 19' yacht tender by Lyman!

My very favorite of the four has to be the 20' utility-custom runabout shown under full power near Detroit. As I mentioned before, this boat was of the non-painted variety and was built originally for Harry Fres, of Detroit, Michigan. She sped along at just over 40 m.p.h. with a big model 152 Scripps engine for power. That 169 h.p. power plant was one of the largest ever mounted into any Lyman utility.

The smaller, less dramatic tender, also included in the magazine article, was a little 15' model which was used as a crew tender for the yacht Kalolah, owned by Keith Dunham of Chicago. This boat was powered by a very small Gray Sea Scout engine whose top speed was just 15 m.p.h. A larger 17' rig with sedan roof was also carried on board the Kalolah but was for the use of the owner and his guests. She sported a Gray 4-49 engine with top speed close to 30 m.p.h. The fourth and final yacht tender we will review is a 19' model equipped with a good ol' Lyman all-weather roof like one of the earlier models had. This 19' tender belonged to a prominent Cleveland gentleman and had a Gray 6-93 engine. Her photo shows her out on Lake Erie cruising in heavy weather.[7]

Lest you are led to believe that Lyman only built yacht tenders for the "idle rich", guess again. I will list the 1934 model line below. All models listed here are inboards. Please don't forget that Lyman offered outboards too.[8]

1934 23½' Lyman hardtop, somewhere on the Great Lakes.

---

[7] "Lyman Tenders and Runabouts", *POWER BOATING*, (Aug. '34), 15.

[8] "Particulars and Prices of Inboard Runabouts", *POWER BOATING*, (June '34), 30.

MODEL	TYPE	LENGTH	ENGINE	SPEED	PRICE
Serv. runa.	open	17' 4"	Gray 57	28	$ 840.00
Util. 17	open	17' 4"	Gray 67	32	$1140.00
Util. 17	open	17' 4"	Gray 57	30	$1060.00
Util. 19*	Db. Cockpit	19'	Gray 93	35	$1545.00
Util. 23*	Db. Cockpit	23'	Gray 125	27	$2575.00

*All-weather hardtop available $150.00 extra.

1935 found Bill Lyman and his all-new "utility" inboard gaining prominence nationwide. Boats were now being sold all over the United States and before long builders like Chris-Craft and others began to offer the open-style inboards because of customer demand. However, it was the persistence of Bill Lyman that made the utility-type speedboat a common sight. Lyman Boat Works built all-wood inboard and outboards up through the early 1970's and even today designs are still based on the old wooden hulls although all production is fiberglass now. The 1935 model lineup was somewhat expanded although some models were dropped while new ones were added. Below is a detailed breakdown of what was available.[9]

MODEL	TYPE	LENGTH	ENGINE	SPEED	PRICE
15	Service	15'	Gray 16 h.p.	15	$ 545.00
15	Runabout	15'	Gray 32 h.p.	28	$ 695.00
17.5*	Runabout	17' 6"	Gray 62 h.p.	28	$ 895.00
17.5*	Util-Runa.	17' 6"	Gray 80 h.p.	32	$1200.00
19.5*	Util-Runa.	19' 6"	Gray 93 h.p.	35	$1545.00
23.5*	Util-Runa.	23' 6"	Gray 125 h.p.	26	$2575.00

*All-weather top optional.

---
[9]"Lyman Specifications", POWER BOATING, (June '35), 34.

1936 custom Lyman 28' cabin cruiser

The mid-thirties were good years at Lyman. 1937 found *RUDDER* magazine giving glowing reviews of all models. A big custom 1937 Lyman shown in the magazine was a 28' cruiser that was unusual in that for power she was equipped with two Gray 6-93 engines connected to one vee-drive. Top speed for this rare model was about 25 m.p.h. This Lyman cruiser was one of few ever built and it did come equipped with full cabin facilities, though crude by today's standards.

The year 1937 was also an important year at Lyman Boat Works because at that time Bill Lyman built an all-new modern plant on some 8 acres of land his family had purchased back in 1928. This new building covered some 18,000 square feet and was fully equipped with all the modern tools available at the time. By adopting the use of electric power tools at an early date Lyman was able to increase its output while still maintaining quality control which was its hallmark. Other additions to the original building would be added over the years as business warranted.

Bird's-eye view of sprawling Lyman plant, about 1950

Another 1937 31' Lyman custom cabin cruiser

Sleek 1938 18' Lyman hardtop runabout

As I mentioned earlier, Lyman boats did not change drastically from year to year. Only subtle modifications were made; rarely was a model dropped or a new one added. 1938 saw Lyman building just two inboards. The smallest was an 18' utility with power supplied by a Gray 4-62 h.p. engine or a larger, more deluxe 20' model with a Gray 6-125 engine that moved out up to 30 m.p.h. By the late 1930's Lyman boats used a rather flat, square style metal-framed windshield. This style would gradually evolve into the wooden-framed "skiff" windshield that became standard on all lapstrake boats up through the 1960's. You will note the nice photo of the 1938 Lyman 18' utility with a hardtop. This boat was again a custom model, one of many turned out over the years at

Clinker Built BY LYMAN ★

The experience gained from sixty-three years of specialized clinker construction is reflected in every Lyman hull. The new 1938 models, while moderately priced, are the finest boats that we can build.

Outboard models in 11, 13 and 15 ft. sizes. Priced from $155.00.

Inboard models in 17, 18, 20, and 24 ft. sizes. Priced from $1075.00.

See them at your dealers, or write for catalogue.

LYMAN BOAT WORKS FOOT OF FIRST STREET SANDUSKY - - - OHIO

1938 Lyman magazine ad

The "Queen" of the 1938 Lyman fleet—a 24' custom runabout

Large open 20' Lyman runabout with rear seat facing aft

1938 18' Lyman custom runabout

Sandusky, Ohio. Three other custom models built during 1938 were as follows: The largest was a 24' custom runabout with all-weather roof. The interesting feature of this boat was the rear seat which was moved about 8' forward, allowing for a large open storage area in the aft section of the boat. There was also a custom 20' runabout with its rear seat facing aft located directly behind the engine box. You may remember from my previous book, THE REAL RUNABOUTS, Volume I, Chris-Craft offered the same type of seating in 1938 in their 19' utility sportsman model. The final boat in the trio was an 18' custom hardtop runabout which also had its stern seat facing aft.

1939 found Lyman offering a more varied line than in past years. For your review, specifications are listed below.[10]

MODEL	LENGTH	ENGINE	H.P.	SPEED
Yacht Tender	15'	Gray	25	18 m.p.h.
Utility	17'	Gray	62	28 m.p.h.
Custom	18'	Gray	103	32 m.p.h.
Custom	20'	Gray	125	35 m.p.h.
Custom	21'	Gray	125	33 m.p.h.
Custom	24'	Gray	125	23 m.p.h.

Just one example of the 1939 fleet is pictured here—a 21' custom sedan shown under full power on Lake Erie.

[10]"Lyman 1939 Specifications", *MOTOR BOATING*, (Jan. '39), 306.

1939 sleek 21' Lyman sedan with Gray 125 h.p. engine

1940 found Lyman offering a new series of low-powered inboards designed strictly for the fisherman. The new 17' "Islander" as it was called, came with a small electric starting Gray Scout engine which allowed for a top speed of just over 10 m.p.h. Other models offered in 1940 would have to include 16', 18', and 19' utilities as well as 21' and 24' custom models. All the new 1940 Lymans featured increased beam and depth plus a more soundproof engine box. The ever popular all-season hardtop had been redesigned with ventilating windshields and a new sliding hatch on the front deck for improved ventilation as well as easy access to the bow area.

1940 18' Lyman with 75 h.p. Gray Phantom, 30 m.p.h.

Clinker Built by LYMAN

Be sure to see the new 1940 Lyman Inboard and Outboard Runabouts at the coming New York Motor Boat Show. New Outboard Models in 11, 13 and 15-ft. sizes. New Utility Inboards in 15, 16, 17 and 18-ft. sizes. New Custom Models in 19½, 21 and 24-ft. sizes. Send for catalogue.

LYMAN BOAT WORKS FOOT OF FIRST ST. SANDUSKY, OHIO

Rare 1940 Lyman magazine ad

7

Lyman did build some models in 1941, but it was their last full year of production prior to the outbreak of World War II. Five inboards ranging from 16' through 24' made up the line. A single example of the 1941 Lyman fleet would be the 18' utility shown here with the 103 h.p. Gray engine.[11] There is little change between it and the 1940 offerings, as you can see.

One of the last boats Lymans built before World War II, 1941

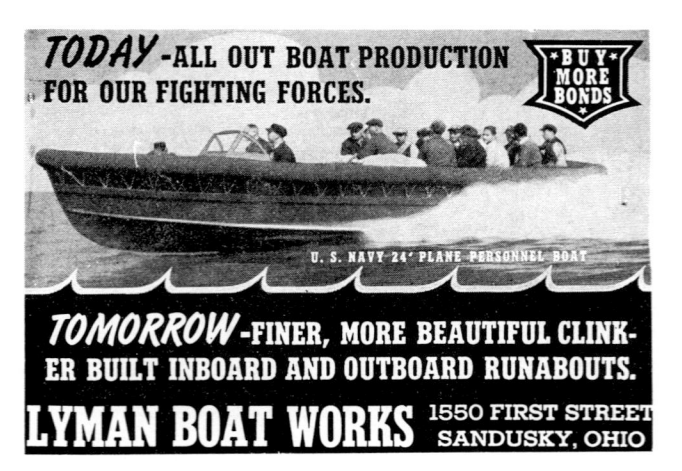

The war years at Lyman Boat Works

During World War II Lyman Boat Works quickly switched production from pleasure craft to war craft. The firm built the following types of craft for the Army-Air Force: 33' plane rearming boats, 24' plane personnel boats and 17' line handling boats as well as a fleet of small 8' sailing dinghies and a group of M-2 assault vessels. Lyman received several government awards for outstanding work through the war and with its final conclusion the firm once more took up where it left off in late 1941. . . .

Several key things were to change at Lyman following production startups after the war. First of all, it seemed before the war that all Lyman boats were built by skilled

1947 Lyman ad

cabinet builders, like Lyman himself. After World War II most of these men retired and few young men came along to fill in their dwindling ranks. For Lyman and other boat builders this meant a change in their building methods. Bill Lyman adopted the use of jigs, molds, etc. for building his boats. As we know from *Volume I*, firms like Chris-Craft, Gar Wood and others used this method as far back as the 1930's. Instead of building boats one at a time, all pieces are made or cut from patterns so they are uniform. Then all parts can be gathered together and the boat assembled, much as an auto. It was a more efficient system and it worked very well. When Bill Lyman's dad began building his boats he used oak for frames and cypress for planking. As time went on, supplies of cypress dwindled and cedar strips were used. In more modern times, five-ply plywood was used for all planking on Lyman lapstrake hulls. Plywood made for a stronger, lighter hull with less leakage, a problem always present with the older planked hulls.[12]

---

[11] "Lyman Lapstrake", *MOTOR BOATING*, (Jan. '41), 14.

[12] Bob Meyers, "They Built a Reputation on Lapstrake Hulls", *MOTOR BOATING*, (Jan. '50), 297.

Big, new 1947 22' Lyman runabout built right after the war

Lyman 18' "Islander" built in 1948 for fishing and cruising

Building new Lymans following World War II

1949 18' Lyman "Islander" with convertible top in use

After World War II, Lyman outboards really caught on. In fact, 1948 found but one Lyman inboard. She was a brand new 18' "Islander" designed not for speed but for cruising and fishing, etc. Her power was a Gray Sea Scout 25 h.p. She did not come equipped standard with a windshield, but a new wooden style skiff windshield was available as an option.

1950 18' Lyman "Islander" inboard

This new boat sported its steering wheel amidships on the starboard side so the captain could fish from his seat while still driving the boat.[13]

For the next few years Lyman offered more outboards than inboards. Only two models were available about 1955 when the firm really began to again expand the inboard portion of its offerings. By 1963 Lyman offered its most varied selection of inboards. Many things were changing at Lyman by the mid 1960's. All models were much wider and deeper with "jazzed up" interiors,

1951 18' Lyman runabout

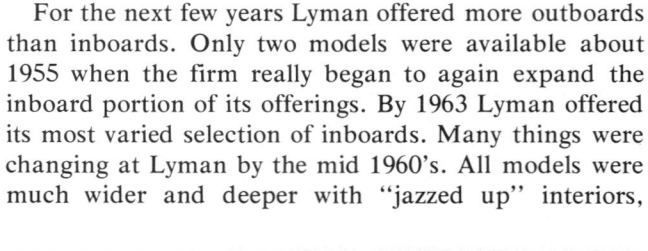

1952 18' Lyman powered by Gray 49

1951 17' Lyman inboard utility

New 1955 20' Lyman inboard designed for cruising, fishing and skiing.

1953 Lyman 18-footer with convertible top and side curtains

---

[13]"Lyman Clinker Boat Models", *MOTOR BOAT*, (Jan. '48), 133.

1954 version of the always-popular Lyman "Islanders"

bright exterior hull paint jobs, etc. A new 28' Islander day cruiser was added to the line at that time and this boat was well suited for use on the Great Lakes. She was equipped with cooking facilities, sink and dinette under hardtop, with a big open rear cockpit astern. The year 1963 also saw the introduction of inboard-outboards in Lyman boats for the first time.

1963 28' Lyman "Islander" day cruiser

The final wooden inboards built by Lyman were built in the early 1970's. By then they were offering such things as a 30' Express Cruiser with flying bridge all made of wood. After this time, production was switched strictly to fiberglass and today the offerings include four different inboards. A fact I do not wish to omit was the death of Wm. E. "Bill" Lyman in the summer of 1952. In his obituary it was mentioned that he was a renowned builder of lapstrake inboard power boats since the end of World War II. It also mentioned that Fred E. Wiehn, former vice president and general manager was going to carry on the business.[14]

---

[14] "Wm. E. Lyman", *MOTOR BOAT*, (Aug. '52), 56.

19' Inboard

The Inboards

18' Islander........from **$2,595** 19' Runabout........from **$2,715**
23' Runabout........from **$3,595**

More of everything you want in an Outboard or Inboard is yours in a 1958 Clinker-built Lyman — and at a price you can afford. Matchless beauty, seaworthiness, roominess, rough water ability, dryness and soft, level riding are all built into the Lyman line. Clinker construction the Lyman way is the answer! There's no substitute for it — no short cuts around it.

The new 15' Outboard with deeper, beamier hull is true-blue beauty in appearance and performance. Lovely to look at — thrilling to ride in — that's the big 19' Inboard, a new addition but already a favorite.

In fairness to yourself, look over the complete Lyman line before you buy any boat. It will be time well spent!

Write today for the free, fully-illustrated Lyman folder — and the name of your nearest dealer.

LYMAN BOAT WORKS — 1619 FIRST STREET, SANDUSKY, OHIO

1958 Lyman inboard ad

In summary, the Lyman Boat Works did play a major role in the development of the wooden lapstrake inboard utility. As mentioned prior, other builders came out with lapstrake inboards too. Names like Chris-Craft, Owens, Gar Wood and many others followed Lyman's example and added their own lines of "clinker" type hulls. Flattery is the highest form of praise. . . . .

I have noticed on some of our larger lakes here in the midwest, like Lake Minnetonka in Minnesota and Lake Geneva in Wisconsin, that the Lyman style clinker inboards are more popular than ever. In visiting with dealers I have found that sales of this type of boat are rising—in fact, demand seems to exceed supply in most areas.

So whenever you see one of those lapstrake runabouts out for a cruise, don't stick your nose in the air or call it an ugly duckling, but appreciate it for what it is. I think then you will see why so many who own this type of "Real Runabout" would have no other. There is a wide selection of photos in this last portion showing various Lyman boats from 1950 on. I hope you enjoy this offering and may it help to show the Lyman story in all its fullness.

Our next firm will be the Higgins Shipyard of New Orleans, Louisiana. Andrew Higgins pioneered mass use of marine plywood in inboard runabouts as well as utilities. From 1947 through the mid 1950's Higgins inboards dotted the waterways and these boats allowed countless families to get into boating after the end of World War II on a level they could afford. No longer was power boating strictly a rich man's sport. I myself still enjoy seeing a colorful Higgins streak by; how about you?

HIGGINS—PIONEERS IN PLYWOOD RUNABOUTS

View of warehouse of Higgins dealer, Touristville Boat Company, Clear Lake, Iowa—1939.

Jammed warehouse with Higgins 1947 models covering floor. Note novel storage racks for runabouts and sailboats.

The story of the Higgins Boat Company is an interesting one, to say the least. I guess my first personal experience with a Higgins inboard must have been when I was about seven or eight years old. One day my dad, brother Art and I drove to Clear Lake, Iowa just to look around. We stopped at the sprawling facilities of the Touristville Boat Company, the local north-Iowa distributor for the complete line of Higgins Boats. I can remember to this day, seeing those neat red and white or blue and white runabouts and utilities tied to the docks or hanging neatly on a row of large overhead boat lifts. It seemed to me, back then in the very early 1950's, that Clear Lake was just crawling with Higgins inboards. Today I doubt if more than one or two still exist there.

Little did I expect then, that someday I would be relating the "rise and fall" of this famous builder to you, my readers. A fact that surprised me was that the Higgins Boat Company actually dated back to 1898 when young A. J. Higgins began building what he called, "sensible" boats good for inland as well as bayou country.[15] In the early days, Higgins built recreational as well as commerical vessels. In fact, Mr. Higgins pioneered what he called the "Eureka", a shallow, bill-bowed craft designed as an early type crew boat popular in the deep South. From around 1937 through the early 1940's, Higgins built fewer and fewer pleasure boats while con-

[15]"The History of Higgins", *MOTOR BOAT*, (July '37), 36.

1938 Higgins "Eureka" work boat

Close-up of Higgins spoon-bill inboard

One of the last 1938 46' custom cruisers ever built by Higgins

The Better Mousetrap

"If a man write a better book, preach a better sermon or build a better mousetrap than his neighbor, though he build his house in the woods, the world will make a beaten path to his door."
Attributed to Emerson

HIGGINS INDUSTRIES, INC., 1755 ST. CHARLES STREET, NEW ORLEANS, LA.

Very unique 1939 Higgins magazine ad featuring the "Eureka" hull.

centrating on filling the numerous orders for Eureka work boats which came in from all over the nation. This photo shows one of the last Higgins cabin cruisers built about 1938 or so. She is a handsome craft, very competitive with boats built at that time by other firms such as Owens, Chris-Craft, etc. In order not to lose out entirely on the New Orleans area pleasure boat business, Higgins built a new, all-modern showroom on St. Charles Street and proceeded to fill it with numerous Chris-Craft cruisers and runabouts.

As I mentioned before, commercial boat building became such a major part of the business for Higgins, that selling other firms' boats was the only way they could stay in the retail boat business.

With the outbreak of World War II, Higgins Industries fell into a similar pattern of boat building that we have seen throughout this book. Over 25,000 craft of all types were built by Higgins for the United States as well as its allies world-wide. The most publicity centered on the now famous Higgins P.T. boats, which were noted worldwide for their excellent design as well as construction. Higgins was a pioneer in the use of plywood in the

13

19' DELUXE RUNABOUT

HARDWARE AND FITTINGS

Controls, Automotive Type
1 Automatic Bailer
1 Chrome Plated Bronze Electric Bow Light & Flag Staff Socket
1 Chrome Plated Bronze Bow Plate & Chock
2 Chrome Plated Bronze Combination Lift Eyes & Cleats
2 Chrome Plated Lock Type Gas Tank Caps
1 Mahogany Combination Flag Staff & Stern Light with Ensign
1 Mahogany Jack Staff with Higgins Pennant
1 Chrome Plated Vee Type Windshield
2 Deck Lines
1 One-Quart Fire Extinguisher
1 Electric Horn
Floor Covering—Linoleum
Rub Rail and Stem Band Trim—Stainless Steel
Trim on Spray Rails—Stainless Steel
Chrome Plated Deck Cleats
Chrome Plated Vents
Stainless Steel Rub Strips (at Cleats)
Chrome Plated Hatch Trim
Set of 5 Instruments Consisting of: Ammeter—Oil Gauge—Temperature Gauge—Tachometer—Fuel Gauge
Upholstery (Naugahyde)
Seats—Box Spring Construction—Lazy Backs Upholstered.

SPECIFICATIONS

Length: 19'
Seating Capacity: 6
Beam: 6' 5"
Draft: 1' 6"
Freeboard Fwd.: 27½"
Freeboard Aft.: 18¼"
Frames: 1⅛" Mahogany
Bottom: ½" Bonded Mahogany
Sides: ⅜" Bonded Mahogany
Deck: ⅜" Bonded Mahogany
Keel 1⅜" x 5½" Laminated Mahogany
Stem: Laminated Mahogany
Chines: 1¼" x 2½" Laminated Mahogany
Sheer Clamps: 1" x 2⅝" Oak
Screws: Silicon Bronze
Bolts: Silicon Bronze
Propeller Shaft: ⅞" Monel
Rudder & Strut: Manganese Bronze
Fuel Capacity—Gallons: 50
Lift Ring, Spacing—Center to Center 16' 7"
Shipping Weight with the Following Engines: (Approximately) Gray Fireball—6 cyl., 140 H. P., 2178 lbs. Gray—6 cyl. 125 H. P., 2198 lbs. Chrysler Crown—6 cyl, 115 H. P., 2285 lbs.
Cradle Weight: (Approximately) 225 lb.

Higgins INCORPORATED NEW ORLEANS

Specifications and Equipment Subject To Change Or Modification

1948 19' Higgins runabout literature

Smooth... Sparkling Speed...

You'll feel like you own the world when you're behind the wheel of the beautiful new Higgins 19-foot Deluxe Runabout. Clips along with power to spare—smooth as a gull's wing—swift as a flash of sunlight on blue water—responding happily to your slightest touch like a rocket under control. Seats six comfortably in two large cockpits *forward* of the engine.
The Higgins 19-foot Deluxe Runabout is *available now for immediate delivery*.
Write for the address of your nearest dealer.

DEALERSHIPS AND DISTRIBUTORSHIPS OPEN IN SOME TERRITORIES FOR HIGGINS CLASS I BOATS. WRITE TO

Higgins INCORPORATED NEW ORLEANS

First true runabout ever offered by Higgins, Inc.—1947

---

building of war vessels. Following the end of the war, a new era in pleasure boats was about to be "launched" by this southern firm.

In December of 1946, Higgins, Inc. ran a full-page color ad in most of the major boat magazines, telling of their very first pleasure craft built by Higgins since the late 1930's. This new boat was to be a 19' Deluxe runabout, twin-cockpit-forward. Oddly enough, Higgins never built another true runabout after 1949. Perhaps you have seen one of these rare runabouts or may even own one. If you are fortunate enough to own one of these beauties, my suggestion to you is this: hang on to it and take good care of it; you have a very rare boat. The boat was finished as follows: red decks, white hull sides, varnished transom and red bottom paint. The 19' Deluxe was a very streamlined craft and was designed along the lines of the famous Higgins P.T.'s of World War II. Plywood was used for planking on these first models and later on, this would prove to be a problem that would plague builder and owners alike. Engine options ranged from 115 h.p. Chrysler up through the Gray Marine 140 h.p. Higgins inboards were lighter than conventional planked speedboats also. This was a plus feature promoted by Higgins through its entire span of production. The 19' Deluxe weighed in at 2,285 pounds.

A copy of the complete 19' Deluxe runabout brochure is printed here for your review. With the excellent acceptance of the first Higgins speedboat, 1948 would see a much expanded line of inboards and small cruisers being offered. The 1948 New York Boat Show featured all the new Higgins boats and they were well accepted by the boat-buying fraternity.[16] The new lineup consisted of the following: the 17' Sport Speedster utility, the 19' Deluxe runabout, a 23' convertible Sport Speedster, as well as a 26' cabin cruiser and several smaller outboard hulls. The 17' Sport Speedster was a brand-new model and it was probably the most popular boat ever built by the firm. It remained in the line in one form or another, right up

---

[16]"Higgins Exhibits Full-Line", *MOTOR BOAT*, (Jan. '48), 136.

4 Beauties

Beauty in hull design is accepted in all Higgins boats... sleek, luxurious lines that instantly catch the eye! There is 'inbuilt' beauty too, in workmanship and durability, a natural heritage of experience gleaned in building famous Higgins battle-tested boats. Couple this to... Beauty in performance... in instant response, with utmost safety at *all* speeds... and you have the epitome of all that is fine in a boat. Choose *yours* from the complete line at your nearest Higgins dealer. Dealers in all principal cities.

Higgins INCORPORATED NEW ORLEANS

Post World War II Higgins magazine ad

1948 17' Higgins sport speedster

Final portion of Higgins runabout assembly line—1948, New Orleans, Louisiana.

17' SPORT SPEEDSTER

SPECIFICATIONS

Length: 17' 0"
Seating Capacity: 6
Beam: 6' 5"
Draft: 1' 6"
Freeboard Fwd.: 27½"
Freeboard Aft.: 21"
Frames: 1⅛" Mahogany
Bottom: ⅜" 5 Ply Bonded Mahogany
Sides: ⅜" 5 Ply Bonded Mahogany
Deck: ⅜" 5 Ply Bonded Mahogany
Keel: 1¾" x 5½" Laminated Mahogany
Stem: Laminated Mahogany
Chines: 1¼" x 2½" Laminated Mahogany
Sheer Clamp: 1" x 2⅜" Oak
Screws: Silicon Bronze
Bolts: Silicon Bronze
Propeller Shaft: ⅞" Monel
Rudder & Strut: Manganese Bronze
Fuel Capacity—Gallons: 25
Lift Ring, Spacing—Center to Center 14' 7"
Shipping Weight with the Following Engines: (Approximately)
Gray Phantom—6— 104 H.P. 1897 Lbs.
Chrysler Ace—6— 92 H.P. 1727 Lbs.
Cradle Weight (Approx.) 225 Lbs.

HARDWARE AND FITTINGS

Controls, Automotive Type
1 Automatic Bailer
1 Chrome Plated Bronze Electric Bow Light & Flag Staff Socket
1 Chrome Plated Bronze Bow Plate & Chock
2 Chrome Plated Bronze Combination Lift Eyes & Cleats
1 Chrome Plated Lock Type Gas Tank Cap
1 Mahogany Combination Flag Staff & Stern Light with Ensign
1 Mahogany Jack Staff with Higgins Pennant
1 Chrome Plated Vee Type Windshield
2 Deck Lines
1 One-quart Fire Extinguisher
1 Electric Horn
Floor Covering—Linoleum (Temporarily substituting non-skid paint)
Stainless Steel Rub Rail Trim—Stainless Steel Stem Band
Stainless Steel Trim on Spray Rails
Set of 5 Instruments Consisting of:
Ammeter—Oil Gauge—Temperature Gauge
Tachometer—Fuel Gauge
Upholstery (Naugahyde)
Seats—Box Spring Construction—Lazy Backs Upholstered.

Higgins INCORPORATED NEW ORLEANS

Specifications and Equipment Subject To Change Or Modification

1948 Higgins 17' utility literature

---

through the 1960's. In order to build larger numbers of 1948 Higgins boats, the firm built an all-new automated factory using the popular assembly line method of construction. You will note the photo taken in late 1948 showing the end of the runabout and utility lines, just before the finished boats are readied for delivery. The larger photo gives you a bird's-eye view of the main assembly area for the cruisers. Off to the far right, you can see some of the smaller speedboats being completed, etc. I have been fortunate in obtaining 1948 brochures on both the 17' Sport Speedster and the 23' utility. I think you will find both of them informative as well as entertaining. . . . .

The huge Higgins assembly line in action, 1948, in New Orleans, Louisiana

1948 23' Higgins speedster literature

23' SPORT SPEEDSTER
Length 23' 0"

SPECIFICATIONS
Seating Capacity: 10 persons
Beam: 8 feet
Draft: 22 inches
Freeboard Forward: 32 inches
Freeboard Aft: 24 inches
Frame: 1⅛" reinforced Mahogany
Bottom: ½" 5-ply Bonded Mahogany
Sides: ½" 5-ply Bonded Mahogany
Deck: ⅜" 5-ply Bonded Mahogany
Keel: 1¼" x 5½" Laminated Mahogany
Stem: Laminated Mahogany
Chines: 1¾" x 3½" Laminated Mahogany
Rub Rail: 1" x 2½" Oak
Screws: Silicon Bronze
Bolts: Silicon Bronze
Propeller Shaft: 1" Monel
Strut: Manganese Bronze
Rudder: Manganese Bronze
Fuel Capacity: 43 gallons
Lift Ring Spacing—Center to Center: 20' 2½"

HARDWARE & FITTINGS
1 Automatic Bailer
1 Chrome Plated Bronze Bow Plate and Chock
1 Chrome Plated Bronze Bow Light—Electric
2 Chrome Plated Bronze Combination Lift Eyes and Cleats
1 Chrome Plated Lock-Type Gas Cap
1 Chrome Plated Bronze Flag Staff Socket
1 Mahogany Combination Flag Staff and Stern Light with Ensign.
1 Mahogany Jack Staff with Higgins Pennant
1 Chrome Plated 3-Piece Safety Glass Windshield
2 Dock Lines
1 One-Qt. Fire Extinguisher
1 Chrome Plated Electric Siren
Floor Covering . . . Linoleum
Stainless Steel Rub Rail Trim
Stainless Steel Stem Band
Stainless Steel Trim on Spray and Quarter Rails
1 Set of Five Instruments consisting of: Tachometer, Fuel Gauge, Ammeter, Oil Gauge and Temperature Gauge
Upholstery—Naugahyde
Seats—Box Spring Construction—Lazy Backs Upholstered

Shipping Weight with following engines:
Gray Super Six 6 cyl-145 H.P.—About 3265 pounds
Chrysler Royal 8 cyl-141 H.P.—About 3350 pounds

CAP. BOB'S BAYSIDE MARINA
505 ALBERT LEA ST.
ALBERT LEA, MINN.

Higgins INCORPORATED NEW ORLEANS

Specifications and Equipment Subject To Change Or Modification

---

Magazine ad in 1948 introducing the new 19' Deluxe Higgins Sport Speedster.

Big Sister TO THE CHAMPION!

. . . . the new, power-packed
Higgins DeLuxe 19' Sport Speedster!

Once you've eased into the cushioned comfort of this sleek, blue-ribbon beauty and felt the first full surge of sustained power, you'll recognize her close kinship to our 17' Class E runabout champion! Yes, this new 19' *DeLuxe Sport Speedster* (seating eight) commands admiring o-o-ohs and a-a-ahs every time she breezes by, first at the finish.

Watch for this newest of Higgins' headliners . . . . These combined characteristics will help you identify her as a Higgins: graceful, gleaming beauty of line and trim; split-second maneuverability and perfect balance at high speed; PT toughness that laughs at repeated poundings, and all the elbow room even a landlubber could ask for. But, best of all, she's priced so moderately you'll want to do business with your nearby Higgins dealer the very minute you've set eyes on this speedster!

Higgins dealers in all major cities.

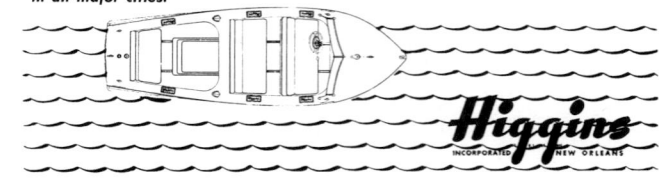

Higgins INCORPORATED NEW ORLEANS

16

1948 Higgins display at Des Moines, Iowa Boat and Sport Show

I am very appreciative to Mrs. Juanita Haddy, daughter of the former owner of Touristville Boat Company, Clear Lake, Iowa. The oblong photo was taken at the 1948 Des Moines, Iowa Sports Show where Juanita and her family had two fine new Higgins inboards on display. The boats were nicely displayed, making for a very attractive booth.

1949 found Higgins again offering basically the same model lineup except the 19' runabout was changed to a 19' Sport Speedster.

This boat was like a runabout except the two seats ahead of the engine were full ones, like the old runabout, while the engine was installed under a padded engine box with a full bench seat behind it in the stern of the boat. Other 1949 models included the 23' Sport Speedster and the 17' Sport Speedster utility. Minor changes occurred in the early Higgins inboards. Nearly every Higgins inboard was painted red and white, or blue and white. You could have custom paint jobs done at the factory or by your dealer for a fee. I once saw a pink and black Higgins utility; I am sure that was done by the owner himself. . . .

19' Sport Speedster by Higgins, 1950

1949 23' Higgins Sports Speedster

1949 17' Higgins utility underway

Unusual 3-seat 1949 Higgins 19' Deluxe Sport Speedster

17

1950 Higgins boats on display at Des Moines, Iowa Boat and Sport Show

For 1950, Higgins offered the same basic lineup. It included a 17' stripped-down, lower-priced utility with a 45 h.p. Gray or 92 h.p. Chrysler engine. Other boats offered included the 17' Sport Speedster with three engine options up to 140 h.p. as well as the 23' convertible Sport Speedster. In 19' lengths, both the runabout as well as utility were still being offered.[17]

The Korean War came on the scene and by 1951 Higgins was back full-time building for the Navy. No speedboats were built at all during 1951, and 1952 would also prove to see Higgins limiting its pleasure boat building. At this point I have included two more "Boat Show" type photos, compliments of Mrs. Juanita Haddy, that were taken about 1950 and 1952 showing family displays at the Des Moines, Iowa Sports Show. Mrs. Haddy and a friend appear to be sitting in the 17' Sport Speedster ready for a short spin around the show. You will also note little overall change in the design and finishing of the Higgins inboards during the early years.

Juanita Hady and friend aboard the 17' 1952 Higgins utility

It was announced that Higgins would again offer its famous 17' Sport Speedster in 1952. Because of heavy orders still to be completed for the Navy, only a limited number of speedboats were being offered for sale in that year.[18]

The Higgins Sport Speedster is a 17' fast runabout

1952 also marked the death of the founder of Higgins Industries, Andrew J. Higgins.[19] Mr. Higgins died in August of 1952 at the age of 66. In his obituary it mentioned he originally was in the lumber business in the Midwest and came to New Orleans where he began to build all types of boats, both large and small. One of his early cabin cruisers set a speed record between New Orleans and St. Louis, Missouri which stood for a number of years. The late Mr. Higgins was survived by his widow and four sons.

1953 found Higgins Industries building no pleasure craft, rather concentrating on building ten laminated wood non-metallic mine sweepers.[20] Plans were to launch one completed vessel every six weeks. Over 600 employees and friends gathered on April 10, 1953 to watch the first vessel being launched.

---

[17]"Higgins", *MOTOR BOATING*, (Jan. '50), 118.

[18]"Higgins Building 17' Speedster", *YACHTING*, (Jan. '52), 255.
[19]"Andrew J. Higgins", *MOTOR BOAT*, (Sept. '52), 38.
[20]"Higgins Launches", *MOTOR BOAT*, (June '53), 76.

17' Sport Speedster

Specifications

Length: 17' 0"
Seating Capacity: 6
Beam: 6' 5"
Draft: 1' 6"
Freeboard Fwd: 27½"
Freeboard Aft: 21"
Frames: 1⅛" Cross Banded Mahogany
Bottom: ½" 5 Ply Bonded Mahogany
Sides: ⅜" 5 Ply Bonded Mahogany
Deck: ⅜" 5 Ply Bonded Mahogany
Keel: 1⅞" x 5½" Laminated Mahogany Cross Banded in Center
Stem: Laminated Mahogany

Chines: 1¼" x 2½" Laminated Mahogany
Sheer Clamp: 1" x 2⅜" Oak
Screws: Silicon Bronze
Bolts: Silicon Bronze
Propeller Shaft: ⅞" Monel
Rudder & Strut: Manganese Bronze
Fuel Capacity—Gallons: 25
Lift Ring, Spacing—Center to Center 14' 7"
Shipping Weight with the Following Engines: (Approximately)
Gray Phantom—6— 104 H.P. 1897 Lbs.
Chrysler Ace—6— 92 H.P. 1727 Lbs.
Cradle Weight (Approx.) 225 Lbs.

HARDWARE AND FITTINGS
Controls, Automotive Type
1 Automatic Bailer
1 Chrome Plated Bronze Electric Bow Light & Flag Staff Socket
1 Chrome Plated Bronze Bow Plate & Chock
2 Chrome Plated Bronze Combination Lift Eyes & Cleats
1 Chrome Plated Lock Type Gas Tank Cap
1 Combination Flag Staff & Stern Light with Ensign
1 Jack Staff with Higgins Pennant
1 Chrome Plated Vee Type Windshield
2 Deck Lines
1 One-quart Fire Extinguisher
1 Electric Horn
Floor Covering—Linoleum
Stainless Steel Rub Rail Trim—Stainless Steel Stem Band
Stainless Steel Trim on Spray Rails
Chrome-plated Brass Panel consisting of: Ammeter—Tachometer—Fuel Gauge Temperature Gauge—Oil Gauge
Upholstery (Naugahyde)
Seats—Box Spring Construction— Lazy Backs Upholstered

Specifications and Equipment Subject To Change Or Modification Without Notice

1954 17' Higgins utility literature

Higgins offered several small runabouts in 1954. One was a 17' Sport Speedster, identical to those offered earlier, except now powered with smaller, less-expensive engines. Outboard runabouts by 1954 were becoming quite popular and Higgins was trying to hold on to their market by offering boats that were competitive with new outboards being built by other builders. We mentioned earlier the problem Higgins experienced because of the use of plywood in boats. . . . Higgins suffered from a stigma created by the trouble they had with plywood used in their early boats. It seems it was the wrong type and many of the first Higgins speedboats had bottoms drop out, rot out, etc. Dealers had to replace many bottoms in the first boats and this problem did not help Higgins establish a sound reputation among boat owners. To improve the company image in 1955, Higgins announced numerous news-worthy plans which management felt would return Higgins inboards to favor with U.S. boat buyers. Let's delve into some of the firm's plans and see how successful they were. 1955 was to be a big year for Higgins and here are some of the reasons.

To comfort potential Higgins buyers for 1955, the firm offered an all-new five-year warranty on all wood used in the construction of its boats. They were so sure they had the old nemesis of plywood trouble under control, every new 1955 boat sold was covered by the warranty. A funny thing also happened in 1955: It seems the first few runabouts built by the firm following the end of the Korean War were modified equipment-wise, part way through the model year. The ol' reliable 17' Sport Speedster first came out equipped with a stylish metal-framed "V" windshield. The boat itself had received some styling changes such as, modern two-tone upholstery, jazzier paint job and large engines. A sleek new bow light was also added along with modern style cleats, chocks, etc. Please note the two photos showing the 1955 17' Sport Speedster with the old style windshield as well as the new wraparound plexiglass version offered by Higgins. The later 1955 models also came powered with the Chrysler

1955 17' Higgins Sport Speedster with old style "V" windshield.

Full speed ahead! in a 1955 Higgins Sports Speedster.

1955 23' Higgins convertible runabout powered by Chrysler 211 h.p. V-8 engine

125 h.p. engine. The only runabout built in 1955 was the 23' convertible model which came equipped with bucket seats up front with a three-quarter seat ahead of the engine box and a full stern seat aft. The largest engine available in this boat was a 200 h.p. Chrysler Imperial V-8. Sliding windows, adjustable windshields and all-mahogany window frames made the 23-footer a popular boat on larger waterways as well as "ride boats" for concession operators. Higgins advised potential buyers that all wood used in their boats was now being treated by "Penta" wood preservatives, thus protecting all wood from deterioration. It was also mentioned that the 17' Speedster had been redesigned so as not to "nose dive" when slowing down. Her top speed had been increased to 38 m.p.h. All new 1955 Higgins boats also came equipped with foot feeds, and the reverse gearshift lever mounted on the steering column, just like the passenger cars of the day. Yes, it looked like Higgins had really gotten off to a great start and it would be nothing but good times from then on. . . . Well, as most of us know, life is never so simple.[21]

Higgins prospered in 1955, adding many new dealers and fans nationwide. Here in the upper Midwest, nearly every area where there were larger lakes and rivers could almost guarantee your seeing the familiar "Higgins" logo proudly hanging in a showroom full of flashy Higgins speedboats. In fact, at Clear Lake, Iowa, Higgins was the best seller of the big three in runabouts through about 1957. Higgins boats seemed to fill a void created by other builders who offered only the more costly mahogany inboards or those who were switching from wood to that new miracle fabric, fiberglass. As it so happened, Higgins stubbornly held out building wood boats, never changing, but continuing to offer all-wood craft—no aluminum or fiberglass as others were doing. The Higgins inboard was popular with the younger buyer, or first time buyers, who could buy a nice used Higgins for about the same price or even less than similar new outboard powered boats which were really coming on in 1955 or so.

1956 saw no change in Higgins runabouts. The 17' Sport Speedster was now powered by a 185 h.p. Dearborn Interceptor, and listed out at $4,295.00. 1956 also saw the end of the 17' Higgins Sport Speedster as we knew it for 10 years.

The Higgins 1957 fleet was completely redesigned to compete against the ever increasing numbers of small, trailerable outboard runabouts which appeared to be swiftly taking over most of the under-17' pleasure boat business in those days. I can personally remember the 1957 Higgins speedboats as I first saw them at a boat show held in Minneapolis, Minnesota in early October. Great crowds seemed to hover around the local Higgins dealer's display which included the all-new Higgins

---

[21]"Higgins Returns to Pleasure Craft", BOATS, (Jan. '55), 61.

"Magnum". As Higgins officials put it, the Magnum was built for those who really know boats. . . . "color styled for those who demand the last word". The new Magnum, as it was called, was more elaborate than its old predecessor, the Sport Speedster. The new hull sported a fancy two-tone paint job in such colors as Baltic Blue, Sunset Red, Deep Mahogany or other colors of the owner's choice, accented with Gull White trim. Interiors on all Magnum models were far more deluxe than the older Higgins speedboats.

Sleek Higgins Magnum model about to fly into space.

Standard equipment lists were longer than ever. The action photo of the 1957 Magnum shown here pretty much tells the story. Note her crisp lines, great planing angle and the jazzy bow rails which adorned her decks. Needless to say, the Magnum took the country by storm and dealers recorded record orders for the spring of 1957. A 23' sport cruiser as well as a 30' flying bridge cabin cruiser also received design changes and looked far more streamlined than in earlier years. If your "cup of tea" was a smaller, less deluxe utility for 1957, Higgins also offered the all-new 16' open boat powered with just a 70 h.p. Gray engine. This model also could be obtained in an outboard version.

1958 Higgins 16' utility

By 1957, Higgins Industries had built an all-new shipyard on the Industrial Canal in New Orleans, Louisiana. The firm by this time was being run by the sons of the founder who still stuck with wood boats, as the popularity of fiberglass became greater and greater with each passing season. A lot of activity of Higgins in the late 1950's was directed toward commercial ship, tug, barge building, repairs, etc.

The most outstanding speedboat probably ever offered by Higgins came along in 1960. She was 18' long and called the "Mandalay", a last ditch, all-out effort of the firm to remain in the inboard runabout market. She was destined to rival the offerings of other firms such as Chris-Craft, Century, Correct Craft, etc. In many ways she may have even been a better boat than others offered in 1960. This new 18' hull was not a "warmed over" version of the old Magnum, but an all-new design sporting small rear tail fins and several colorful paint jobs which were very attractive. The Mandalay came in blue and white, gold and black, or white and gold. Decks were all varnished and bottoms were painted copper. Engine sizes ranged from 125 h.p. through the big 240 h.p. V-8 Chrysler which pushed her along at an impressive 46 m.p.h. Without a doubt, the Mandalay was the finest and most deluxe Higgins ever built. Strangely

Sleek, 1960 Higgins Mandalay 18' in a power-slide

enough, it was the last real well-built runabout the firm would ever build.

There are still quite a few of these boats in use today and I feel they will become more popular with collectors as time goes on. Two years ago I had the privilege to view a Mandalay in perfect condition, a boat that was a proud possession of its skipper and still drew attention when it pulled up to a dock.

1960 Higgins Port Royal utility

A somewhat less deluxe 1960 model was the 17' Port Royal utility. Not nearly as plain as the 1957 and 1958 models, this boat seemed to strike a happy medium, as it was nicely finished inside as well as out, and sold very well as a mid-price range inboard. From 1960 on, we saw fewer and fewer Higgins inboard speedboats coming out of the New Orleans complex. The shipyard itself swung more toward commercial repair, building, etc., and with Vietnam becoming a major conflict, most output of Higgins was of a war nature. The very last year Higgins even advertised concerning pleasure boats was early 1963. Shortly into 1963, the firm ceased building pleasure craft altogether. The firm suffered from a number of things which finally caused its demise in 1963. Let's look at these happenings at this time.

Following the death of Andrew Higgins in 1952, the firm began to lose numerous government contracts that the elder Higgins had built up over the years, beginning with World War II. President Eisenhower cancelled all ship and war craft contracts shortly after he took office, leaving Higgins and other builders with no work or income to speak of. This blow almost caused the complete folding of many builders, but Higgins was able to continue. With increasing slumps in wooden boat sales and not wanting to change to fiberglass boats, which were very much the trend from the late 1950's on, the firm tried several other ventures which completely caused them to go bankrupt. One of the sons decided they should switch into the manufacturing of wooden floors for homes, offices, etc. Millions of dollars were poured into this project and it turned out to be a total flop. This event, along with some family problems among the sons of the late Mr. Higgins, finally caused all operations to cease in 1963.

Today, barely a small handful of Higgins speedboats still exist. I have talked with many dealers who told me in the early 1960's, when so many old Higgins inboards were being traded in on new fiberglass boats, it was even hard to give them away, much less try and sell one. Everyone thought that since so many Higgins inboards were once in use, we would never reach the time when they would become what we shall call "endangered species". I still enjoy the view of a smart Higgins utility or runabout out for a fast spin. We all look forward to the day when more Higgins inboards will be restored and put back into regular service. . . One dealer told me he considered them to be the "Volkswagon" of motorboats! Could he have been correct?

Now we shall move on to another builder who played a big role in the rise of inboard speedboats—Horace E. Dodge Boat & Plane Company of Newport News, Virginia. Dodge boats were and still are among the most prized and rare of all antique runabouts. This firm pioneered many "firsts" in the industry which we shall now look at in more detail.

DODGE—THE WORLD'S LOWEST PRICED FINE MOTOR BOATS

The famous Horace E. Dodge Boat & Plane Company —originally of Detroit, Michigan and later of Newport News, Virginia—built some natty motor boats for about twenty-five years. Dodge boats today are beginning to re-appear on the scene once more, though harder to restore as old hardware, parts, etc. seem to be harder to find.

The Dodge Boat Company was founded by the late Dodge brothers, Horace and John, about 1920. Both brothers were famous for operating the former Dodge Car Company that bore their name. When they entered the boat business, the two brothers assembled a team of specialists to help shape their firm and it appears they had followed the right plan. . . .

The firm was incorporated in February of 1924 and first built a 22' Watercar. In the early years, few models were offered. Most were of the type having the engine mounted forward with cockpit seating in the aft. For 1926, Dodge announced four new models. They were as follows: The smaller hull was 22½' long and had a single cockpit aft with a special-built 20 h.p. Dodge Brothers engine for power. This small boat could also be ordered with a larger 50 h.p. engine that would boost its speed from 20 up to 37 m.p.h. If the buyer preferred a larger runabout, a longer 26½' double-cockpit model was also available. The very same engines were used in the 26½' boat as in the smaller one. Prices for the 1926 Dodge "Watercars", as they were called, ranged from $2,475 to $3,475 for the deluxe 26½' version.[22]

Horace Dodge and his brother John both died within months of each other. Horace's son Horace Dodge Jr. was running the then Detroit-based firm by 1925 and doing an outstanding job for such a young man. Horace Jr. spent much of his free time as a boy around the plant and learned the boat building business under the watchful eye of his dad Horace Sr. In 1925, the old plant was enlarged to 75,000 square feet located on two floors where the boats were built, stored and sold all under one roof.[23]

Young Horace Dodge, Jr. announced in late 1925 that his firm was then turning out five boats a day with additional output being planned. Before 1926, the Watercar came mainly in 22' lengths. The two runabouts we mentioned earlier by Dodge were both new and featured many design advances for that era. The early Dodge inboards were of the all-varnished variety with green copper bottoms and white water lines. Mr. George F. Crouch was appointed vice-president in charge of all design and production and his genius showed forth in the design of the famous Dodge racing craft that was to come some years later.[24]

Young & Hall, Inc. of 522 Fifth Avenue, New York City, N.Y. was appointed exclusive Dodge distributor for New York State, as well as part of Florida. Dodge was still quite a small firm back in the mid 1920's compared to Chris-Craft, Hacker, etc. However, though small, they adopted the assembly line method of construction but did not have a large dealer network as other builders of that period did. From 1926 on, Dodge Boats would mushroom into one of the largest speedboat builders in the world. For 1927, Watercars were built in three sizes. They were 22½', 26' and 30' long. The largest, a model 426, was a 30' custom-built model with only 25 being built for that model year. There are several photos shown here of 1926 and 1927 Dodge Watercars. You will note that each had its engine mounted forward with cockpits towards the stern. The two boats shown are almost identical with older inboards except the older boats tended to have less streamlined windshields than did the newer models.

1927 Dodge model 442 runabout

DODGE RUNABOUTS
Built of the very finest mahogany, technically designed, with a high record of performance to back them, all three Dodge Runabout models are offered at these outstanding prices.

$1595 $3265 $7800

HORACE E. DODGE BOAT WORKS, INC.
562 Lycaste Avenue   Detroit, Michigan

1928 Dodge magazine ad

1926 25' Dodge Watercar

1929 26' Dodge police boat, Detroit, Michigan

---
[22]"Horace E. Dodge Announces Two New Watercars", *MOTOR BOATING*, (Nov. '25), 98.
[23]"Watercars Improved", *MOTOR BOATING*, (Nov. '25), 140.
[24]*Ibid*.

By 1929 most Dodge speedboats looked like the more modern styles offered by most other builders of that era. The photo of the big 1929 26' three-cockpit runabout will pretty well sum it all up. That boat had its engine mounted amidships with seating fore as well as aft. Note the words, "DODGE WATERCAR" painted diagonally across the bow.

Before we move on to a review of the 1930 Dodge boats, I feel we should become acquainted with Horace E. Dodge, Jr. Mr. Dodge died on December 23, 1963 at the age of 63 because of heart failure. It seems Horace often made more news because of his private life rather than his boat building. . . . Dodge was married five times and divorced four. It is not the duty of this book to judge Horace, but only relate some events that helped to shape his rather colorful, but short life.

His 93-year-old mother, Mrs. Horace E. Dodge was very fond of her son and, sadly enough, did not reach his deathbed until it was too late. Mrs. Dodge accepted her son's fate and went ahead planning the funeral the way she thought he would like it done himself. Horace never really had to work for a living throughout his life. Horace Sr. had left a massive fortune to his widow who in turn provided a fine "allowance" for her son. The younger Dodge maintained several very elaborate homes both here and abroad. Friends estimated Dodge spent over $1,000,000 trying to become a famous speedboat racer like his business competitor, Gar Wood.[25] Some years Dodge had numerous boats entered in the major boat races, although in most cases he was never that successful. . . . Dodge named all his major racing boats after his only sister, Mrs. Delphine Dodge Cromwell Baker Goode, who died back in 1943 when she was living in New York City.[26] Thus we have seen a slight glimpse of the rather unusual life of Horace Dodge Jr; a life that would make him a famous man for various reasons. Now, let's move on to review the Dodge pleasure boats built between 1930 and 1935.

---

[25]"Death Last Headline on Horace Dodge", THE DETROIT NEWS, (Dec. 22, '63), 2.
[26]Ibid.

1929 21' Dodge Watercar under full power

1930 16' Dodge runabout

1930 was the first year we shall review. At that time, the Dodge fleet was smaller than it would be later on. A new and popular model for 1930 was a trim 16' split-cockpit runabout. The boat came equipped with a 40 h.p. Lycoming four-cylinder engine and reached speeds of 25 m.p.h. The boat was not a stripped-down model, but deluxe in every manner. Recently, a number of these small gems have surfaced here in Minnesota and I look forward to seeing them when they have been restored. Nearly all Dodge inboards had blue upholstery and all-varnished hulls and decks. Though a little underpowered, the little 16' model allowed hundreds of Americans to own a true inboard for under $1,000 complete.

Complete 1930 Dodge runabout fleet

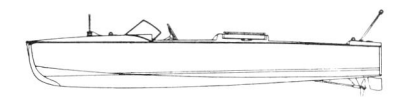

THE 16 FOOT RUNABOUT

Just like larger Dodge Runabouts in all-mahogany, double-bottom quality, the Dodge 16 foot Runabout, powered by Lycoming with a 4-cylinder, 40 h.p. motor, seating five, makes 25 miles an hour. Price. F. O. B. factory, fully equipped, $945.

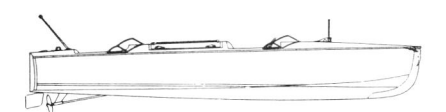

THE 21 FOOT RUNABOUT

A miracle of performance. Rides any water, and makes 35 miles an hour with its Lycoming straight eight, 115 h.p. motor. Seats six and sells for $2100, F. O. B. factory.

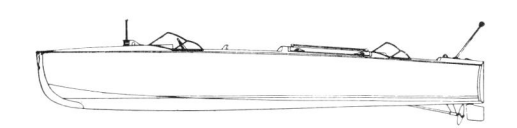

THE 25 FOOT RUNABOUT

There are three 25 foot models, all powered by Lycoming straight eight motors. Model 3, 125 h.p., speed 32 miles an hour, price $2500. Model 4, seats seven, 165 h.p., speed 38 miles an hour, price $3200. Model 10, seats seven, the Sedan, 165 h.p., 34 miles an hour, price, F. O. B. factory, $3900.

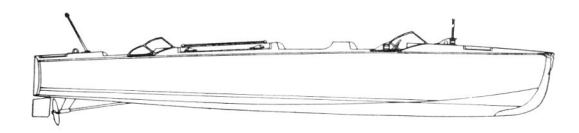

THE 28 FOOT RUNABOUT

Three 28 foot models offer a wide choice of speeds. All are powered by Lycoming. Model 5, seats ten, 165 h.p., straight 8, speed 32 miles an hour, $3700. Model 6, seats ten, 300 h.p. V-12, makes 45 miles an hour, $4500. Model 11, the deluxe sedan, 300 h.p. V-12 motor, speeds 38 miles an hour, $5300. All prices F.O.B. factory.

1930—21' 6" twin cockpit runabout with 115 h.p. Lycoming—$2,100 f.o.b. factory.

My favorite of all Dodge runabouts appeared in the line only in 1930 and 1931. The 21' 6" split-cockpit runabout was unique in many ways. Last summer I had the rare privilege of riding in the finely appointed runabout of Todd Warner. Upon looking over Todd's 21' you would think it is a three-cockpit model when really, it is just two. Both cockpits have their own folding glass windshields, which is "real class". Looking over that Dodge of Warner's, I am keenly aware of the fine workmanship that was always a part of the Dodge operation.

Todd Warner's Exquisite 1930 21' 6" Dodge

For example, the rear cockpit of the 21' runabout has plenty of leg room for passengers, as well as a well constructed wooden storage shelf running all the way across and under the rear deck ahead of the passenger seat. Also a very neat white rubber walkway is located down the center of the twin doors over the engine compartment for safe movement fore and aft. Large, white oval step pads with the name Dodge imprinted on them also were used on every Dodge speedboat. The most famous Dodge trademark has to be their famed "mermaid". This artistic nickel-steel creation first appeared in 1930 and was designed by the then-famous sculptor, Russell G. Crook.[27] Mr. Crook was active in both sculpture and ceramics near Boston, Massachusetts. The Dodge Boat Company expected to start a new trend with boat builders for years to come. It seems though, that the idea of nautical "hood ornaments" never really did catch on in this country. Today the "mermaid" is highly valued and anyone who is fortunate to possess one can be very proud. Elsewhere in this book is mentioned a firm that is making exact replicas of the mermaid cast from an original, in case you need one to complete a Dodge restoration.

[27] "Dodge Figureheads Set Fashion", *POWER BOATING*, (Jan. '30), 34.

Another all-new Dodge runabout for 1930 was the 25' three-cockpit model. This boat also came with twin folding windshields, the mermaid and numerous other pieces of standard equipment. Two models were offered in 1930: a model #3, a 125 h.p. Lycoming Straight eight as well as a model #4 with a 165 h.p. Lycoming. A model #10 with the same 165 h.p. engine and a sedan hardtop rounded out the line. Speeds were to 38 m.p.h. and prices ranged from $2,500 to $3,900 for the sedan versions.

Model #5 Dodge 28' triple cockpit runabout, Lycoming 165 h.p.—$3,700.

The ultimate of all 1930 Dodge speedboats was the big 28' model. This boat was built in three models in 1930 and came in the following ways: Model #5 had a Lycoming Straight eight 165 h.p. engine while the second version, model #6, sported the massive Lycoming 12-cylinder 300 h.p. engine which helped to speed the boat along at 45 m.p.h. The third and final model was #11, and the major difference in this boat over the two others was its custom hardtop sedan roof. All Dodge runabouts came with an outstanding list of standard items. Examples would be cigar lighters and Duesenberg-type steering wheels, to name a couple. Dodge used a very unique custom-made bow light, which was so made to act as a mooring cleat, as well as running light. Also, small engine air vents were styled like the line of a wave for

1930 30' Custom Dodge runabout with sedan roof

added sleekness and style. All Dodge boats were well built and equipped for ultimate boating pleasure regardless of their length, engine size, etc. It is such a pity that more of those fine boats were not saved from ultimate destruction in some back lot or burned for fire wood years ago. . . . Having ridden in a 21' 6" twin-cockpit Dodge, I can attest to their smooth ride and ease of handling. Many Dodge speedboats rode rather "bow high" compared to other runabouts but visibility was adequate once the boat planed out and got moving. The Lycoming engine put out a rather loud, spitting-type exhaust unlike any other I have ever heard. Perhaps being a descendent of aircraft engines caused that phenomonen? A final, less known Dodge for 1930 that few of us probably were aware of, was a big 45' cruiser that was custom-built and powered by two 300 h.p. Lycoming engines. The price tag on that model was $27,500 which was a very high price in those days. Only a handful of the big cruisers were ever built.

An air view of the Horace E. Dodge Boat and Plane Corporation plant at Newport News, Virginia

The boat storage shed has capacity to absorb weeks of production pending the demand for boats in the spring.

Ever popular 16' Dodge runabout with 45 h.p. Lycoming engine, 1931.

Let's now move on to 1931 and look over the Dodge "fleet" that proved to be a very interesting one at that. The biggest news in 1931 was the move of the complete Dodge Boat Company east to Newport News, Virginia where the firm built the world's largest motor boat plant of that era.[28]

Newport was chosen as the new plant location because of its convenience to railroads, highways and access to steamship routes. Complete test sites were located right off the end of the factory where every boat was water tested before delivery to dealers. The assembly line method of construction was used in the Dodge plant also. The most modern methods of building, finishing and storing completed boats were used.

Another interesting event staged by the Dodge Boat Company was a 50-mile race sweepstakes for Dodge 16' runabouts only. There is an interesting photo in this section which shows a "wave" of boats leaving the starting line.

The 1931 Dodge lineup began with the same 16' split-cockpit runabout which was unchanged from the 1930 one. The price of the 1931 16-footer crept up to $1,095 complete. The ol' reliable 21' 6" twin-cockpit runabout was equipped with a larger engine for 1931, a Straight eight 125 h.p. Lycoming. Some new standard equipment items were added to the boat also: 2 boat hooks, 4 cork fenders and twin cockpit covers, to name just a few. The 21' 6" hull was able to reach a higher speed of 35 m.p.h. in 1931 while the price rose to $2,295. The three-cockpit 25' runabout also was virtually the same as in 1930. Three versions were being offered. The first was model #3, selling for $2,595 powered by a 125 h.p. Straight eight Lycoming. Model #4 sold for $3,195 and had the Lycoming 165; and the final model, #10, was a sedan hardtop and sold for a hefty $3,895. There was one brand new Dodge runabout for 1931 and it was a 25½' three-cockpit version with deeper and wider specifications for larger bodies of water. Power for this new runabout was a Lycoming V-12 which developed 300 h.p. and featured 12-volt ignition and lighting systems. Top speed of the 25½' was 47 m.p.h. and her price tag reached $4,795 f.o.b. factory.[29] The "queen" of the 1931

1931, 50-mile Dodge Sweepstakes for 16' Dodge runabouts

---

[28]"The World's Largest Motor Boat Plant", *DODGE 1931 Catalog.* 2.

[29]"The Dodge Special 25½'", *DODGE 1931 Catalog.* 7.

27

Dodge boat showrooms, downtown New York City in 1931

Dodge fleet was the luxury 28' three-cockpit runabout with twin windshields. No major changes in this boat occurred since 1930. Three models, including two open runabouts as well as the sedan, were being offered for 1931. Prices ranged from $3,695 up to $5,795 for the sedan version.

1931 also found Dodge using photos of their spacious New York City showrooms in many of its magazine ads. The motif was Spanish and the sleek creations of the Dodge firm were shown in displays straight out of old Mexico.

1932 saw Dodge begin to offer new painted utility models selling at prices from $695 and up. By that time, the Depression was in full swing and Dodge was attempting to cope with conditions and still sell some boats. Below are listed all of the 1932 Dodge models. Utility boats will be listed first, followed by the mahogany runabouts.[30]

MODEL #	LENGTH	BEAM	SEATING CAPACITY	FINISH	ENGINE H.P.	SPEED
202 U*	19'	6' 2½"	8	White marine paint	Lycoming 45	18
203 U*	19'	6' 2½"	8	Philippine Mahogany	Lycoming 45	18
201 R*	16' 3"	5' 3"	5	African Mahogany	Lycoming 45	30
204 R*	19' 5"	6' 6½"	9	Philippine Mahogany	Lycoming 90	34
205 R*	19' 5"	6' 6½"	6	Philippine Mahogany	Lycoming 115	36
206 R*	23' 5"	6' 8"	9	Philippine Mahogany	Lycoming 90	32
207 R*	23' 5"	6' 8"	9	Philippine Mahogany	Lycoming 125	34
208 R*	25' 6"	6' 8"	9	Philippine Mahogany	Lycoming 165	37
208-S R*	25' 6"	6' 8"	8	African Mahogany	Lycoming 165	33
209 R*	25' 6"	6' 8"	9	African Mahogany	Lycoming 325	48
210 R*	28' 6"	7' 5"	11	African Mahogany	Lycoming 165	34
210-S R*	28' 6"	7' 5"	10	African Mahogany	Lycoming 165	32
211 R*	28' 6"	7' 5"	11	African Mahogany	Lycoming 325	46
211-S R*	28' 6"	7' 5"	10	African Mahogany	Lycoming 325	43

U*-utility   R*-runabout   S-sedan top

---

[30]"Detailed Specifications", *DODGE 1932 Catalog,* 10.

Dodge 1932 19' utility

Front cover of Dodge 1932 Catalog

Dodge 1932 poster announcing its new 16' utility

1932 saw Dodge Boats offer its first true lapstrake utility called the "all-purpose", a lower priced open model with painted or varnished hulls. Power was from a small 45 h.p. Lycoming which propelled the craft at just over 15 m.p.h. The boat was designed to attract possible buyers who, because of the Depression, could no longer afford buying the bigger, more expensive runabouts that Dodge had been most famous for. The first lapstrake model was a huge success, its price tag being only $650 complete. The next model year, 1933, would see a very big increase in numbers and types of utilities being offered by Dodge.

1932 19½' Dodge runabout

1932 16' Dodge runabout

1932 23½' Dodge runabout

1932 28' Dodge Sedan runabout

Main show room of Dodge Boat Company in New York City, 1933

Some revisions were made in the Dodge runabout lineup for 1932. The most notable change was an all-new 19½' three-cockpit runabout which had a 90 h.p. Lycoming but only a single windshield. The smaller 16' split-cockpit model was slightly modified equipment-wise and her price reduced from $1,095 to $840. The 21' 6" runabout was dropped and in its place a longer 23½' runabout was added. The new boat could seat three or more passengers and also had three larger engine options available. The big 28' open and sedan runabout remained unchanged in 1932, except the engine size rose to 325 h.p. in a new Lycoming V-12.

More views taken in the New York Dodge showroom also appeared in 1932 magazine ads. It appears the photo shows a large sedan and a small 16' runabout in the foreground. 1932 was a big year at Dodge; in fact, one of its very biggest ever. As we will see in 1933, Dodge again really expanded into the utility field in a very big way.

Below is another complete breakdown of all 1933 Dodge inboards for your review.[31]

MODEL #		LENGTH	BEAM	SEATING CAPACITY	FINISH	ENGINE H.P.	SPEED
301	U*	16'	5' 10"	7	White paint	Lycoming 45	25
202	U*	19'	6' 2½"	10	White paint	Lycoming 45	18
202-G	U*	19'	6' 2½"	10	White paint	Lycoming 66	24
202-GK	U*	19'	6' 2½"	9	White paint	Lycoming 66	22
201	R*	16' 3"	5' 3"	5	Natural finish	Lycoming 45	30
203	R*	19'	6' 2½"	10	Natural finish	Lycoming 45	18
204	R*	19'	6' 6½"	9	Natural finish	Lycoming 90	34
207	R*	25'	6' 3¼"	10	Natural finish	Lycoming 115	32
208	R*	25' 6"	6' 8"	8	Natural finish	Lycoming 165	37
208-S	R*	25' 6"	6' 8"	8	Natural finish	Lycoming 165	33
210	R*	28' 7"	7' 5"	11	Natural finish	Lycoming 165	34
210-S	R*	28' 7"	7' 5"	10	Natural finish	Lycoming 165	32
211	R*	28' 7"	7' 5"	11	Natural finish	Lycoming 325	46
211-S	R*	28' 7"	7' 5"	10	Natural finish	Lycoming 325	43

U*-utility R*-runabout S-sedan top

[31]"Detailed Specifications", *DODGE 1932 Catalog*, 12.

Dodge Boats added several more painted utility type inboards to its lineup in 1933. The smallest was the model #301, a 16' utility first offered in 1932 with a four-cylinder 45 h.p. engine. The 1932 model with a 19' hull was continued in 1933, with new engine options ranging from 45 through 66 h.p. each. The most deluxe 1933 utility was a 19' model with cabin-type roof. This largest of all three utilities sold for $1,095 complete.

1933 16' Dodge utility, 25 m.p.h., $545.

19' 1933 Dodge utility speeds to 18 m.p.h.

1933 Dodge 19' Sedan utility

The 1933 runabout lineup was as follows: The very popular 16' split-cockpit runabout was still in the line. Her power was the same old 45 Lycoming but her price dropped another $50 down to $795. The next runabout, the 19½' three-cockpit model was also the very same even right down to its price—$1385.00. The 25' and 25½' runabouts were also still in the line for 1933, but no longer could you order the 25½' with the large V-12 325 h.p. engine. The 25½' rig could be ordered open or with a sedan hardtop also. The 28' sedan also was unchanged from 1932. The largest of all Dodge speedboats sold for $3,695.00 to $6,895.00 complete. 1933 did see Dodge expand its selection of open, less expensive utility-type craft to cope with economic conditions while the mahogany runabouts remained exactly the same as in the past years.

1933 16' Dodge runabout

1933 19½' Dodge runabout

1933 25' Dodge runabout

1933 Dodge 25½' runabout

31

Dodge showroom in downtown New York City, 1933. Note model ships on display in glass cases.

1933 28' Dodge Sedan runabout

1934 saw a tremendous change in Dodge inboards. Three separate series of inboards appeared; two were open utility types and the other was the famous mahogany speedboat. Let's review the complete breakdown of the 1934 Dodge boats and then look more at specific models.[32]

I think you will agree with me, the 1934 Dodge model selection was the biggest in its long history. As we mentioned earlier, the acceptance of the new painted utility had been excellent in both 1932 and 1933, so more models were added for 1934. The biggest change was that standard as well as deluxe utilities were begun. The eight standard utilities ranged from a small 16' through two 25' models and all had white painted hulls and less deluxe appointments. Most of the smaller standard models did not have upholstered seats, while deluxe versions were varnished rather than painted and did have blue upholstery and very nicely styled windshields. 1934 also saw Dodge introduce the use of an all-new bottom called "the Dodge Multiple-Vee Double Bottom", which meant the following: each bottom plank laps over the next plank's edge and is fastened through three thicknesses of solid mahogany planking.[33] The sweep from stem to stern of the raised edges reduces side spray and insures dry riding under all conditions. If you will remember from *Volume I*, Century used a similar bottom style.

Of the 35 models offered by Dodge in 1934, 25 were open painted or varnished utility-type craft. It seems the Dodge utility had met with enthusiasm worldwide as the

---

[32]"Detailed Specifications", *DODGE 1934 Catalog*, 7.

[33]"Dodge Presents 35 Models for 1934", *DODGE 1934 Catalog*, 2.

MODEL #	LENGTH	BEAM	SEATING CAPACITY	FINISH	ENGINE H.P.	SPEED
301 U*	16'	5' 10"	7	White paint	Lycoming 45	25
202 U*	19'	6' 2½"	10	White paint	Lycoming 45	18
202-A U*	19'	6' 2½"	10	White paint	Gray 62	25
401 U*	20'	6' 6"	10	White paint	Lycoming 45	22
401-A U*	20'	6' 6"	10	White paint	Gray 62	25
401-B U*	20'	6' 6"	10	White paint	Gray 93	28
501 U*	25' 4"	7' 2"	15	White paint	Lycoming 115	28
501-A U*	25' 4"	7' 2"	15	White paint	Lycoming 165	32
302 U*	16'	5' 10"	7	Natural finish	Lycoming 45	29
402 U*	20'	6' 6"	10	Natural finish	Lycoming 45	24
402-A U*	20'	6' 6"	10	Natural finish	Gray 62	28
402-B U*	20'	6' 6"	10	Natural finish	Gray 93	32
502 U*	25' 4"	7' 2"	15	Natural finish	Lycoming 115	32
502-A U*	25' 4"	7' 2"	15	Natural finish	Lycoming 165	35
201 R*	16' 3"	5' 3"	5	Natural finish	Lycoming 45	30
204 R*	19' 5"	6' 6½"	9	Natural finish	Gray 93	34
207 R*	25' 0"	6' 4"	10	Natural finish	Lycoming 115	32
208 R*	25' 6"	6' 8"	10	Natural finish	Lycoming 165	35
208-S R*	25' 6"	6' 8"	8	Natural finish	Lycoming 165	33
210 R*	28' 7"	7' 5"	11	Natural finish	Lycoming 165	34
210-S R*	28' 7"	7' 5"	10	Natural finish	Lycoming 165	32
211 R*	28' 7"	7' 5"	11	Natural finish	Lycoming 325	47
211-S R*	28' 7"	7' 5"	10	Natural finish	Lycoming 325	45

U*-utility S-sedan R*-runabout

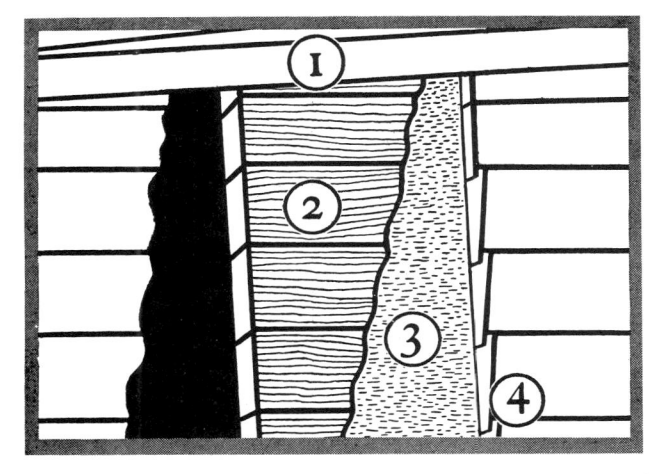

Cut-away view of Dodge Boat Hull showing: (1) Stout oak keel supporting oak frame timbers. (2) Inner butt-joint mahogany planking. (3) Cloth skin firmly fastened with waterproof glue to inside planking and to (4) wedge-shaped solid mahogany planking of the sensational new lap strake Multiple-Vee* Bottom.

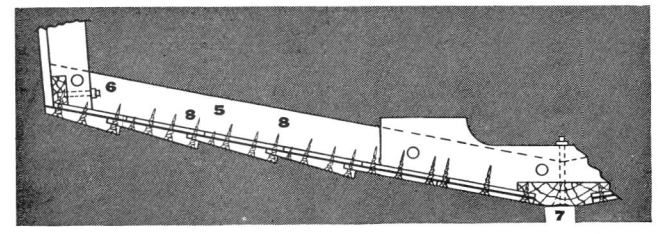

Cross-section of bottom planking, showing: (5) Stout frame timber of solid oak. (6) Bronze Bolt fastening frame and rib to chine. (7) Bronze bolt fastening keel to oak frame. (8) Brass screws, driven through outer hull lap joint, cloth skin, inner hull — butt jointed — and into oak frame. Note that screws pass through three thicknesses of outer planking.

Dodge multiple-Vee bottom, 1931

boats were not just being sold in the United States. My own personal favorite of the 1934 Dodge utilities was the 20' special model. She had an all-varnished hull and deck with a very nice two-piece windshield, complete upholstery and the deluxe hardware package. The largest engine in that boat was a 93 h.p. six-cylinder Gray Marine. Not all the utility craft were designed for high-speed running or racing but rather for fishing, cruising, picnics, and surfboarding.

The 1934 runabout lineup was exactly the same as in 1933. Sizes were from 16' through the big 28' sedan with the V-12 325 h.p. Lycoming. 1935 would see a general reduction in models offered by Dodge, as well as two entirely new types of boats. Twenty-two models were offered by Dodge in 1935. Changes did occur in all sections so, for your convenience, all the 1935 models are listed below.[34]

---
[34]"Detailed Specifications", *DODGE 1935 Catalog*, 2.

MODEL #	LENGTH	BEAM	SEATING CAPACITY	FINISH	ENGINE	H.P.	SPEED
101 U*	16'	5' 8½"	5	Natural finish	Dodge	35	25
301 U*	16'	5' 10"	7	White paint	Lycoming	45	25
401 U*	20'	6' 6"	10	White paint	Lycoming	45	22
401-A U*	20'	6' 6"	10	White paint	Gray	62	25
401-B U*	20'	6' 6"	10	White paint	Gray	97	28
302 U*	16'	5' 10"	7	Natural finish	Lycoming	45	29
402 U*	20'	6' 6"	10	Natural finish	Lycoming	45	24
402-A U*	20'	6' 6"	10	Natural finish	Gray	62	28
402-B U*	20'	6' 6"	10	Natural finish	Gray	97	32
102 R*	17'	6' 1½"	6	Natural finish	Gray	80	35
102-A R*	17'	6' 1½"	6	Natural finish	Gray	115	40
103 R*	17'	5' 10"	6	Natural finish	Gray	60	32
104 R*	19' 5"	6' 6"	6	Natural finish	Gray	97	36
208 R*	25' 6"	6' 8"	10	Natural finish	Lycoming	165	35
208-S R*	25' 6"	6' 8"	8	Natural finish	Lycoming	165	33
210 R*	28' 6"	7' 5"	11	Natural finish	Lycoming	165	34
210-S R*	28' 6"	7' 5"	10	Natural finish	Lycoming	165	32
211 R*	28' 6"	7' 5"	11	Natural finish	Lycoming	325	47
211-S R*	28' 6"	7' 5"	10	Natural finish	Lycoming	325	45
50 C*	26'	8' 5"		White hull, natural finish Cabin & deck trim	Gray	80	18
51 C*	26'	8' 5"		White hull, natural finish Cabin & deck trim	Gray	60	14
25 S.B.*	18'	7'		Sail area 165 sq. feet			

U*-utility   R*-runabout   S-sedan   C*-cabin cruiser   S.B.*-sail boat

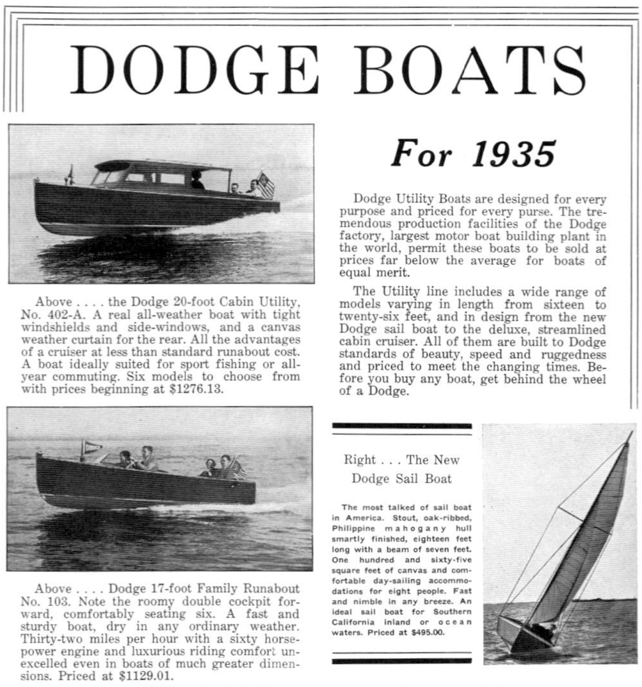

DODGE BOATS
For 1935

Dodge Utility Boats are designed for every purpose and priced for every purse. The tremendous production facilities of the Dodge factory, largest motor boat building plant in the world, permit these boats to be sold at prices far below the average for boats of equal merit.

The Utility line includes a wide range of models varying in length from sixteen to twenty-six feet, and in design from the new Dodge sail boat to the deluxe, streamlined cabin cruiser. All of them are built to Dodge standards of beauty, speed and ruggedness and priced to meet the changing times. Before you buy any boat, get behind the wheel of a Dodge.

Above.... the Dodge 20-foot Cabin Utility, No. 402-A. A real all-weather boat with tight windshields and side-windows, and a canvas weather curtain for the rear. All the advantages of a cruiser at less than standard runabout cost. A boat ideally suited for sport fishing or all-year commuting. Six models to choose from with prices beginning at $1276.13.

Above.... Dodge 17-foot Family Runabout No. 103. Note the roomy double cockpit forward, comfortably seating six. A fast and sturdy boat, dry in any ordinary weather. Thirty-two miles per hour with a sixty horsepower engine and luxurious riding comfort unexcelled even in boats of much greater dimensions. Priced at $1129.01.

Right ... The New Dodge Sail Boat

The most talked of sail boat in America. Stout, oak-ribbed, Philippine mahogany hull smartly finished, eighteen feet long with a beam of seven feet. One hundred and sixty-five square feet of canvas and comfortable day-sailing accommodations for eight people. Fast and nimble in any breeze. An ideal sail boat for Southern California inland or ocean waters. Priced at $495.00.

All Prices F. O. B. Newport Beach, Including Cover and Tax

1935 Dodge magazine ad

New 1935 Dodge 17' runabout on display at New York Boat Show.

One of the new 1935 Dodge boats was a sailboat, the first ever offered by the firm. A rather sleek 26' inboard cabin cruiser also appeared. The sailboat was a Sea Gull knock-about class and was very popular along the Eastern Seaboard in the early 1930's. The hull was of all-mahogany with varnished sides and decks covered with canvas. The owner was allowed to choose from a variety of colors for the deck.

The 26' cabin cruiser was very well designed and equipped. There were comfortable "V" bunks for two, as well as cook stove, head, ice box and plenty of storage space. A painted lapstrake hull was used on the cruiser which seemed to work very well in rough water conditions. To show you exactly how well the Dodge cruiser came equipped, I am listing its full accompaniment of standard equipment at this time (from the '35 catalog).

40-pound anchor	Galley sink
150' of line	Fresh water tank (20 gal)
Anchor locker	Ice box (25 lbs.)
Auto. drag link steering	Linoleum floors
Bell	Mirror
Bilge vents (2)	Rack (for dishes, silverware)
Boat hook	Spring berths
Cabin dome light	Running lights
Deck house dome light	Stove
Electric signal horn	Soap dish
Fire extinguisher	Safety starter control on engine
Flagpole and burgee	Self bailing cockpit
Flagpole and ensign	Side curtains in deck house
Fog horn	Toilet
Hand rails (silver-nickel)	Tie lines (2-25')
	Towel rack

You will agree that this boat came with about everything an owner might ever need.

The only real change in the utility fleet for 1935 was a new 16' fishing boat, varnished but no windshield or upholstery; the special-built Dodge 35 h.p. engine was standard.

1935 saw quite a shakeup in Dodge mahogany speedboats. The old reliable 16' split-cockpit disappeared and was replaced by two new 17' models. The first was model 103, a twin-cockpit-forward model with a 60 h.p. engine. The sleeker, faster model 102-A was a 17' split-cockpit rig which could be ordered with a 225 cubic inch 115 h.p. engine for speeds of 40 m.p.h. on the measured mile. That split-cockpit version was well-accepted, as by 1935 people were again beginning to purchase larger, more deluxe speedboats and the era of the $1,000 or less mahogany inboard was gone forever. The other new boat for 1935 was a very nice 19½' twin-cockpit-forward runabout. It appeared to have a long, sloping rear deck and a very nice "V" windshield with glass side panels for added protection. The 19½' model won a number of local and regional races in its class in 1935. The other runabouts—the 25½', 28' open, and 28' sedan—were virtually the same as in the past. So 1935 saw probably the greatest amount of change in Dodge runabouts in the last six years. Dodge, unlike other speedboat builders, tended to keep their line pretty much unchanged from year to year. New models would appear every so often,

Complete 1935 Dodge runabout fleet

DODGE 17 FT. MODEL 103
Family Runabout, double cockpit forward. 32 m.p.h.
Price $945.

DODGE 17 FT. RACING MODELS
Speedster models, with 225 cu. in. racing type engine.
Speeds 35 and 40 m.p.h. Prices, $1195 and $1395.

DODGE 19½ FT. RUNABOUT
New type double-cockpit forward runabout, engine installed under after deck. 35 m.p.h. Price $1495.

DODGE 25½ FT. RUNABOUT
Carries eight, straight-eight 165 h.p. engine, 35 m.p.h.
Price $3395.

DODGE 28 FT. RUNABOUT
32 m.p.h. with 165 h.p. engine, 45 m.p.h. with 325 h.p., V-12 engine. $3845 and $5795.

16 FT. FISHERMAN'S BOAT
Natural Philippine mahogany, special Fisherman's throttle for speeds of 1 to 24 m. p. h. Price $565.

16 FT. UTILITY RUNABOUT
Natural Philippine mahogany hull. With white painted hull, less windshield and upholstery, at slightly lower prices. Speed 26 m. p. h. Price $795

20 FT. UTILITY RUNABOUTS
Natural Philippine mahogany hull. With white painted hull, less windshield and upholstery, at slightly lower prices. Two power plants, speeds 18 & 28 m. p. h. Factory built cabin enclosure as illustrated $200 extra. Prices $975 to $1125.

17 FT. FAMILY RUNABOUT
Double cockpit forward model. Natural Philippine mahogany, speed 29 m. p. h. Price $945.

17 FT. RUNABOUT
Two power plants, including 225 cu. in. racing type engine. Natural Philippine mahogany. Speeds 35 and 40 m.p.h. Price, $1195 & $1395.

19½ FT. RUNABOUT
Double cockpit forward model, natural Philippine mahogany. Speed, 33 m. p. h. Price, $1495.

25½ FT. RUNABOUT
Natural finish African mahogany, straight eight engine, speed 34 m. p. h. Price $3395. With custom built Sedan enclosure, $4195.

28 FT. RUNABOUT
Shown with custom built Sedan enclosure, the 28 ft. model in African mahogany is offered with choice of two power plants, speeds 32 to 45 m. p. h. Prices range from $3845 to $6895.

1936 Dodge speed boats

Deluxe 1936 Dodge 25½' runabout

Model 104 Dodge 19½' runabout

but it was not common practice. For some yet unexplained reason, little was ever heard about Dodge boats after 1935. I found one lone magazine ad for Dodge in 1936 and it showed the exact same lineup as 1935.

I understand the Boat Works were closed down in the late 1930's, but 1941 saw Horace open them up once more for work on national defense contracts. As far as I know, no pleasure boats were ever built again after World War II ended. It is a true shame that a firm which built boats as well finished, etc., as Dodge, did not stay in business longer than the approximate 25 years they did operate.

As I said, Dodge boats are beginning to appear a little more frequently each year. I believe myself that there are probably still quite a few around, but it is a real problem to find old parts, hardware, etc., as the firm has been out of business so long and few original Dodge dealers are still in business.

Now let's move on to another firm, Ventnor Boat Company of Atlantic City, New Jersey. Having built boats from the very early 1900's, Ventnor did much to change power boats and later on, following the end of World War II, had great influence on the development of inboard runabouts for pleasure as we know them now.

VENTNOR—FINE RACING AND PLEASURE BOATS SINCE 1902

The name Ventnor Boats to some readers will mean little or nothing. If this is the case for you, I think you shall find the material on this builder of great interest. My first "encounter" with a Ventnor inboard happened when I was about 8 or 9 years old. I remember showing my dad a 1948 Ventnor ad which appeared in "Holiday" magazine. Wow! Did that boat look like a spaceship—complete with rear tail fin and the works! I guess America was not quite ready for such boats but those remaining today still draw "ohs" and "ahs" all the time. In fact, later in this section we shall review several Ventnor "masterpieces" which are among the rarest speedboats still in existence. As was the case with many of the other firms we have reviewed, Ventnor went the way of the "Iron Horse" and completely disappeared years ago. I would like to thank several people for providing me material on the Ventnor "dream boats". More about these men and their boats later on. . . .

Surprisingly, Ventnor Boat Company goes back a long way. The firm was founded in 1902 in Ventnor, New Jersey, thus the reason for the company's name.[35] A Mr. Adolph Apel was the proud founder of the business and during those early years was a pioneer in the design and building of the new-fangled gasoline-powered boats. It seems Apel and his firm soon gained the reputation for building fast racing craft. His boats were raced nationwide and their speeds set all types of speed records year in and year out.

Ventnor Boat Company actually covered two distinct eras. First of all, from 1902 up through 1942, the vast majority of production was inboard racing boats. Following World War II the firm switched almost totally to pleasure craft rather than racing boats.

We shall now look at the early Ventnor offerings, when "speed" was their main goal. I have located the 1935 specifications for Ventnor boats which will show you, the reader, exactly what the firm built. You will note that all three boats are strictly racing craft.[36]

MODEL	TYPE	LENGTH	ENGINE	SPEED
90	Racing hydro.	13'	Special	50 m.p.h.
135	Cubic inch class	16'	Gray-90	50 m.p.h.
225	Cubic inch class	16'	Special -150	60 m.p.h.

[35] "Ventnor—Speed Merchants", *MOTOR BOATING*, (Oct. '47), 99.
[36] "1935 Specifications", *POWER BOATING*, (June '35), 33.

1934 Ventnor 125 cubic inch champion

A typical Ventnor "speedster" shown here is the 1934 125 cubic inch champion of its day, "The Emancipator III". During trials at the national class championships in late August, 1934 she sped along at almost 51 m.p.h.—no small feat for a 16' craft powered by a 90 h.p. engine.[37] In reviewing this 1934 Ventnor, we first become aware that the driver and mechanic rode behind the engine as in the pleasure craft built by other builders back in the early 1920's through about 1930 or so. Ventnor pretty much styled all their racing craft along similar lines. Speed was the name of the game and everything humanly possible was done to streamline all hulls for optimum performance. I suppose that little 16' racing craft looks quite boxy and very unstreamlined by our standards, but back in 1934 few, if any, other builders offered anything as sleek in comparison.

A second newsworthy Ventnor racing craft we shall look at made news in the year 1936. This boat, a 19' 6" 225 cubic inch racing craft, was powered by a six-cylinder Lycoming engine. In looking at this unusual boat you will note the great amount of streamlining present in her design. From the side, she resembles a tri-hull or modern "V" hull speedboat. She also used a new-fangled "outboard stern drive".[38] "Why," you ask, "was the stern drive used on this craft?" Well, Adolph Apel felt the new unit would allow lower center of gravity and higher speeds.

He was correct on both accounts. However, no reports were given as to the boat's top speed. Later that year, Ventnor officials announced that particular boat hit a high of just over 65 m.p.h. A 12" by 18" racing prop turning at 5,300 r.p.m.'s did the trick.

[37]"Auerbach Retains Class Title", POWER BOATING, (Sept. '34), 42.
[38]"New 225 Class Racer Shows High Speed", POWER BOATING, (March '36), 63.

Numerous racing craft were built at Ventnor Boat Company in the early years. A partial list of the boats will suffice to show you these people knew how to build fast boats! Boats like Miss Peps V, Tempo VI, My Sin, So Long, Lady Glen IV, Hi-Ho II, Eagle, Senorita, plus others were just some boats built in the 1930's. Just prior

Sleek 2-seat Ventnor, 135 cubic inch, race boat

Revolutionary Ventnor hydroplane—1936

Sleek 1937 Ventnor racer

Another Ventnor speedster—1937 style!

Note sponsons on sides of Ventnor record-setting hydroplane

to World War II, Ventnor ran a series of colorful magazine ads featuring famous Ventnor racing boats of the times. As it said in the ads, "History in the Making", is what all these boats had in common. Even though some years passed since the early Ventnor racing crafts were built, basic hull styles were pretty much the same. I guess the biggest difference would be that all were true hydroplane hulls now, with sponsons on each side for added stability. New classes were being added as interest in racing grew nationwide. Here in the Midwest, inboard boat races were big sport in the 1930's and 1940's. At one time, we even had inboard speedboat races here on my hometown lake, but that was before my time. My favorite of the racers shown was the little Class B service runabout, Eagle. Her top speed was just under 33 m.p.h. but she sported a small cockpit ahead of the driver and mechanic for a passenger or two. I'll bet it was a thrill to sit in that little speedster and feel the wind in your face as you sped around the race course! In those years, Ventnor did, on occasion, turn out a custom pleasure boat or two but they were quite rare. Even their pleasure boats looked much like their racing craft. By 1939, 225 class speed records were up to over 65 m.p.h.

The successor to Emancipator III. Note the style changes. . . .

39

Unique Pre-World War II Ventnor ads
1939

History in the Making!

August 24, 1940:—Approaching the close of the first year of World War II, Hitler tries to blast England out of the war with the first 1,000-plane raids in history. At Red Bank, N.J., on this day a Ventnor-built boat, Eagle, blasted the existing 5-mile world record for Class B Service Runabouts with a new mark of 32.490 m.p.h. This is another of many unbroken records that have made Ventnor the world's most renowned racing boat.

VENTNOR HOLDS MORE WORLD'S RECORDS THAN ANY OTHER BOAT

Building Today for Victory in War—Tomorrow for Victory on the Race Course
It's not too early for discussion of plans for your new racing boat.

VENTNOR BOAT WORKS, Inc.
VENTNOR, ATLANTIC CITY, N.J.

PIONEER BUILDERS AND DESIGNERS OF WORLD-RECORD-HOLDING RACE BOATS

History in the Making!

September 29, 1940: The big news story of the day is the Jap's boast that they together with Germany and Italy "are ready to display the power of their military alliance." In the sports world the big event of the day is the new world's mile-trial record of 58.395 m.p.h. for class E Racing Runabouts made by the Ventnor-built Hi-Ho II at Havre de Grace, Md., with its owner George Ward, Jr., at the controls.

VENTNOR HOLDS MORE WORLD'S RECORDS THAN ANY OTHER BOAT

Building Today for Victory in War—Tomorrow for Victory on the Race Course
It's not too early for discussion of plans for your new racing boat.

VENTNOR BOAT WORKS, Inc.
VENTNOR, ATLANTIC CITY, N.J.

PIONEER BUILDERS AND DESIGNERS OF WORLD-RECORD-HOLDING RACE BOATS

More Ventnor ads!

VENTNOR

Custom Built

RACE BOATS

*Holds World Record in 225 Class of 75.52 M.P.H.
Owned and driven by Jack Cooper*

Following another year of unusual success "Ventnor" announces their new 1939 models into which have been incorporated further improvements in speed and seaworthiness.... A new 91 cu. in. model that will attain 50 M.P.H.; a new 135 cu. in. model that will attain 60 M.P.H.; and an improved 225 cu. in. model that will attain 75 M.P.H. Also, racing runabouts that will attain 55 to 65 M.P.H., 17 ft. and 22 ft. lengths. These runabouts are particularly designed and built not only for racing but to serve as yacht tenders and for pleasure riding at thrilling speeds.

If you have the urge to race and win with a "Ventnor," then write or wire us today for all detailed information.

VENTNOR BOAT WORKS, Inc.
New Ventnor, Atlantic City, N. J.
Canadian Associates: Minett-Shields, Ltd., Bracebridge, Ontario
PIONEER BUILDERS AND DESIGNERS OF WORLD-RECORD-HOLDING RACE BOATS

1939 magazine ad

and that was with the standard inboard drive, not the experimental inboard-outboard we viewed earlier. Another event in history was going to alter the history of Ventnor Boat Works when in 1941, the United States entered World War II.

Late 1930's—Ventnor racing runabout

Ventnor, like all other boat builders in the 1940's, discontinued racing craft and switched over to strictly military work. In order to produce larger numbers of war craft, Ventnor moved their entire operation to Atlantic City, New Jersey where they had complete testing, as well as manufacturing facilities second to none. From racing boats to war ships was a big switch, but Ventnor employees were up to the challenge and soon began turning out the following types of vessels: A large number of 83-foot and 104-foot aircraft rescue craft for the Army, as well as 110-foot sub-chasers for the Navy rolled off the waves at Atlantic City. Because of their excellent work throughout the war years, Ventnor received the Army-Navy "E" award in late 1946.

The war taught Ventnor much about building quality boats in fewer hours. Mr. Apel and his staff had big plans for the future using these principles in their operation. Apel began to surround himself with new faces, and he and his main management wanted to change the image of Ventnor from a race craft builder to a pleasure boat manufacturer. Quite a few headlines and stories began to appear in late 1946 about Mr. Apel and his Ventnor Boat Works.

The first new official added at Ventnor in 1947 was Jack Schrefer. Jack was appointed manager-superintendent in charge of all production activities. In the past years Schrefer worked for such firms as Consolidated Shipbuilding, Elco Boat Company, and most recently with the defunct Dee Wite Boat Company.[39] Only one model was introduced for 1947. That single boat was a rather "plain-Jane" type 18-foot deluxe utility runabout.

1947—view of new Ventnor plant, Atlantic City, New Jersey.

1947 18' Ventnor Deluxe utility

**18 Foot
DELUXE UTILITY RUNABOUT**
High speed V Bottom is just one of the great features found in this model. Superb fittings designed to give the utmost in extra speed. New type engine box for increased comfort and capacity.
Immediate delivery on this beauty.

1947 Ventnor 18' utility

---

[39]"Ventnor Appointment", *MOTOR BOAT*, (Nov. '47), 63.

42

Ventnor runabouts on display in Milwaukee, Wisconsin showroom—1947

Sales were such that orders were coming in faster than boats could be delivered. The new model sped along at 44 m.p.h. and many new Ventnor dealers were being appointed by Mr. Apel nationwide. 1947 was a good year at Ventnor and 1948 loomed high on the horizon with the firm planning to market its first complete line of inboards in its long history.[40]

1948 was to dawn a very special year at Ventnor Boat Works. 1948 marked the first full year of pleasure boat building by this innovative concern. Another new face at Ventnor in 1948 was that of Comdr. Walter Leveau, new general manager, formerly chief designer for the Horace E. Dodge Boat & Plane Corporation of Newport News, Virginia.[41] Both Mr. Leveau and Mr. Apel planned to pull out all the stops when they introduced their new 1948 models to an anxious, buying public. All new 1948 Ventnor boats were water-tested on the ocean close by the factory. Let's first take a look at the complete list of all 1948 Ventnor boats and then review certain models in more detail.[42]

MODEL	LENGTH	TYPE		
Inboard	16'	Utility	Plywood	
Inboard	16'	Utility	Planked	
Inboard	18'	Deluxe utility	Planked	
Inboard	20' 6"	Deluxe runabout	Planked	
Inboard	22' 9"	Custom runabout	Planked	Two Gray Marine engines

1948 15' 6" Ventnor utility

Rough and Ready!

...favored by sportsmen!

When the big ones are biting... when hunting is good .. the new HUNTSMAN by Ventnor is a boat you can depend upon to take you there .. and bring you back! Light, sturdy, fast and backed by Ventnor's fame for speed and performance.

$1295
Length - 15'6"
Draft - 17"
Beam - 5'6"
Seats 5 - 7 Persons
up to 25 M. P. H.
with 25 H. P. Motor

SINCE 1902 **VENTNOR**

Builders of Champion Craft
VENTNOR BOAT CORPORATION
WEST ATLANTIC CITY, NEW JERSEY

I realize the listing is not that well illustrated, but hopefully the following information on the 1948 models should help. . . .

Ventnor showed one of each of the above models at the 1948 New York National Boat Show and the crowds really liked what they saw. Boating magazines gave glowing accounts of the boats, some of which I will share with you now. The smallest and most simple of all Ventnor inboards on display was the 15½' plywood utility. She was a simple open craft, no frills, not even cushions or a windshield. Aimed at the fisherman and hunters, her main duty was dependable transportation to and from the hunt or ol' fishing hole. She only sported a small 25 h.p. engine and list price in 1948 for that model was $1,295.00 complete. Ventnor, along with Higgins, were some early boat-builders using plywood, a by-product of the war years.

If you preferred your new Ventnor a little more deluxe, the 16' deluxe utility was your "cup of tea". This boat was much more deluxe in its appointments, etc. She came equipped with upholstered seats, varnished decks and transom, white hull sides or pale blue on special

---

[40]"Ventnor Beats Market on Delivery", *MOTOR BOAT*, (Jan. '47), 68.

[41]"Ventnor—Speed Merchants", *MOTOR BOATING*, (Oct. '47), 100.

[42]"New Boats", *MOTOR BOAT*, (Jan. '48), 66.

1948 16' Ventnor Deluxe utility

order. Engine options ranged from 75 through 150 h.p. This 16' utility compared favorably with Chris-Craft, Century, etc., of the same era. An even more deluxe utility offered by Ventnor was an 18' deluxe model. This boat was finished completely natural, boasting five coats of hand-rubbed spar varnish. Under the rear deck of the 18' model one would find a nifty built-in fish compartment or a small ice box. If you ordered this boat with a hardtop, it came equipped with an all-new Formica-plastic ceiling. This allowed for easier cleaning and was claimed to be fireproof.

Probably the most famous portion of the 1948 Ventnor fleet had to be the runabouts. Not contented to copy other builders of that time, Apel and his staff embarked on an ambitious program and stunned the boating fraternity with three highly-styled true runabouts in 1948. If you have ever heard of Ventnor boats, you are probably most familiar with the runabouts that sported those wild dorsal fins. Evidently most Ventnor runabouts built in 1948 were of the painted variety. I have seen four to date in various stages of repair and all had the varnished decks, white hull sides and white rear fins. Two photos of

1948 20' Ventnor finned runabout

a 20' Ventnor are shown here. This boat has been totally restored and is in grand shape. I do not believe the twin windshields were standard equipment, but they do add to the look, don't you agree? The stern of the boat is square across the back while the rear deck comes to a point which allows for a very streamlined effect. I call it the "bumble-bee" design transom. Six people could ride fairly comfortably in the 18' runabout. The 18' runabout was called the "Sport Speedster" and came with a 160 h.p. Gray Fire-ball engine.[43]

Ventnor runabout still to be restored

Side view of twin windshield on restored Ventnor

Since I have been researching Ventnor, I have come in contact with several folks who own Ventnor runabouts and each boat is different. You will note the various photos of the all-varnished Ventnor shown at anchor, as well as under power. Well, its owner, Bob Langell of Michigan has been unable to find any serial number or identification tag on his boat. The story of the redoing of this boat is a very notable one. The "dorsal fin" on this boat does not resemble any I have ever seen, but the

---

[43]"New Ventnors", *MOTOR BOAT*, (Nov. '47), 57.

Completely restored 1948 Ventnor runabout

Rare Ventnor without fin

Bob Langell's completely restored Ventnor

Beautiful all-restored Ventnor runabout—1977 view

Rear view of beautiful Ventnor

Overall view of restored Ventnor runabout

The finished product!

1948 Ventnor magazine ad

1948

VENTNOR '23' DELUXE RUNABOUT

Here's 23 feet of streamlined beauty for those who insist on the best in a modern Sport Runabout. VENTNOR offers the ultimate in speed, appearance and comfort in this new model which seats 8. Two power plants with speeds in excess of 50 MPH. Write for descriptive folder.

SINCE 1902 **Ventnor**

VENTNOR BOAT CORPORATION
West Atlantic City, N. J.

VENTNOR 1948 FLEET – 15½ ft. Economy Utility ★ 18 ft. Deluxe Runabout ★ 20 ft. Deluxe Runabout
16 ft. Deluxe Utility ★ 18 ft. Runabout ★ 23 ft. Deluxe Runabout ★ 23 ft. Cruiser

owner swears it's still original. His color scheme is a great one, with red upholstery and a red bottom with white boot top.

The ultimate Ventnor in 1948 had to be the big 23' deluxe runabout. She is a true three-point suspension hydroplane and had just one purpose—SPEED. I have only seen one of these boats and that was some ten years ago. All I can say is, wherever that boat stopped, a crowd was soon to gather. . . . She also was an all-varnished model with two-toned mahogany decks, dorsal fins and lots of other "goodies". Standard power was twin 150 h.p. Gray Fire-ball engines. Top speed was conservatively set at 55 m.p.h. Some other Ventnor features in 1948 included non-trip chines for safer, faster cornering. All battery boxes were lead-lined and special reinforced frames were installed under all engines. Little things like these added up to true quality in Ventnor boats.[44] As an interesting sidelight, I have discovered just recently that the 20' Ventnor could be ordered with a Tucker auto engine as an option. I believe it was about 180 h.p. or so. I wonder how many of these were ever sold?

One other man who played a big role in the affairs at Ventnor in 1948 was Frank J. Reyers, Jr. He was the new general sales manager and before World War II, operated a large boat dealership in Louisiana. He had experience in retail selling, as well as dealer setup, purchasing, building and service. Reyers vowed that "service" would be his main duty to dealers as well as customers.[45] New dealers were being added to the Ventnor family all over the country. In fact, Reyers wanted to triple the number of Ventnor dealers from what there were before World War II. With such a large number of new key employees and fresh hull styles, one wonders how Ventnor was to fare in the years ahead. . . . We shall study their rise and fall in the concluding portion of this section.

It seems that although the Ventnor streamlined inboards were well accepted at the boat shows and by the magazines, buyers were hesitant to purchase a boat so unusual compared to other builders' offerings. The old adage applied once more—everyone loved the Ventnor, but no one bought it. . . . It seems today, in 1978, that Adolph Apel's firm was years ahead of itself when it offered these dorsal finned runabouts to the public back in '48. Chris-Craft introduced its dorsal finned Chris-Craft "Cobra" some 17 years later, which also drew "ohs" and "ahs", but never was a big selling boat. Consequently, it was dropped from the line in just one short season. Other reasons given for the low interest in the Ventnor fin-equipped runabouts were the following: One dealer who sold Ventnor boats back in those days said, "the 18' and 20' runabouts were poor performers". Both boats appeared to be underpowered and did not plane properly. They seemed to "mush" along, with bows pointed toward the sky. Another former owner told me that the Ventnor boats tended to have a leakage problem and they never seemed to really seal up after a proper soaking. These problems helped spell the eventual demise of Ventnor. Their gamble with the far-out 1948 designs failed and new boat buyers seemed at that time to prefer the more conservative speedboats offered by Chris-Craft, Hacker, etc.

1949 18' deluxe Ventnor utility

1950 19' Ventnor runabout

The rest of the 1940's and the very early 1950's found Ventnor building various types of the inboard speedboat.

The "fins" eventually disappeared altogether and Ventnor built more conventional types of speedboats. The mid-1950's showed Ventnor building numerous twin-cockpit-forward models. I have seen two examples—one was an 18' Ventnor, all-varnished hull with very streamlined rear deck powered with a 200 h.p. V-8 Chrysler engine. The other was a 1955 19' twin-cockpit runabout with a fancy two-tone red and white hull and varnished deck. This boat also had the very slanted rear deck, similar to the earlier racing craft Ventnor built back in the 1930's.

From that time on, the name Ventnor seemed to more or less disappear. By 1960 the firm no longer was in operation as such, and had switched to a new location—Egg

---
[44] "Ventnor Facts", *MOTOR BOAT*, (Jan. '48), 29.
[45] "Ventnor Appoints Reyers", *MOTOR BOAT*, (March '48), 69.

INTRODUCING: THE 1960 VENTNOR 28

- DOUBLE BOTTOM SKIFF CRUISER INCORPORATES THE HIGHEST STANDARDS OF YACHT CONSTRUCTION.
- SAFETY ENGINEERED FOR TOP SPEED AND SEAWORTHINESS; SAFETY GLASS THROUGHOUT.
- SLEEPS FOUR. CASTRO CONVERTIBLE AND TWO 74" BUNKS. SIX FOOT GALLEY WITH 3 BURNER PROPANE STOVE.
- SPEEDS TO 39 M.P.H. PRICED MODERATELY FROM $8495.00.

Look for the exciting new Ventnor at these fine dealers

MARINE CENTER
LINDENHURST, L. I.

DUNHAM'S SHIPYARD
CITY ISLAND, N. Y.

OR WRITE FOR FURTHER INFORMATION TO
Ventnor BOAT CORP. • EGG HARBOR, N.J.

1960 Ventnor cruiser

Harbor, New Jersey. Only the firm's old logo still remained, as at that time they were offering a 28' lapstrake cabin cruiser. This type of building went on up to at least 1967, when cabin cruisers still made up the entire fleet. Speedboats were no longer built and the name "Ventnor" would no longer be synonymous with high speed, stylish inboards as in the past. . . .

Again, another speedboat builder had departed the ranks and we, the boating public, are probably worse off. If you are lucky enough to have seen any of the Ventnor inboards or own one, hang on to it, restore it and maintain it, as they are among the least frequently seen boats anywhere.

Now, let's move on to another builder and see what he offered during his "heyday". We shall now travel from New Jersey down to sunny Florida and review a firm whose inboards did as much for water skiing and Cypress Gardens as any one thing could. That firm was the Pinecastle Boat & Construction Company which eventually became known by its modern, shorter name—Correct Craft.

Last of the Ventnors!

VENTNOR '67

28' Ventnor Hardtop Express

See the 21 to 30 footers on display
See us before you buy

CORRECT CRAFT—FOR GREATER PERFORMANCE AT LOWER PRICES BUY CORRECT CRAFT

Correct Craft inboards have been around for over fifty years; though styles and construction materials have changed, the same basic demand for excellence in a ski boat goes on. It is interesting to this writer that for 1978 the complete Correct Craft fleet, while now built entirely of fiberglass, is all straight inboards—no inboard-outboards, jets or outboard units. Few firms today can boast such a long tradition of building and selling inboard boats all over the United States as well as nearly every other nation on the face of this earth.

To review this interesting firm with you, I must briefly cover some of the early historical facts, dates, etc., to put the story into context. I am not going to attempt a year by year history of the firm as that has already been done by a recent new book which I highly recommend to all my readers. The book, *SAVED FROM BANKRUPTCY*, by David and Dorothy Enlow, traces the good as well as bad years experienced by the Meloon family and their famous boat company. In the rear of this book you will find where to order the above book if you wish to delve further into this interesting concern.

One thing always remained foremost in the lives of the Meloon family and that was their very sincere love of God and belief in the "golden rule". Later I will mention just one example of how management of Correct Craft put God ahead of money and what happened in the meantime to them.

Walter Crawford Meloon, originally from New Hampshire, moved with his wife and three sons to Duncan Lake, Florida where in 1925 he founded the Florida Variety Boat Company. Young W. C. Meloon felt since there appeared to be such a lack of boats in the state of Florida that boat building would be a good occupation.[46]

The first plant was located in Pine Castle, Florida which remained the firm's headquarters ever since.

Those first few years in the late 1920's were tough ones and by 1930, Mr. Meloon changed the firm's name to Pinecastle Boat & Construction Company. It would be 1938 before the name "Correct Craft" would be used for the name of Meloon's power boats.[47] In those harried years during the Depression the Meloon family suffered numerous setbacks, including three bank failures which swallowed up all the family's meager savings. Undaunted W. C. kept going, selling most of his boats from the roof of his car while traveling around the East Coast and elsewhere, often having to demonstrate the features of his boat to gain a sale. I now will pick up the story on Correct Craft about 1939 and take it through the mid-1960's when the firm totally ceased all-wood boat building.

Top—1939 21' day cruiser. Bottom—1937 17' deluxe runabout.

Trailering a Correct Craft—1939 style

Inboard racing 91 cubic inch hydroplane, powered with Gray, speed up to 50 m.p.h. Price, $795.

1939 15½' deluxe and standard utilities

---
[46] Dorothy and David Enlow, *SAVED FROM BANKRUPTCY*, (Chicago, '75), 27.
[47] *Ibid.*

Correct Craft at full speed

1939 deluxe 17' Correct Craft

Boats leaving our factory by truck and trailer to all parts of the country.

By 1939, the Pinecastle Boat & Construction Company was turning out a rather complete selection of both power and powered craft—everything from rowing dories to 91 cubic inch hydroplanes to inboard speedboats and cruisers. I wish to thank Mr. Ralph Meloon for providing the interesting late-1930 views of Correct Craft boats shown here. I myself was very surprised to see the stylish-looking all-mahogany utilities the firm built prior to the start of World War II. Here in the Midwest, few Correct Craft from that era still exist. A friend recently showed me a photo of a very neat 1939 17' Correct Craft which was completely restored at Lake Tahoe, California.

With the beginning of the war, Correct Craft switched all boat building from pleasure to defensive. During those years the firm built numerous pontoon boats for bridges—all from plywood. With the extreme amount of experience the firm gained in plywood boat building

Delivery of new Correct Crafts—1947 style

during the war, it seemed only natural that in 1947 new, plywood constructed boats would be put on the market. My own personal recollection of Correct Craft inboards began about the early 1950's. As a young boy one of my most remembered speedboat rides was aboard a sleek 1948 19' racing runabout on Lake Minnetonka west of Minneapolis, Minnesota. Though my dad never bought the boat, I can to this day, still remember the "bark" of that Packard engine as we sped down the lake. . . .

1948 19' custom runabout by Correct Craft

The firm at which we tried that racing runabout—Cochrane's Boat Yard at Excelsior, Minnesota—was probably the largest Correct Craft dealer-distributor in this portion of the Midwest. They had a big truck-mounted crane to launch and retrieve boats right at their location and offered complete dockage, storage and service, too. Some other good friends of mine at Clear Lake, Iowa also sold quite a few Correct Crafts in the mid-1950's through the 1960's.

With the war being over just prior to the 1947 model year, the first Correct Crafts of the assembly lines were

1948 21' streamlined sedan by Correct Craft

mostly of the painted, plywood variety. 1948 was to find the firm offering more all-mahogany inboards, including both the 19' racing runabout as well as a 19' custom runabout. Other varnished sedans, open hulls and smaller plywood ski boats were also available. By 1949 over 16 different models were being built from small 15' 6" Junior utilities up through 32' cabin cruisers. The popular 19' racing runabout was still very much in the line and was popular as ever.

15' 6" Junior utility by Correct Craft

1949 18' Correct Craft utility

1949 19' racing runabout—125 h.p.

1950 proved to be a big year at Correct Craft with the Florida builder offering an all-new 14' Atom 25 plywood utility. Even at that early date the outboard motor was becoming larger and less difficult to operate and this was an attempt by the firm to compete in the lower price ranges, as the Atom came with a 25 h.p. Universal engine and sold on the market for $1,095 at the factory. A new runabout first offered in 1950 by Correct Craft

14' Correct Craft with 25 h.p. engine—new in 1950

17' twin cockpit runabout called Dart by Correct Craft for 1950

was called the 17' Dart. Power was supplied by a four-cylinder, 45 h.p. engine and the boats sold for just over $1600. Most Correct Crafts in those days were the open utility types, made famous as well as popular by the then world-renowned Cypress Gardens, a mecca for tourists the year around. The first Correct Craft inboards were used back about 1940 and from then on, more and more of these powerful little boats could be seen towing rafts of skiers daily throughout the park. The untold exposure gained by the use of Correct Crafts in those shows helped spread the name "Correct Craft" nationwide, making it a common household word. About this same time, the famous Esther Williams made a 2½ million dollar

Fun aboard a 1950 15' 6" Junior by Correct Craft

51

Close-up of 1950 19' 6" Correct Craft racing runabout

1950 18' utility, 75 h.p.—$2,481

1950 19' 6" deluxe custom runabout

movie, "Easy to Love", at Cypress Gardens and she and her co-star, Van Johnson, thrilled thousands as they skied through the Gardens pulled by you know what? Correct Craft inboards, what else![48]

As a kid in grade school I can remember seeing that movie along with my dad and my brother Art. The most exciting sequence of all showed forty-six skiers being towed by eight 18' Correct Craft ski boats. That was a real sight and shots taken from the air above showed a giant "V" spread out behind the boats, all pulling in perfect unison, thus allowing for a spectacular shot. Again Correct Craft inboards, painted in their familiar blue and white paint jobs, received untold public exposure. The public loved what they saw and expressed their interest in increased purchases of Correct Craft boats of all sizes.

By 1952, the Korean conflict had about run its course and Correct Craft offered one of its largest, most varied fleets of all time. Models ranged from a small 12' plywood outboard to a super luxurious 50' yacht, of which few were ever built. I have photos of nearly every runabout offered in 1952. The little 14' Atom had been restyled with an all-natural finish, more deluxe windshield, hardware, etc., and was as easy to trail as any outboard boat of the day. Several nicely finished utilities on the larger side were also offered, starting with the 15½' Junior ski boat up through the posh 23' Capri,

---
[48]Dick Pope, Sr., *WATER SKIING*, (Englewood Cliffs, N.J., '57), 192.

which could seat 10 passengers in style. The 17' Dart runabout and a new 18' Collegian twin-cockpit-forward runabout were also added in 1952. 1952 was one of the biggest years in the history of the Pinecastle, Florida firm, of all its 27 years of boat making.

Easily trailerable, 1952 14' Correct Craft Atom utility

Cute little 14' Atom at full speed

1952 15½' Junior ski boat by Correct Craft

1952 18' utility commuter

21' Pompano utility sedan by Correct Craft—1952

Luxury 23' 3-seat utility Capri by Correct Craft

1952 17' Dart runabout with 75 h.p.

1952 18' Correct Craft Collegian, 165 h.p.

Minor changes would occur in the firm's line from then on. Many models remained in the line year in and year out while others were dropped along the way. By 1955, fiberglass outboard boats were making major inroads on the sale of wooden inboard boats. Correct Craft tried to counter this by offering new, more jazzed up models but competition was plenty tough. Some of the 1955 models are shown here and you will see styling changes designed to "hypo" slumping sales of wood boats. By late 1956 the firm began to suffer from harder times. Sales were down from the past and government contracts for building wood boats which used to be very beneficial to the firm now began to be a thorn in their side. For example, government inspectors who had to inspect all hulls built for other nations suddenly began to find fault with the most minor blemish; thus hundreds of boats had to be reworked at added cost, thereby cutting down on the firm's cash income from such work.

1954 18-foot Commuter utility and 21' Baca Raton utility

RUN A BOUTS

14' 6" ATOM SKIER

18' COMMUTER

19' HURRICANE

17' AQUA SKIER

Correct Craft 15' 6" Junior deluxe at rest, 1955

1955 19' Hurricane twin cockpit runabout

It seems the problems all arose when officials at Correct Craft refused to bribe or "pay off" inspectors as almost all other builders were doing at the time. But not giving up, the Meloons had faith in God and a number of almost miraculous events occurred which eventually saw the proud rise of a strong Correct Craft Boat Company. To see what events those were, you will have to read about the firm in the book that I mentioned at the opening of this section. . . . .

Around 1956 or so the Correct Craft Aqua Skier, a sleek 17' 2" utility build by the firm and used at Cypress Gardens was a big seller. The hulls were painted white with varnished decks and deluxe interiors. Other plywood skinned hulls included the Atom Skier, a shorter 14'

1955 Correct Craft speed boats

version of the Aqua Skier. By 1957, lots of changes were coming to Correct Craft. The number of models offered had been lowered with most large cruisers no longer being built. The 1957 17' Star-Flite utility was the ultimate boat of its type built by Correct Craft. Rather unpretentious tail fins began to make their appearance as well as new wraparound windshields and two-tone paint jobs, etc. The Star-Flite could be ordered with up to a 215 h.p. V-8 engine for ultimate performance. Another popular model in 1957 was the 20' Debonaire utility. It, too, had been restyled with snappier interiors, larger engines, etc.

Custom Correct Craft speedster—late 50's era

Correct Crafts towing 12 skiers at Cypress Gardens

1956—14' Atom Skier and 17' Aqua Skier by Correct Craft

Two 1956 Correct Craft utilities

1957 Star-Flite runabout by Correct Craft

1957 20' Debonnaire utility by Correct Craft

55

1958 18' Collegian runabout

1961 Correct Craft utility, towards the end of the wood boat era

1957 18' Correct Craft Rocket Skier

1960 15' 4" Atom Skier Deluxe by Correct Craft. Note the tail fins.

In 1958 Correct Craft built its last true runabout—the 18' Collegian—a real honey of a boat. The hull was finished with two-tone decks as well as two-tone hull sides and beautiful light blue seats and interior. I remember seeing a colored photo of that very boat in 1958 on a cover of a boating magazine and it stood out over every other boat on the scene. A third plywood-hulled ski boat also built at that time and painted like the other two already mentioned was called the Rocket Skier, an 18' open boat also seen in use at Cypress Gardens. From 1960 on, Correct Craft built all utility models with tail fins much in evidence, especially in 1960 and 1961. Most hulls were now plywood planked, although varnished except for the most expensive models which were still mahogany planked.

1962 found the Orlando firm building some 8 different wood utilities from a small 15' Compact Skier up through a deluxe 20' Collegian which sold for $4656 with V-8 power. You will note that some of the 1962 models still sported tail fins while others did not. Shortly after that time, the firm offered one small 16' all-fiberglass utility which soon caught on and within a few years various "all-glass" models would make up the complete line. The firm eventually got back onto its feet after some shakey financial days and today the total Correct Craft fleet is all straight inboards—no jets, outboards or inboard-outboards, as mentioned earlier. Correct Craft fiberglass inboards are used at all major major ski tournaments nationwide, even worldwide. There have been three or four imitations of the Correct Craft but nothing has come along to remove it from its important place in water ski tournaments.

It is amusing to me that so many kids growing up today think skiing behind an inboard is so neat and so much fun. They think they were the first people to ever ski behind an inboard and are surprised when you tell them that you skied behind one also when you were their age, but it might have been a Correct Craft, Higgins, Chris-Craft, etc.—and it was made of wood, not plastic. Again, we see where good design and construction in a boat built years ago can still be popular to this day even if it is built out of an all new material, namely, fiberglass. Correct Craft boats thus far have not been overly popular with antique boat buffs but I see increased interest in them; and if the right models can be found and restored and preserved, we will be fortunate in being able to enjoy their uniqueness.

The next firm we shall look at is the little-known Truscott Boat Company of Michigan. You will be surprised when you see some of their "offerings" which were introduced shortly after the end of World War II.

1962 20' Collegian—from $4656

16' Atom Skier Deluxe—1962—from $2896

1962 18' Aqua Deluxe

1962 18' Star Flite by Correct Craft

57

TRUSCOTT—BUILDERS OF FINE BOATS
SINCE 1885

Following the conclusion of World War II a lot of major changes affected the boat building industry here in the United States. For example, some of the old-line builders like Gar Wood, Elco and others never did get fully back onto the track. Quietly they folded their tents and stole off into the night, never to be heard of again. Others—such as Truscott Boat and Dock Company of St. Joseph, Michigan—received a "transfusion" of management and ideas which took the inboard market by surprise in 1948. Let's take a closer look at Truscott and see exactly what their plans were and how well they actually succeeded.

As some boat builders closed, key personnel were absorbed into other existing firms or entirely new names and boats came on the scene. As far as Truscott was concerned, the first example given was the case. In late October of '47 it was announced that Truscott Boat and Dock Company was again entering pleasure boat construction and the new general manager of the firm was to be Ed Hancock, who for over 23 years was high up in the management of Gar Wood.[49] Truscott dated back to 1885 when it began building small craft of all types on a rather limited basis. By 1900, Truscott was well established and advertised nationally, extolling the virtues of their row boats, launches and sail boats. The small ad accompanying this section was from an early 1900 ad placed by Truscott in a leading magazine of that day.

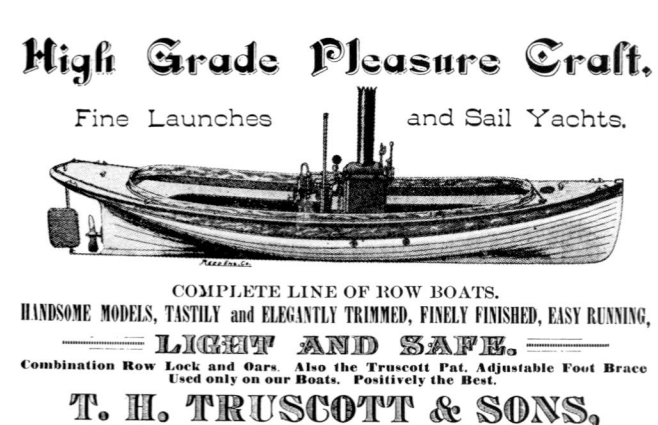

High Grade Pleasure Craft.
Fine Launches and Sail Yachts.

COMPLETE LINE OF ROW BOATS.
HANDSOME MODELS, TASTILY and ELEGANTLY TRIMMED, FINELY FINISHED, EASY RUNNING,
LIGHT AND SAFE.
Combination Row Lock and Oars. Also the Truscott Pat. Adjustable Foot Brace Used only on our Boats. Positively the Best.
T. H. TRUSCOTT & SONS,
ST. JOSEPH, - - - MICH.

Truscott dated back to the early 1900's

Truscott, over the years, built all types of pleasure as well as commercial vessels, thanks to their strategic location on the Great Lakes. During World War II, the yard built and serviced many types of naval craft from all over the country. After the war, management wished to get back quickly into the pleasure boat business in a big way. By hiring Mr. Hancock, it felt it would be well on its way to becoming a leader in the post-war boating scene. We must remember that Truscott offered a varied selection of cabin cruisers also in 1948, but we shall only review their speedboat offerings at this time.

Glowing press releases announced that Truscott would begin introducing its all-new 1948 models of both cruisers and speedboats by late November of 1947. The new speedboats were to range in size from 16' through 25' in length and most would sport varnished hulls with numerous style and construction features shared by no other builder. It was planned that the total line of speedboats was to be built at St. Joseph, Michigan in the hometown plant, while cruisers were to built over at Benton Harbor where excellent facilities for the building of larger craft were available.

My own experiences with Truscott speedboats were quite limited. Some fifteen years ago, a man moved to my hometown from Michigan who owned a rather nice 22' Truscott sedan runabout. The boat was quite gracious in appearance with a heavily padded hardtop roof covering a split front seat, a three-quarter seat ahead of the large engine box, and a full stern bench seat in the rear. The boat was painted white with varnished decks and transom. As I remember, the deck hardware was stylish and of the firm's own design. At that particular time I guess I was not as interested in speedboats so I never bothered to get even a good photo of the boat. It originally belonged to the State of Minnesota or the Conservation Commission, and the owner bought it at a surplus auction for a very reasonable price. I am not sure what size engine the craft had, but speed was under 20 m.p.h. It was rather an impressive boat as it would plane by, throwing a small wake behind with a neat wave peeling off each side of the bow, back and away from the hull.

To get back to the 1948 Truscotts, let's view each model by itself and compare it to others offered by other builders from that era. The smallest model offered by the Michigan-based firm was a neat little 16' utility called the 16' All-about. This boat was very similar to the Chris-Craft, Century, etc. of the era and offered seating in comfort for five adults.

Other features of the 16' All-about included its all-varnished hull and decks and very colorful two-toned plastic upholstery. Top speed was to be 35 m.p.h. and the boat's vital statistics were as follows: 16' 3" in length with a beam of 6' and a draft while at rest in the water of 1' 7½". I must not fail to mention that the complete 1948 Truscott fleet was designed by the then noted

---

[49]"Hancock Announces New Truscotts", *MOTOR BOAT*, (Oct. '47), 62.

designer, J. Gordon Lippencott, who preferred the clipper bow along with the straight sheer on all his "creations".[50]

Aerial view of Truscott plant at St. Joseph, Michigan—1944

1948 16' All-About by Truscott

Deluxe 1948 18' All-About Truscott speedboat

Sleek, 1948 Truscott 18' utility

[50]"Truscott for 1948", *MOTOR BOAT*, (Jan. '48), 138.

For those wishing a larger utility, Truscott also introduced a new 18' model that looked very much like the Gar Wood utilities offered at the last before the firm closed down. I think we will have to admit that Mr. Hancock, formerly of Gar Wood, probably had quite an effect also on what styles and designs were finally built at the Truscott plants. . . . . The 18' Truscotter as the boat was called featured several unique ideas. Probably the neatest thing was the three-quarter front seat which allowed for easy movement from the bow to the stern without crawling over seat backs, etc. The complete interior was of deluxe design with more two-tone upholstery available in colors of the new owner's choice. The inside cockpit walls were covered by nicely varnished mahogany, and dark-stained decks added a nice touch with the varnished hull sides and red bottom paint. A big 115 h.p. engine propelled the boat at speeds in excess of 35 m.p.h.—plenty of speed for surf boarding, water skiing or just a fast ride for the whole family to nowhere in general.

The 18' utility sported a length of 18' 9" with a beam of 6' 9" and finally a draft of 1' 8". Although Truscott built mostly utilities, the firm did offer one truly deluxe runabout. In fact, of the total 1948 lineup, this boat was my all-time favorite. Maybe it's yours also?

I have been very fortunate in obtaining two excellent views of the 19' Truscott runabout. Again I feel the runabout especially resembles the 1947 19' Gar Wood runabout pictured on page 53 of THE REAL RUNABOUTS, Volume I. In the photo taken from above, looking down on the 19-footer, we can see the large amount of tumble home or curvature on the transom of this speedboat. The set of bow and stern deck rails adds a little "pazazz" to the boat too. This Truscott sped along at 38 m.p.h. and was the "queen" of the 1948 Truscott fleet. Heavily upholstered seats for six people were among the long line of standard equipment on this speedboat. You will note the two square transom vents on the rear of the boat. They were designed to ventilate the bilge area as well as to act as an overflow drain for the gas tank. On the front deck, Truscott "adopted" the old familiar Gar Wood "anchor" styled deck hardware which consisted of one lifting ring at the top of the anchor piece as well as a chrome chock out at the tip of each side of the anchor fluke. A very stylish feature that Gar Wood used after the war was only slightly modified by Truscott for their own use. The safety glass "V" windshield and brackets were also very much in the former Gar Wood tradition. All in all, Truscott did offer a stylish-looking speedboat but the number of boats built was never very great and today I am sure only a few of these good-looking boats still exist and even fewer yet are still in use.

The final 1948 Truscott we shall look at was a massive 24' "All-about" that came with painted rather than varnished hull sides. This big boat could seat nine adults; its engine was mounted beneath the rear cockpit floor, thus removing the space-robbing engine box. A lot of these boats became popular with the Great Lakes fishermen and with those who operated water taxi or speedboat ride operations. This Truscott was the "beamiest" offered as it was 7' 8" and drew 1' 10" of water while at rest. As I mentioned earlier, Truscott added the above runabouts to supplement their already existing line of cabin cruisers.

In my researching of the firm I stumbled onto a list of 1948 Truscott dealers which is reprinted in this review. It is interesting to me that their only 1948 dealer in Minnesota was located in downtown Minneapolis on the 12th floor of the Foshay Tower Building. This building consists of mainly office space so most likely boats were displayed at another location, possibly Lake Minnetonka. In trying to find out more about the Mariner Company, the local Truscott dealers, I ran into a brick wall. Perhaps one of you readers can tell me about sales of Truscott here in Minnesota? Good friends of mine in Clear Lake, Iowa who had sold Gar Wood, took on Truscott to replace Gar Wood but sold few boats as they found the line to be poorly accepted on their particular lake.

In conclusion, Truscott, with the aid of experienced personnel from former successful speedboat firms, hoped to take over where "giants" like Gar Wood left off. However, this never happened as Truscott also soon

1948 20' Truscott runabout, twin cockpit forward

See Your TRUSCOTT Dealer

ALABAMA
G. E. BARNES CO., INC.
50-60 So. Broad St.
Mobile

CALIFORNIA
FOSTER & SONS
920 Coast Highway
Newport Beach

MODERN APPLIANCE CO.
111 So. Ellsworth Ave.
San Mateo

NATIONAL MOTOR SALES
421 National Avenue
National City

SUNSET BOAT COMPANY
9130 Sunset Blvd.
Los Angeles 46

CANADA
JOHN K. STOREY
Thetis Island, Box 176
Chemainus, B. C.

FLORIDA
R. S. EVANS
1622 N. E. Second Ave.
Miami 36

OCEAN MOTOR COMPANY
133 S. E. 2nd Street and
1600 S. E. 8th Street
Fort Lauderdale

SELLHORN SALES & SERVICE
Payne Terminal
Sarasota

ILLINOIS
LITTLE GIANT PRODUCTS, INC.
1530-50 North Adams Street
Peoria 3

F. E. LUDOLPH
2257 Silverton Way
Chicago

IOWA
AUSTIN CRABBS, INC.
P.O. Box 816
Davenport

KENTUCKY
WM. G. NASH
303 N. 16th St.
Murray

MEXICO
ALEJANDRO HERNANDEZ
Av. Morelos 29
Mexico, D. F.

MICHIGAN
CHRYSLER BOAT COMPANY
9303 E. Jefferson
Detroit 14

GITZEN COMPANY
44 Dodge Street
Houghton

ROGER MOTOR SALES
905 N. Third Street
Muskegon

MINNESOTA
MARINER COMPANY
1220 Foshay Tower
Minneapolis 2

MISSISSIPPI
GULF BOAT & SUPPLY CO.
P. O. Box 471
Gulfport

MISSOURI
CRANE & EQUIPMENT CO.
706 Chestnut Street
St. Louis 1

DR. ERIC A. CUNNINGHAM
122 South Third Street
Louisiana

NEVADA
THE SPORTSMAN, INC.
406 Fremont
Las Vegas

NEW YORK
WM. M. BARNEY
c/o Hyde Boat Yard
Watervliet

HAMILTON YACHT & MARINE CO.
974 Amherst Street
Buffalo 16

ST. LAWRENCE MARINE SALES & SERVICE COMPANY
Clayton, 1000 Islands

SYRACUSE MARINE SALES & SERVICE, INC.
317 State Tower Building
Syracuse

NEW YORK OFFICE
J. S. HICKS
607 Fifth Avenue
New York

NORTH CAROLINA
MOREHEAD CITY YACHT BASIN
Morehead City

OHIO
MOTORBOATS, INC.
515 Williamson Building
Cleveland

OHIO TRAILER & BOAT COMPANY
1502 Madison Ave.
Toledo 2

OREGON
WALLY'S MARINE SALES & SERVICE
State Street
Oswego

PENNSYLVANIA
MARINE MART
108 Walnut St.
Philadelphia

S. W. RAWSON
Erie

RHODE ISLAND
MOE ENGINEERS
Central St.
Pontiac

TEXAS
GENERAL BOAT COMPANY
1015 Capitol Avenue
Houston

LAKE TEXOMA BOAT & MARINE COMPANY
P. O. Box 619
Sherman

WASHINGTON
COVE MARINA
North Wenatchee Ave.
Wenatchee

MARINA MART, INC.
1550 Westlake, N.
Seattle

TACOMA BOAT MART
2315 Ruston Way
Tacoma

WASHINGTON, D. C.
NATIONAL MOTOR BOAT SALES
800 Maine Avenue, S. W.

WISCONSIN
VALLEY BOAT MART
P. O. Box 454
Green Bay

TRUSCOTT PLEASURE CRAFT SINCE 1895 — *Truscott Boat and Dock Co.*
ST. JOSEPH, MICHIGAN   NEW YORK CITY OFFICE 607 FIFTH AVENUE

1948 list of Truscott dealers nationwide

1948 Truscott 24' All-About utility

Rare view of 19' 6" Truscott runabout out for a cruise

disappeared without really ever becoming the leader it hoped it would be. As was the case with nearly every builder we have studied in this book and *Volume I*, most people never thought to save any—or at the most, just a handful—of the boats built by the numerous boat companies in this country. When we did realize what was happening it was almost too late to save any. However, today I am happy to say that many of our "endangered species" are now beginning to reappear, which is a truly great thing.

Now let's move on to another national speedboat builder and see what their claim to fame might have been. . . . Sea-Lyon Boat Company of City Island, New York built fine wooden inboards in numerous sizes up until 1933 or so. In those few years, most boats were sold factory-direct to keep prices low and production figures were also low to keep quality up. Few Sea-Lyons still are in operation today but, like any other antique boat, models can be found; however, gathering parts and restoration material on a small builder really causes headaches for those involved. I am sure you will appreciate the Sea-Lyon runabouts after reading about them and viewing them in the next section.

SEA-LYON—THE ARISTOCRAT OF THE FLEET

A firm that operated in the later 1920's through about 1933 was the Lyon-Tuttle Shipyard located on City Island in New York City. I have been unable to find a lot of material on this firm other than that, at one time Mr. Howard Lyon, owner, was a Gar Wood merchant in New York City and later went into the boat business on his own. According to "natives" on City Island, Mr. Lyon took over the old Kyle Shipyard but no one really remembers just what year.[51] The Sea-Lyon boats were much in evidence by 1928. At that time a rare 42' Commuter was being offered. These boats were few and far between and I doubt today that even one remains in existence. The "bread and butter" of Sea-Lyon was its runabouts. Four models were offered in 1929, one being the big Commuter we already mentioned. The biggest was a 30-footer and one of the more popular versions was the 24' three-cockpit model shown here. The photos show good detailed features of Sea-Lyon boats, such as oval

[51]B. Stevonic, "Letter", New York Public Library, (March '78).

Rare view of 1928 42' Sea-Lyon Commuter

1929 24' Sea-Lyon runabout

Sea-Lyon owned by Wm. C. Smith of New York

Another view of 1929 24' Sea-Lyon

24' 1929 Sea-Lyon with 100 h.p. 6-cylinder Chrysler motor

Another view of 1929 24' Sea-Lyon runabout

1929 Sea-Lyon magazine ad

Significant!
84% Are Experienced Yachtsmen

OF those who have purchased Sea-Lyon runabouts so far this season exactly 84% are yachtsmen who have owned from one to ten boats in past years. Men who know runabout performance intimately, who have had the opportunity to learn what to look for, what to expect and what to avoid, are buying Sea-Lyons this year.

For Sea-Lyons are incomparably finer boats, designed and built to win the choice of a most discriminating clientele. More expensively constructed than any other standardized runabouts, they have set a pace in design, workmanship and performance that is years ahead of all competition in the opinion of those qualified to judge.

Sea-Lyon quality is more than skin deep. It embodies not only new grace in lines and finish but also a perfection of hull design, balance and power plant installation that results in greater speed, smoother riding, better seaworthiness, easier handling and longer service.

Immediate Deliveries — Seven Models — $2,975 to $30,000
f.o.b. New York

For eastern buyers the location of our plant in New York City is a distinct advantage for prompt delivery and for competent service throughout the life of the boat.

Take a ride in a Sea-Lyon and judge its performance for yourself. Write or telephone—

HOWARD W. LYON
INCORPORATED
HOTEL BARCLAY   NEW YORK
532 Lexington Avenue (at 49th Street)
Telephone: Vanderbilt 4445—4446
Plant and Service Station:
City Island 1645—1646

SEA-LYON

62

1929 Sea-Lyons on parade!

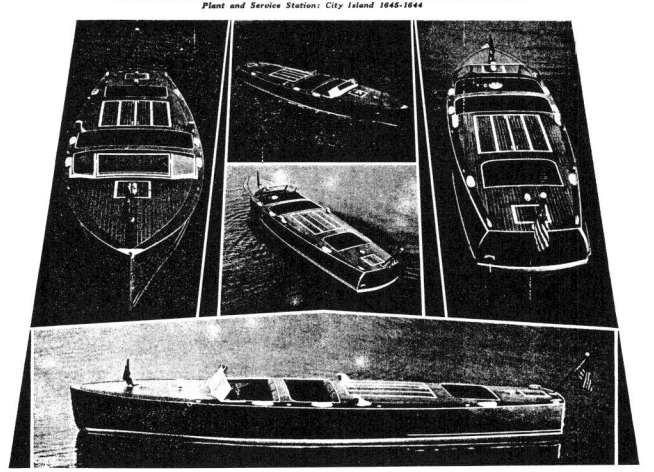

1930 Sea-Lyon magazine ad

1930 Sea-Lyon magazine ad

Out for a fun day in 1930 aboard a Sea-Lyon!

step pads and a rather plain type upholstery package. By 1930, Sea-Lyon offered six speedboats and the Commuter. Models were designated as follows and sold for the prices shown below:[52]

   SEA-LYON "30" $2,675.00
   SEA-LYON "35" $2,975.00
   SEA-LYON "40" $4,650.00
   SEA-LYON "45" $6,500.00
   SEA-LYON "46" $6,500.00
   SEA-LYON "60" $12,500.00
   SEA-LYON Commuter $30,000.00

Lyon's method of sale was factory-direct, thus keeping prices down as there was no middleman to take care of.

In 1931 Howard W. Lyon took some rather drastic steps to keep his Sea-Lyon boats in business. As you will remember, the Depression was well underway by then so many boat builders just folded—but not Howard. By powering his boats with larger engines and watching production costs, etc., Sea-Lyon was able to lower prices, build six models from 20' through 30' with the same dimensions as the past without cutting any quality features. I have selected views of the 1931 28' Sea-Lyon as well as the largest Sea-Lyon runabout of all—the 30' three-cockpit model.

Customers could view a number of new Sea-Lyons in downtown New York at the Graybar Building in Manhattan. Sleek models were displayed at rakish angles among potted palms and men in pin-striped suits were waiting to help you select your new runabout. 1932 was the final real year of Sea-Lyon inboards. In that year, the following models were offered at all-time low prices:[53]

24' SEA-LYON	125 h.p. Chrysler "Imperial"	35 m.p.h.	$2,500.00
28' SEA-LYON	225 h.p. Kermath "Sea Wolf"	44 m.p.h.	$4,000.00
28' SEA-LYON	325 h.p. Lycoming "12"	52 m.p.h.	$7,000.00
30' SEA-LYON	225 h.p. Sterling "Petrel"	52 m.p.h.	$5,000.00
30' SEA-LYON	300 h.p. Hall Scott "Invader"	48 m.p.h.	$7,500.00

---

[52] 1930 magazine ad.

[53] *RUDDER MAGAZINE*, (Feb. '32), 87.

The 28-foot Sea-Lyon runabout skims along with a full load of eight passengers.

Slightly larger, the 30-foot Sea-Lyon has greater capacity and more speed.

24' 1932 Sea-Lyon runabout, 125 h.p. Chrysler, 35 m.p.h.—$2,500.

Downtown Sea-Lyon showroom—1932—in New York City

1932 28' Sea-Lyon runabout, 225 h.p. Kermath, 44 m.p.h.—$4,000

1932 28' Sea-Lyon did 52 m.p.h. with 12-cylinder 325 Lycoming engine—$7,000.

1932 30' Sea-Lyon with 225 h.p. Sterling Petrel, 42 m.p.h.—$5,000

30' Sea-Lyon with 300 h.p. Hall-Scott Invader engine in 1932— $7,500.

Although these prices sounded really great, we have to remember most people in 1932 had barely money enough for food, much less $7,500.00 for a new speedboat. . . . So shortly after that time Sea-Lyon boats quietly departed the scene. Today, there are a few Sea-Lyons still in use and more being restored for use in the future.

Howard W. Lyon died in 1962 and his obituary mentioned his operation of the Lyon-Tuttle yards as well as building and selling Sea-Lyon runabouts and Commuters. In the 1920's, Howard competed in many famous boat races such as the Gold Cup of 1925 and 1926. He raced along the seacoast off Cuba in power boat races in those early years also. His last years were spent cruising along our southern coasts, enjoying a more leisurely pace. Sea-Lyons have always been a favorite of mine as I hope they are of yours. Perhaps it is because I could find so little about the firm.

Chapter Two of this book will deal with nine speedboat builders who sold their boats mostly right near where they were built. In other words, the next firms are called "Regional builders" and most were much smaller in size than some of the "biggies" we have just finished looking over.

Our first firm will be Mariner Boat Company of Michigan. This firm can honestly trace their ancestry back to the old Gar Wood Boat Company as their first jigs, molds, etc., belonged to that builder until they ceased production.

CHAPTER II
MORE REGIONAL BUILDERS

MARINER OF MICHIGAN—QUEEN OF THE SEA

A firm which built mahogany speedboats until the mid 1960's was Mariner Boat Company of Algonac, Michigan. Not a whole lot of material has been unearthed on the firm, but what I did find should be of interest to you, my readers.

When Gar Wood Industries stopped building boats it seems that a Mr. Edward Kaunitz bought all their jigs, molds, forms, etc., and moved into an old roller-skating rink at Roberts Landing, two miles north of Algonac. Not much could be found concerning those early years at Mariner, except the boats greatly resembled the old Gar Woods with barrel bows and sterns. All boats built in the early years were custom models, each built to the owner's specifications. Some years after the firm's beginning, two other plants were set up at New Baltimore and Marine City, Michigan.

Little was heard of the firm until about 1956 when a small two-color folder was issued describing the 1956 line, which included the following models:

Model 19 Sports Utility

95 h.p.	Chrysler	$3,608.00
125 h.p.	Interceptor	$4,032.00
145 h.p.	Interceptor	$4,084.00
165 h.p.	Interceptor	$4,236.00
185 h.p.	Interceptor	$4,440.00

Model 20 Deluxe Utility

125 h.p.	Interceptor	$4,580.00
145 h.p.	Interceptor	$4,628.00
165 h.p.	Interceptor	$4,784.00
185 h.p.	Interceptor	$4,992.00

The above utility models were complete, ready for the water. A good assortment of equipment came on each boat and all were water tested before delivery. If the above prices were too high, the buyer had two other choices by which to obtain a Mariner inboard. First of all, there was what the firm called a "Model 19 complete-it-yourself" which consisted of an assembled hull with decks, covering boards, instrument panel, floor boards, seat frames less paint and varnish. This boat sold for $1,472.00. A more elaborate offering included all the above-mentioned features plus the following: a cutwater, sheer moldings, quarter rail moldings and transom trim. This hull came completely painted and varnished, ready for an engine, for $1,768.00. All deck hardware, windshields, upholstery, etc., was additional. The hull used in the 1956 Mariner boats looked just like a Gar Wood from the late 1940's.

1957 saw the firm offer a more modern-looking inboard called the Mariner Deluxe Utility. Her dimensions were: length, 19' 6", beam, 81". Five Dearborn Interceptor engines were offered, ranging in size from 125 h.p. through the big 215 h.p. model. My first personal experience with a Mariner was 1957, when one of these utilities was displayed at the Minneapolis Boat Show. I can remember the boat so well, since it was about the only all-wood boat in a "sea" of fiberglass and aluminum models. The color scheme was a little weird as I remember. . . .would you believe the covering boards and king planks were done in a *dark green* stain! The 1957 model still resembled the Gar Woods, except it now had a modern wrap-around windshield and a fancy auto-type steering wheel, split front seats, and a glove box. Evidently the "do-it-yourself" boats were quite unpopu-

The 19' 6" Deluxe utility by Mariner for 1957

66

lar as no such model was offered in 1957. There are a series of photos at this point which illustrate nicely the 1957 Mariner in greater detail.

Stern view of the Mariner deluxe utility—1957

Front cockpit on 1957 19' 6" Mariner utility

About to install deck on 1957 Mariner utility

Carefully preparing the mahogany decks before varnishing

Planking a 1957 Mariner 19' 6" deluxe utility

In the fall of 1958, Mariner made the news when it was announced a new plant was being built at Marine City, Michigan and all operations would move to the new location by the first part of 1959. Dr. Joseph Davidson, one of the firm's owners, said that the new plant would employ 10 to 15 people when production reached its peak by mid-March. Mariner was merging at that time with a smaller builder of cruisers from Ohio to offer a more complete model selection. Orders for new 1959 Mariner boats were coming in at a good rate and Davidson expected many more boats to be sold from the new location as compared to years past. 1959 saw Mariner offer an all-new 20' utility called "Typhoon" which could reach 60 m.p.h. with a V-8 power plant. The only other Mariners I came across were a very roomy 1961 23' three-seat utility and a rare 1962 lapstrake utility which was built by Mariner for the County of Sandusky, Ohio, as a police boat.

NEW! TYPHOON 20

NOW! 60 M.P.H. plus!

Flashing performance and high maneuverability are the reasons for Mariner's big success in racing—leading all the way in three major 1958 races at Buffalo, Cincinnati and Miami. The new Mariners are redesigned—they're wider, plane better at low speeds, don't submarine when you cut the power. All that performance and the best in construction too. Planking is solid center cut mahogany, oak battens and seams, double planked bottom. Hydraulic steering standard, Marmac throttle and clutch controls. Tempered safety glass. More luxurious too—new upholstery, trim and hardware. Call or write today. Phone RO 2-6421.

MARINER BOAT CO., INC.   MARINE CITY, MICH.

Describing the 1959 Mariner 20' Typhoon

Cockpit of 1961 Mariner 23' utility

1963 20' Mariner Cyclone police boat for Sandusky County, Ohio—215 h.p. Interceptor.

Custom 1961 23' Mariner deluxe utility, 3-seater

In the mid-1960's, Mariner ceased all building. I understand that many of the hulls that were built were sold without engines. A few of these fine boats still exist in and around Cincinnati, Ohio. It seems some of the men who were involved with the firm in those earlier years live near Cincinnati now, and a Mariner or two can be seen on the Ohio River every once in awhile.

I am going to try and find out more about Mariner boats as their connection with the former Gar Wood operation makes them unique in speedboats; and any that are still in use or restorable should be of value.

Now we shall move across the country from Michigan to Tacoma, Washington and take a close look at the Fairliner "Torpedo" runabouts which caused such a stir among runabout owners back in the late 1940's through the mid-1950's or so.

FAIRLINER—BUILT WITH CUSTOM-CARE FOR PEAK PERFORMANCE

WESTERN BOAT BUILDING COMPANY

Soon after the end of World War II, Western Boat Building Company in Tacoma, Washington, hired a noted designer, Dair Long, to draw up plans for a totally new and stylish 17' inboard speedboat. The Fairliner Torpedo was the result. That sleek little gem was styled after the old Hacker and Dee Wite Torpedos we viewed in *Volume I*. The first Fairliners came out in late 1946. It appears from early photos taken at the time of their introduction that the boats were somewhat stubby and boxy-looking. You, the reader, can decide for yourself. After the first boats came out, subtle modifications were made to the point where the boats appeared more racy and stylish. Only about 35 boats were ever built and the last model rolled off the line in late 1956. No others were built after that date, as production costs had risen to the point where it was no longer possible to build and sell a Torpedo competitively with the fiberglass and aluminum boats that were flooding the market at that time. Perhaps, had it not been for a serious fire that occurred in the mid-1960's, Western Boat Building Company may have gone on to build other Torpedos. In that fire, the firm lost all jigs, plans, etc., for the Fairliner. Upon rebuilding the new plant, the firm went strictly into the production of larger fiberglass cruisers that it still builds to this very day.

Nearly all the Fairliners were 17' long with twin-cockpit-forward seating. The standard model in 1950 sold for

1947 17' speedster built by Western Boat Building Company, Tacoma, Washington.

1949 17' Fairliner Torpedo

1947 Fairliner Torpedo 17' in length. Note unique hull design.

1950 17' Fairliner Torpedo

Stock 1950 18' Torpedo. Designed by Dair Long.

Custom 1950 Fairliner at rest, single seat.

Custom 18' Fairliner inboard at rest. Note double-ended design.

18' Torpedo at full speed

about $3,600 and came equipped with a 106 h.p. Gray engine. Top speed was quoted to be 36 m.p.h. As was the case with nearly every boat builder, a few custom models were built. I am indebted to Gean Arenz of Wisconsin for providing me with photos and historical data on his own "one-of-a-kind" Torpedo.[1]

Gean tells me that his boat was built in April of 1950 at Tacoma and its original owner, a Mr. Lunde, ordered several custom options. First of all, the boat was to be built with only a single cockpit, offering seating for two people. This allowed for a long, racy-looking rear deck which really added style to such a small boat. Secondly, a bigger, six-cylinder Chris-Craft racing engine with triple carburetors was installed at the plant. This extra horsepower pushed Gean's boat at speeds over 40 m.p.h. Enjoy the photos in this rather short review. I think you will agree with the author, the 17' Fairliner Torpedo by Western Boat Building Company of Tacoma, Washington was quite a boat! At this time I would guess less than half a dozen of these masterpieces still exist. If you know of one or have one yourself, restore it, enjoy it and let others see and enjoy it with you. It is really sad that there will never be boats built like this again.

The next firm we shall visit is just down the coast from Fairliner in Burbank and Piru, California, locations of the former Mercury Boat Company of West Coast fame. The owner, Bill Nollenberger, still operates at the old location, but no longer turning out sleek inboards of all sizes. I think you will like what follows concerning Mercury inboards.

---
[1] Gean H. Arenz, "letter", (June 18, '77).

MERCURY OF CALIFORNIA—THE FINEST NAME IN SOLID MAHOGANY PLANKED BOATS

Another important regional speedboat builder from the West Coast we must not forget is Mercury Boat Company of Piru, California. Many of you East Coast devotees may not be familiar with this particular line, while we here west of the Mississippi have enjoyed Mercury inboards since way back in 1933.

It seems way back in 1933, a young Bill Nollenberger began building small wooden outboard hulls designed for tiny electric outboard motors.[2] After a short time of building this type of craft, Bill decided to switch to building plywood outboard fishing boats for Sears and Wards. Figuring out that the cheap boat business was still not his bag, Nollenberger switched over to experimenting with all-mahogany inboards. That move was a wise one, as from that time on orders always far exceeded output. Even into the mid-1960's, Bill and his crew held on, still building excellent wooden utilities and runabouts even though fiberglass boats had almost taken over in the pleasure boat business. A special thanks to Mr. Nollenberger for digging through old records of his firm and providing me with a wealth of old photos to use in this section. I have in my collection three Mercury brochures for 1954, 1959 and 1960, from which many of the other photos used to illustrate this section came. Now, let's return to the early 1930's, when Mercury Boat Company had its start out in Burbank, California.

I am fortunate in having a photo taken in 1934 showing Bill Nollenberger testing his very first 18' twin-cockpit-forward runabout. That particular boat was powered by an 85 h.p. Ford V-8 engine and did a satisfactory job. That early photo was taken before hardware, windshield and upholstery had been installed in the boat. From the photo it appears she planed along at a very nice angle. Bill told me he was the first man to build a runabout 18' long with a 6' beam. This was known as the three to one beam ratio.[3]

First test of 18' Mercury runabout—1934

A companion runabout to the large 18' model was a sleek, smaller 14' version of the same basic model. The next photo shows a recently completed Mercury runabout next to Bill's home. This little gem was powered by a converted Ford 60 h.p. V-8. In those early days, Ford conversions were used in Mercury boats exclusively. From then on, Mercury Boat Company build all types and sizes of runabouts and utilities as well as cabin cruisers up through World War II. Boats built by Nollenberger were pretty much on a custom basis to begin with. It was not until the late 1940's that he actually came out with a series of models for each year. Other old photos included in this early history of Mercury date from the late 1930's and early 1940's.

Late 1930's era 14' Mercury runabout with Ford 60 h.p. engine.

Early 14' Mercury utility about 1940

---

[2] "Mercury Boats", *BOATS*, (June '54), 63.
[3] "Letter", Bill Nollenberger, (Feb. '78), 1.

71

Sleek 1940's era—Mercury runabout, 17'

Two of my favorite early Mercury runabouts were built about 1940 or so. The first one was a very stylish 17' twin-cockpit-forward runabout called Skyliner. Her very curved transom and rear deck, plus the shiny varnish job, really made her an eye-catcher. By then, most of the Mercury boats were being powered by Gray Marine engines, which was a practice carried on through 1964 when the firm stopped boat-building altogether.

1940 21' Mercury Barrel-Bow runabout

Probably the nicest of all Mercury runabouts built before World War II was the 21' speedboat shown with the two girls in the front seat. Her barrel bow and stern were very similar to the Chris-Craft designs of that era, but please note the unusual chrome cutwater on the front of this boat. It comes down the nose like all others, but then two small strips shoot back about 16" on both sides for a neat little style feature. We shall later see a smaller version of this boat that was built in 1948 also. There are several other examples of pre-World War II Mercury boats shown here too. From all of these first views you, the reader, can obtain a good idea of exactly what Bill Nollenberger was trying to do out in California. Only one other builder—Philbrick Boat Company from Oakland, California—built wooden inboards in that state back in the 1930's. We shall review Philbrick boats later in this work.

When the firm resumed boat building in late 1947, they began to offer an organized fleet of boats for each model year. No longer did they build boats basically on custom basis. That first lineup in 1948 consisted of seven models. All boats were of mahogany with the "V" bottom except for one 16' hydroplane that was designed strictly for the racing scene. My own favorite of the 1948 Mercury offerings was a very sleek 19' runabout which came powered with a 160 h.p. Gray engine. This boat was designed along the lines of the 1940 model except more hardware was installed on this model and the boat was shortened. Over the years almost all Mercury boats were of the open or utility variety.

In 1949, Mercury boats were advertised nationwide in all the major boat magazines. The firm proudly announced its 1949 lineup as follows. Truly, more models and sizes were being added as time went by.[4]

1940's 17' utility early model

1940's era—19' Mercury runabout

---

[4] "Mercury Specifications", *MOTOR BOAT*, (Jan. '49), 84.

72

Very rare 1948 19' Mercury 160 h.p. inboard runabout

MODEL	LENGTH	SEATS	H.P.	MODEL NAME
Inboard	16'	6	45	Standard Utility
Inboard	16'	6	6-cyl. 104 Gray	Deluxe Utility
Inboard	18'	6	6-cyl. 104 Gray	Standard Sportsman
Inboard	18'	6	6-cyl. 150 Gray	Deluxe Sportsman
Inboard	22'	8	Two 6-cyl. 150 Gray	Sportsman Utility
Inboard	17'	6	6-cyl. 150 Gray	Custom Runabout
Inboard	19'	6	6-cyl. 150 Gray	Custom Runabout

As you can see, that was quite a model lineup. I am fortunate to have four photos of 1949 Mercury inboards. The smallest is a sharp little 16' utility that came with the standard Gray 4-75 engine or the 6-104 for additional power and speed. This boat again reminds me of the 1949 16' Chris-Craft utilities. Both the standard as well

1949 16' Mercury utility with Gray 4-75 engine

Nicely styled 18' Mercury standard utility under full power

73

Streamlined, 18' deluxe Mercury utility—1949

as deluxe 18' utilities were special in every way. The interior appointments, hardware and finish add up to very deluxe-looking inboards. Perhaps the wildest Mercury for 1949 was a big 22' utility equipped with twin 150 h.p. engines. She was very popular along the West Coast for use on the ocean, as well as on the larger inland lakes of the west. Though a big boat, she clipped along at over 45 m.p.h. It appears that the big engine boxes took up lots of seating room, but still the boat was popular.

Each year saw new boats added and others removed from the line. In 1950 Mercury offered six models, the most noteworthy being the all-new 18' Racer model which came equipped with a big 160 h.p. engine. Her sleek lines, long front deck and semi-curved windshield added up to lots of good looks and high speed. The boat

1949 Mercury twin engine 22' utility

1950 Mercury 18' "Racer" very sleek with speeds over 40 m.p.h.

1950 18' Mercury deluxe utility

74

Two 1950 Mercury utilities in action, 22' and 18' in size

1952 18' Mercury "Racer", Gray-Super 6-330 engine

Cute little 14' Ski-Tug by Mercury for 1954

1954 16' Sabre "hottest" Mercury of them all!

1954 18' Super Sportsman utility by Mercury Boats of California

was actually designed to be raced in the Class-E Service Runabout division of The American Power Boat Association.[5] I was unable to find any results concerning the Racer model's racing circuit ranking, but I am sure it did very well. Other 1950 models shown here that did not change were the 18' deluxe utility and the 22' Sport Utility. With the conflict in Korea, few boats appeared in 1951, so it was early in 1952 when Mercury introduced new photos of its 1952 18' Racer. This boat was similar to the 1950 model except it now had a new Gray Super 6-130 engine.

The first time I personally became familiar with Mercury boats was when I sent a postcard to Burbank, California, site of their new factory built several years earlier, seeking the 1954 brochure. Sometime later, the nice black and white folder arrived showing five new models. My own favorite was the all-new 14' Ski Tug, designed for the water skier exclusively. This new boat came with a 90 h.p. Gray engine but tipped the scales at a mere 900 pounds. She was as easy to trail as any outboard of the day and did not cost any more. A more deluxe version with upholstered motor box, seats, etc., was also offered. This Ski Tug was to prove popular and was a good seller on the West Coast. Again, it compared favorably with the then popular Correct Craft Atom-Skier. Another new 1954 model was called the 16' Sabre.[6] This boat featured a new streamlined bow with the wraparound plastic windshield. She was advertised as the "hottest" true pleasure boat offered by Mercury for 1954. The 18' Racer remained in the line, now powered by a 165 h.p. Gray engine. The other new 1954 model was an 18' Super Sportsman which had a new style wooden skiff windshield. She also came with the 115 h.p. Gray Marine engine.

That new Super Sportsman for 1954 got lots of use in the open water along the California coastline. Many changes were occurring at Mercury by 1955. In that year

a sleek new 18' Mustang utility was added. This boat came with V-8 power and sold new for $3,770.00 at that time. In 1955, another "first"—Mercury began to cover the hull of their boats with a plastic type of varnish which reduced even more the yearly chore of varnishing your Mercury. From 1955 on, the number and variety of

1955 18' Mercury Mustang

1959 16' Mercury Sabre—one of two models that year

1959 18' Mercury Mustang—a real beauty

---
[5]"Mercury Specifications", *MOTOR BOAT*, (Jan. '50), 64.
[6]"Mercury Boats", *BOATS*, (June '54), 63.

76

16' 1959 Mercury mahogany plywood utility

Mercury inboards was reduced. Two models made up the main part of the line by 1959. The smallest model was again a 16' Sabre but now it featured a truly curved wraparound windshield and a large 361 cubic inch engine converted by Mercury's own staff was being used. The Sabre had powder blue seats with white vinyl cockpit liners. The other main model in the line was a wild 18' Sabre that also had been redesigned. That boat sported Sea Foam green seats along with the white cockpit liner and the big 430 V-8 power plant. 1959 also was the last year for the truly all-varnished Mercury. From then on, a little more white vinyl appeared on decks, transoms, etc. Some smaller plywood utilities were also being built from about 1958 through 1960. A variety of these boats is shown along with a larger cabin cruiser, turned out about 1960.

Again in 1960, Mercury offered just two models. The major changes were that rear decks, the center section of the front decks and trim sections on the hull sides now were covered by white vinyl. The boat also had been redesigned by Nollenberger with what he called, a "Flying Wedge" which helped the boats to take off quickly from the water without their transoms going down into the water and their bows skyward. The firm also used a V-drive on some models of their own design. The 1960 Sabre had all-white upholstery but only partial white covering boards in its cockpit. The larger, more deluxe 18' Mustang had pale blue interior with a 225 h.p. Gray Marine power plant. For the next several seasons, these two models changed only slightly.

Now powered by V-8 engine in 1960—Mercury 16' Sabre

Very deluxe 18' Mustang by Mercury in 1960

Mercury inboard being planked at Piru, California plant—1960

Small 16' Mercury plywood utility

1960 16' Crown Custom

1960 Mercury 17' Super Sport plywood hull ski boat

1960's era 16' Mercury utility

1961 Super Sabre entering a sharp corner

Sleek Mercury 18' utility streaking across the lake—1961

Head-on view of one of the last Mercury Super Sabres built in 1961

The very last Mercury inboard I ever was aware of, was built in 1961 and was called the 17' Super Sabre. From all appearances this boat looked much like a Century from the same era. The Sabre used the V-drive we mentioned before as well as a potent 250 h.p. V-8 to produce top speeds of 44 m.p.h. Seating was a little different, as a full front seat was standard along with a three-quarter seat ahead of the engine box that filled the rest of the cockpit area. A single-lever Morse control was used to handle shift and speed controls on this boat. The front deck was totally covered in vinyl, as was a major portion of the rear deck and transom. Although this boat was excellent in every aspect, West Coast boaters were not that interested in mahogany inboards anymore by 1961 and on, so by 1964 the last Mercury all-wood boat was built. Rising supply costs, labor fees and changes in buyer interest finally forced Bill Nollenberger to close down his operation forever. Today, Bill can be found still working around the Piru plant but he is busy building—of all things—fiberglass diving boards.

I hope you enjoyed this section on Mercury. The chances of Midwestern and Eastern fans ever seeing or finding a Mercury in restorable shape are quite rare. You West Coast folks can scour the boat yards, etc. and maybe you will be able to find a near-mint condition Mercury, or one that is still restorable, that you can buy, fix up and enjoy.

Now, let's move on to another regional builder and see what Dart boats had to offer. Dart inboards were built at Toledo, Ohio and were very popular in the Midwest, especially along the Great Lakes where the boats performed well on the often rough waters of this inland "sea". Dart boats today are few in number, but more and more are beginning to appear as interest in them increases.

1961 Super Sabre going through her paces. Note unusual rear seat.

DART—PIONEER IN ITS CLASS

Forerunner of Dart boats

1927 Dart magazine ad

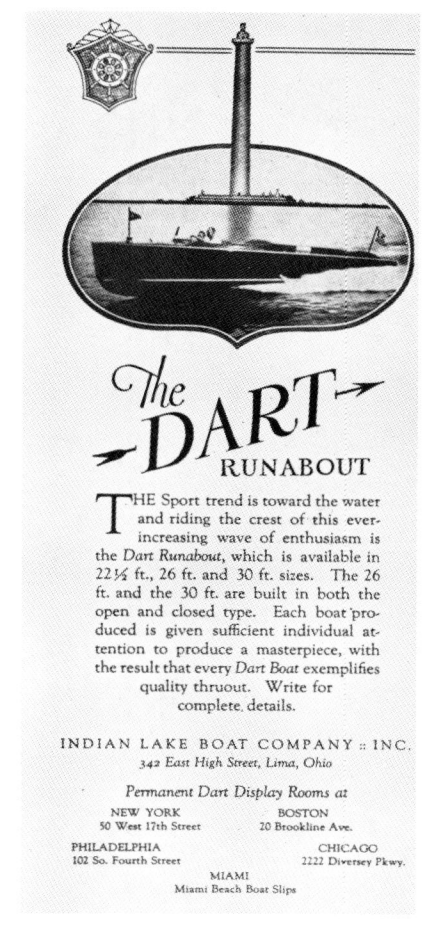

1928 Dart ad

The Dart Boat Company of Toledo, Ohio operated about eight years, but in that time turned out some excellent examples of inboard runabouts.

Originally, the firm was known as the Indian Lake Boat Company, Inc. of Lima, Ohio, a sleepy little resort city on the lake. The firm, beginning in the early 1920's, built all types of rowboats, outboards and inboard speedboats. I feel fortunate to have a view of an old 1926 28' Indian Lake launch taken from above. Most boats built at the Lima plant were smaller fishing boats and outboard runabouts. It was announced in October, 1928 that the rights to build all Dart runabouts had been purchased by a group of businessmen headed by Lieutenant Commander Webb C. Hayes, late of the U.S. Navy.[7] The new firm was named Dart Boats, Incorporated and the following officers were elected: Webb C. Hayes, president; F. D. Suydam, vice-president; William Baker, treasurer; and W. L. Hixon, secretary. Plans were to build an all-new modern plant in Toledo along the banks of the Maumee River. Production was expected to get underway by January of 1929. Webb Hayes stated the company was going to follow the policies set up by the former Indian Lake Boat Company as far as service to customers was concerned, and build about the same basic models, at least to start with. Dart Boats, Incorporated also was going to repair, restore and sell Dart boats in the Toledo area, according to company reports. The old Indian Lake Boat Company was going to remain very much in operation building outboard runabouts and fishing boats only. In fact, Indian Lake would continue

---
[7]"Dart Runabouts Change Hands", *POWER BOATING*, (Sept. '28), 34.

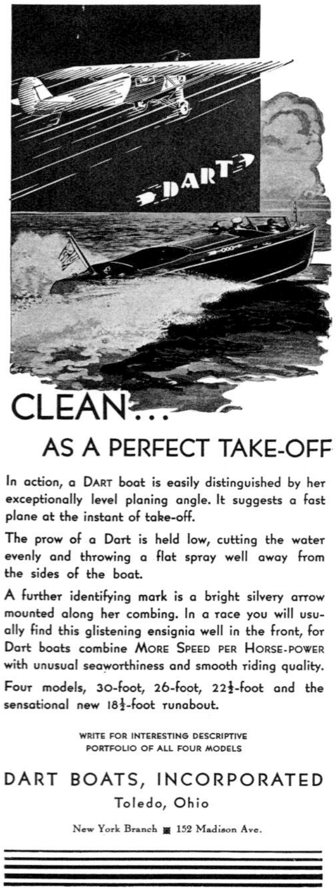

CLEAN...
AS A PERFECT TAKE-OFF

In action, a Dart boat is easily distinguished by her exceptionally level planing angle. It suggests a fast plane at the instant of take-off.

The prow of a Dart is held low, cutting the water evenly and throwing a flat spray well away from the sides of the boat.

A further identifying mark is a bright silvery arrow mounted along her combing. In a race you will usually find this glistening ensignia well in the front, for Dart boats combine MORE SPEED PER HORSE-POWER with unusual seaworthiness and smooth riding quality.

Four models, 30-foot, 26-foot, 22½-foot and the sensational new 18½-foot runabout.

WRITE FOR INTERESTING DESCRIPTIVE PORTFOLIO OF ALL FOUR MODELS

DART BOATS, INCORPORATED
Toledo, Ohio

New York Branch ■ 152 Madison Ave.

1930 Dart magazine ad

1930 18½' Dart magazine ad

Another 1930 Dart magazine ad

HERE is an unretouched photograph of the beautiful new 18½ foot Dart. Looks just like the larger Dart models, and has the same exceptional qualities of smooth riding, seaworthiness and additional speed per horsepower. All mahogany with a six-cylinder inboard motor that will go 30 miles per hour. Can be operated easily by anyone who drives a car. Regular automobile type of steering and controls, self-starter and positive reverse gears. If you live or vacation on any lake or river, you will add beyond measure to your summer's enjoyment by owning this new Dart Runabout. For commuting, fishing, pleasure jaunts or extended trips, there is no small boat to be compared with it. No cranking, no mixing of oil with gas, no fussing . . . just press the starter and away you go for a new thrill in motor boating. The price is $1595.00 f. o. b. Toledo. And purchase can be made on our convenient deferred payment plan.

DART BOATS, Incorporated ▲▲ **TOLEDO, OHIO**
NEW YORK OFFICE, 11 W. 42ND ST. CHICKERING 5611

MORE SPEED
▲▲▲▲▲ PER HORSE POWER

When you buy a runabout you want a fast craft. Not necessarily a racing boat but one that you can depend on to get you there in a hurry and then take you back the same way.

Dart boats are designed to give this extra bit of speed for the amount of horse power exerted—and in actual tests they do.

And it's one of the oddities of boat building that the craft capable of attaining a little greater speed always proves a bit more seaworthy.

This may seem strange but the fact is that a boat must ride smoothly, plane evenly and overcome pounding in order to go fast, and these same attributes are the essentials of seaworthiness.

These facts apply to every Dart Runabout. We make or develop no special boats for racing purposes, yet the impressive list of Dart victories speaks for itself.

Dart Boats—22½ ft., 26 ft., and 30 ft. open or closed models. Deferred payments if desired.

DART BOATS • *Inc.* • **TOLEDO, OHIO**
New York Office: - - - 11 West 42nd Street

---

in business until the mid-1950's, when they finally ceased building molded plywood runabouts, with the increased interest shown in fiberglass at that time.

In late December of 1928 the Toledo newspaper announced the opening of the all-new Dart Boats plant. The report mentioned output was planned to be three finished boats per day with the possibility of more when orders required it. The all-new building cost $60,000 with a 300-foot frontage and a depth of 60 feet. It featured open-span construction with concrete floors, brick walls and glass skylight-type roof.[8]

Being a small regional builder, Dart did not advertise to any great degree, so finding material on 1929 models was quite hard. I do have a photo of a typical 1929 25½' Dart runabout that used to, and still may, operate in Northern Minnesota.

1930 saw the real growth of Dart as a leader in building semi-custom mahogany speedboats, by then being sold by a rather large dealer network. Magazine ads began to appear in such publications as *MOTOR BOATING, POWER BOATING, YACHTING*, etc. I have a varied selection of 1930 ads scattered throughout

---

[8]"Dart Runabouts Change Hands", *POWER BOATING*, (Sept. '28), 34.

1929 25½" Dart 1961 view taken in northern Minnesota

HERE are the 1930 models of Dart Speed Boats—more dashing, more beautiful, more luxurious than ever before—but embodying the same principles of sturdy construction and careful workmanship that have made Dart the quality standard of the runabout industry.

As in the past, the new Darts offer more speed per horse power, smoother riding quality and additional seaworthiness at prices no higher

-DART-

DART BOATS · INCORPORATED
TOLEDO, OHIO

than other runabouts of their same type.

If you have the opportunity, see the new Darts at the Motor Boat Show; otherwise write us and we will tell you where these boats may be viewed and give you other information and specifications.

Four models 18½′ (upper left), 22½′ (upper right), 26′ (lower left) and 30′ (lower right.) Sedan type if desired in the larger models.

Total 1930 Dart fleet shown in magazine ad

this portion of the review. Dart announced they were offering an all-new 18½′ runabout selling for $1,595 f.o.b. Toledo.[9] The boat was to be of the split-cockpit style with a 60 h.p. Gray engine. Construction included all-mahogany planking, brass and copper fastenings and top speed was to be 30 m.p.h. With the introduction of

---
[9] "Dart Produces New Runabout", *POWER BOATING*, (Sept. '29), 50.

this small model, Dart was competing with other giant firms such as Chris-Craft, Gar Wood, Dodge, and many others for the small boat market.

The 1930 Dart lineup consisted of four models. The smallest was the 18½′ runabout we described earlier. The second was the 22½′ three-cockpit model followed by a 26′ and 30′ open or sedan model. All boats were basically styled alike and each featured the long, chrome Dart "arrow" running along the raised deck of the

81

engine compartments. The name "Dart" also was painted diagonally along the bow of each speedster, similar to that done by Dodge Watercars.

Famous race between Dart and English Flying Scotsman train. The Dart won! 1930 Dart advertisement.

An event that grabbed national headlines for Dart Boats occurred in England, when in 1929 a 26' Dart runabout raced the famous "Flying Scotsman" along the River Ouse. Of course, the Dart won hands-down. Pictures of the event soon appeared in many of the national boat magazines as well as the 1931 Dart catalog. I would like to thank Pete Henkle who loaned me a copy of his mint 1931 Dart catalog, from which much of the material for this section came.

Very late in the 1930 model year, Webb C. Hayes, II, revealed plans for his firm to offer an all-new 22½' yacht tender for 1931. Several unusual refinements and innovations were planned for the new boat whose debut would be early in 1931. A little later in this section, we shall take a closer look at the sleek and somewhat rare tender.

Mr. Webb also advised the public that 1930 had been a banner year with sales for the first three months of 1930 exceeding by several hundred percent their volume for the same period of 1929.[10] So many new orders had been sent to Dart for 1931 models, Mr. Webb expected to hire two additional crews and operate 24 hours a day to get caught up. With those expectations we shall begin a review of Dart for 1931.

As I mentioned earlier, Dart offered a fine 18-page black and white catalog for 1931. The outside cover was unusual in that on it, the only word that appeared was "DART" and it was done in all-black background with silver and pink writing and trim. Inside the front cover was a great view of the two Dart buildings taken shortly after their completion. A copy of that photo is shown at this point. The smallest 1931 Dart was the 18½' split-

[10]"Dart Announces New Speed Tender", *POWER BOATING*, (May '30), 37.

View of new Dart Boats factory, 1931, in Toledo, Ohio

cockpit we mentioned earlier. The new boat was pretty much unchanged except for a larger, new 75 h.p. Chrysler Crown which upped her speed to 32 m.p.h. Excellent overall views of every 1931 Dart were shown in the large catalog. Some of those views are shown in this section.

1931 18½' Dart Runabout

A race which caused international comment between a Dart Runabout and the Flying Scotsman, the fastest train in England—pictured again in 1931 Dart catalog.

Dart Boats are sold all over the world. This crated runabout was shipped to Jerusalem, and was the first speedboat to be used on the Dead Sea.

82

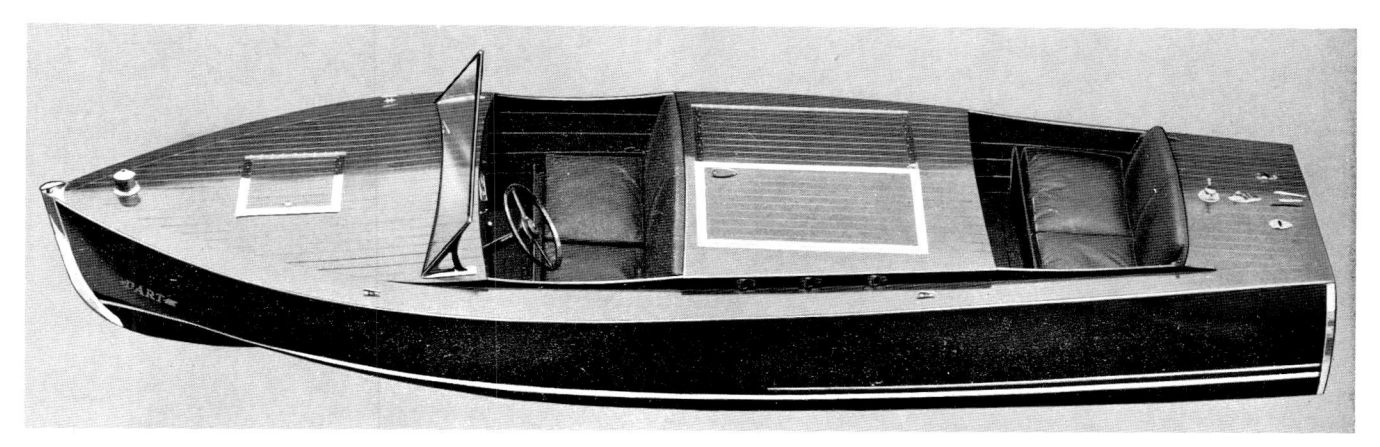

1931 18½ Dart split-cockpit runabout

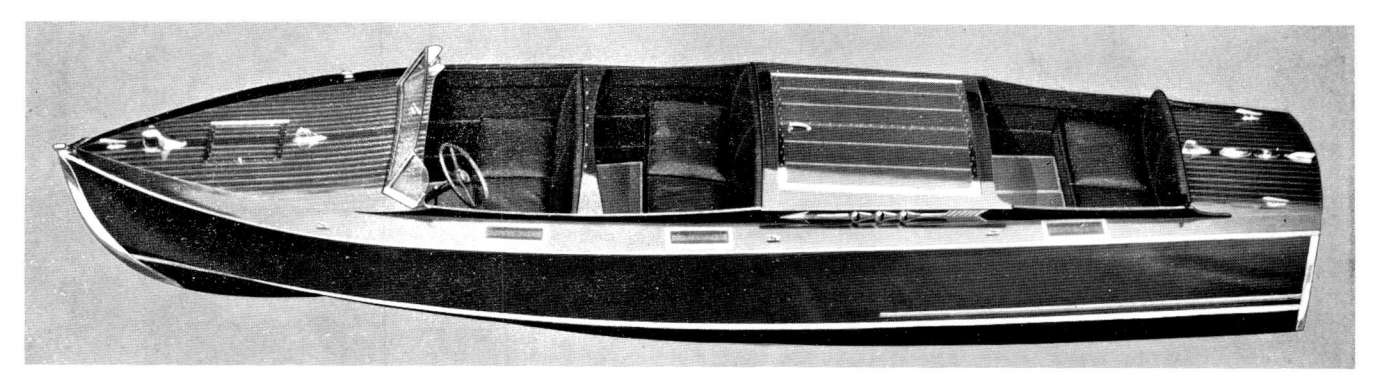

1931 24' "Red Dart" deluxe runabout

A 26-foot Dart with collapsible, automobile-type top. These tops, with curtains, are available as optional equipment on all models.

Dart runabout "in frame"—1931

Dart runabout having deck installed—1931

An interesting practice of Dart on its other 1931 Darts was to give each model a name all its own. The 1931 22½' runabout was called The Red Dart. This model was a three-cockpit flyer and a real beauty. She sported a double bottom consisting of an inner and outer bottom between which had been interspersed a layer of heavy duck canvas impregnated with waterproof glue. Only brass screws and rivets were used throughout every Red Dart as well as the finest sawed white ash frames and all white oak keel and chines. Expertly selected mahogany was used in all deck and hull planking. The 22½' came with three engine choices including the Chrysler Crown 75, 82 h.p. Chrysler Royal, and finally the 125 h.p. Chrysler Imperial. This big Chrysler could speed the boat over 35 m.p.h.

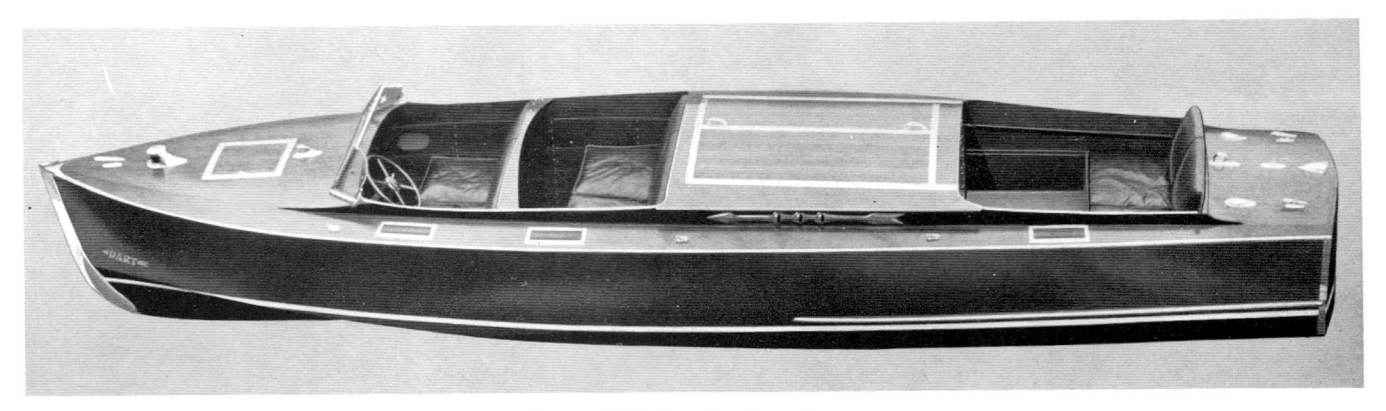

1931 Dart 26' "Silver Dart" runabout

"Queen" of the 1931 Dart runabout fleet, 30' long

The 26-foot Dart Sedan has all the luxury and beauty of the higher priced limousine motor car. A flat lounging deck amidships is an exclusive Dart.

30' "Golden Dart" about to take off

The next Dart runabout for 1931 was called the Silver Dart and was 26' long. It was offered as both an open three-cockpit runabout as well as a sedan model. The same fine selection of materials went into the construction of the Silver Dart as all the other models. Two Chrysler engines were available in 1931 for the 26' runabout, either the smaller six-cylinder 125 h.p. Imperial or the Chrysler Majestic 150 h.p. model. The big runabout could reach speeds of nearly 45 m.p.h. with the 150 h.p. engine. It too featured the traditional Silver Dart running along the raised engine hatch on both sides. The queen of the Dart fleet in 1931 was the big 30' Golden Dart. This boat was also a three-cockpit model, styled very much along the lines of Hacker Craft, right down to the three-piece windshield. Several interesting engine options were listed for the Golden Dart also. The standard engine for 1931 was to be a Sterling Petrol six-cylinder 200 h.p. or, for the sportsman who craved additional speed, a larger 400 h.p. Capitol Liberty was also available. A final twin-screw power option was also offered which consisted of two opposite-rotating 125 h.p. Chrysler Imperial engines. This twin-engine rig would reach speeds of 38 m.p.h. Finally, a very deluxe sedan commuter model in a 30' runabout was also available with the same engine options already mentioned. Perhaps the most unique boat ever offered by Dart was the 22½' Speed Commuter or Tender. The hull is the same as the standard 22½' Dart except for the addition of the all-new streamlined coupe top. Six passengers

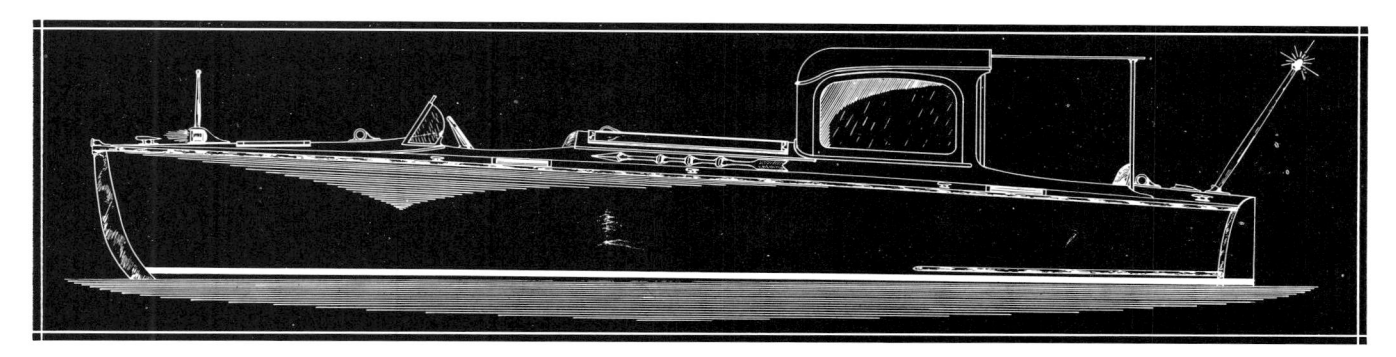

Posh, 1931 22½' Dart speed tender

This graceful 30-footer is largest of the Dart fleet. It will do 50 miles with 400 h.p.

could ride comfortably in the rear covered area while a crewman could ride forward to drive. In inclement weather, a convertible top and curtains could be added for the driver's comfort. The Dart tender came with a 125 h.p. Chrysler Imperial for 1931. That winds up the year 1931 and Dart.

1931 was the last year the Dart Boat Company was in existence. The same set of officers ran the firm as when it started and it seems their dream for expanding their production with lots of new models was never to be. The villain, the Depression, killed off this talented builder and never after 1932 would we see the beautiful Dart arrow running down the side of a sleek runabout built in Toledo, Ohio. . . .

Well, so much for the famed Dart line. Now let's look at another regional builder and see what the company had to offer.

ENSIGN—FOR DISCRIMINATING SPORTSMEN

Never heard of Ensign Boats you say? Well, I doubt if many others ever did either. Just the same, they, and other small concerns just like them, filled a void in power boating just after the conclusion of World War II. As we noted before, following the war's end, Americans were crazy for new boats and builders could hardly keep ahead of incoming orders. Now not everyone could buy, or wanted to buy a boat built by the big builders like Chris-Craft, Car Wood and others, so small local builders took up the slack and turned out speedboats to suit local tastes.

One such firm, Ensign Boats of Holland, Michigan announced that for 1947 they were offering two small wooden utility models. Mr. Merlin K. Disbrow, then owner of the company, reported that a new 16' utility was being added to the line along with the original 14' version first built in late 1946.[11] Thank you, Jack Kinn, Wisconsin dealer-collector for loaning me a copy of the 1947 Ensign brochure describing the all-new models. The 16' utility sported white hull sides, varnished decks, and deluxe vinyl interiors. The power plant for the new 16' model consisted of a 45 h.p. Gray Marine engine and the boat was claimed to be as well-built and stylish as anything then on the market. I think the 16' looks a lot like the small Century or Chris-Craft utilities from that era.

Ensign 16' inboard utility

[11] "16' Utility Inboard Boat Added to '47 Ensign Line", *BOATING INDUSTRY*, (Dec. '46), 45.

85

1947 brochure of 14' Ensign utility

The smaller 14' model also shown in this section was somewhat boxier in design and came with a 25 h.p. Kermath engine. Both boats had running lights, windshields, lifting rings, cushions, etc.

Though Ensign only lasted a few years, they did play a part in power boating and I doubt if today more than a handful of their creations still exist. I, for one, am glad to have the chance to show the Ensign in this book. I hope you readers enjoy it also.

From the tiny Ensign Boat Company another small firm, Globe-Mastercraft, will be reviewed. Some of my first inboard rides were taken in a Globe and I was part-owner of one of the little 14' gems about eight years ago. Let's see what you think of the Mastercraft after you read about them in the next section.

GLOBE MASTERCRAFT—
ACTION-A-PLENTY BY GLOBE

There was a small 14' split-cockpit inboard built at Lake Geneva, Wisconsin in the early 1950's which proved to be a boat much ahead of its time. You may or may not have heard of the "Globe", but after reading the following report perhaps you will wish you had....

It seems in the latter part of 1948, Mr. Millard E. Mogg, founder of the Inland Marine Boat Company, announced plans to build an all-new plant at Williams Bay, Wisconsin for the manufacture and sale of small inboard and outboard motor boats.[12] Mr. Mogg along with George F. Getz, owner of the Globe Corporation, were to join forces in the new boat-building firm. Quite a backlog of orders had been received for several small outboard boats the firm planned to offer to dealers in 1948. It soon became apparent to the company that a small, trailerable inboard runabout would be an asset to their line, so in 1949 a new model was "launched" at the New York Boat Show by Globe. I am indebted to the famous industrial designer, Mr. Brooks Stevens for the following information. Brooks told me he was hired by the Globe Corporation back in 1946 to design their entire fleet of boats. The little 14' inboard appeared on the scene in 1949 and was the hit of the 1949 New York Boat Show. Brooks told me that the small runabout was very innovative and the firm was awarded the "Grand Prix" for design at the 1949 show. My own experiences with the Mastercraft go back to about 1954, when a man here in Albert Lea used to give me a ride in his little 14-footer

1950 14' Globe Mastercraft

[12]"New Inland Marine Plant", *MOTOR BOAT*, (July '48), 120.

86

14' Mastercraft under full power of 45 h.p. Gray Marine engine

Local 14' Mastercraft I drove when a young lad

every so often. Even then, I thrilled at a chance to ride and sometimes even steer a real inboard speedboat. In 1972, a good friend of mine bought that ol' Mastercraft which had been in storage for at least ten years and completely refinished the boat. To this day, the boat is still here on Fountain Lake and her little 45 h.p. Gray still hums along as smoothly as ever.

14' Globe Mastercraft inboard

1949 saw the 14' split-cockpit Globe become a very popular boat. A utility was offered, as well as several outboard models, but I cannot personally say I have ever seen one. The model #R-6 Deluxe Runabout was 14' long, 59" wide and weighed 750 pounds with engine.

Please review the photos of the 14' runabout spread throughout this section. Some of its novel features follow. The decks were finished in two-tone, a first of that era. It also sported a swept-down stern profile as well as automobile-like instrumentation and crash padded cockpits. Another feature I can remember was that the shift mechanism was located on the dashboard and it consisted of a chrome lever you pushed in for forward and pulled back for reverse. The little 45 h.p. Gray Phantom four-cylinder fit nicely in the engine compartment and allowed for speeds up to 33 m.p.h. I am sure our little boat did close to 30, but when you rode in the rear cockpit it felt much faster. The windshield was a custom-built all-glass wraparound version that also was way ahead of its time. It made the boat look much newer than it really was.

Construction features included full-sheet, marine-grade, resin-bonded plywood over white oak ribs. The decks and transom were Honduras mahogany. The bottom featured non-trip chines and allowed for sharp corners without the tendency to skip or slide. When slowing down from high speed to idle, the boat showed no tendency to "nose dive" as was the case with other boats of similar design and size. All in all, that little 14' runabout was in a class all by herself. The photo of the 14' runabout tied up was taken by me back in 1960 or so. The boat, even then, looked nowhere near 11 years old. Mr. Stevens also designed a 22' twin-cockpit runabout as well as a 22' utility for Globe. The artist's drawing reproduced here shows how the boats were to look. Brooks still owns both the 14' and the 22' pictured here. Thanks to him for providing me with excellent photos.

22' Mastercraft on trial run on Lake Geneva, Illinois in 1950

1950 22' Mastercraft runabout on test run. Very rare model.

1950 22' utility Globe Mastercraft on Lake Geneva, Illinois

87

Globe ceased all boat building in 1950 with the beginning of the Korean conflict, and never built boats again. I, some day, would very much like to own a 14' Mastercraft as many of my first inboard rides were aboard one.

If you ever see a Mastercraft, you will know it from the pictures here. Years ago, they were quite a common sight here in the Midwest. I am sure, with a little looking, a person could find one to restore and really have a fine, small inboard that is a joy to own as well as to operate.

If it sounds like I am prejudiced toward the Globe, I am. It is an excellent boat for younger fans, or as a boat that can be trailed around on a small trailer modified for an inboard. Although only in business for 6 years, the Globe Corporation did much to advance the cause of inboards, especially in the 5-state midwestern area of the U.S.

All of us antique boat fans connect Algonac, Michigan with such firms as Chris-Craft, Gar Wood, etc., but how about Eckfield Boat Company? I must admit, the firm was a new one to me also, and you may find what they built and who operated it, as interesting to you as it was to me.

Artist's conception of new 1950 Mastercraft 22' runabout

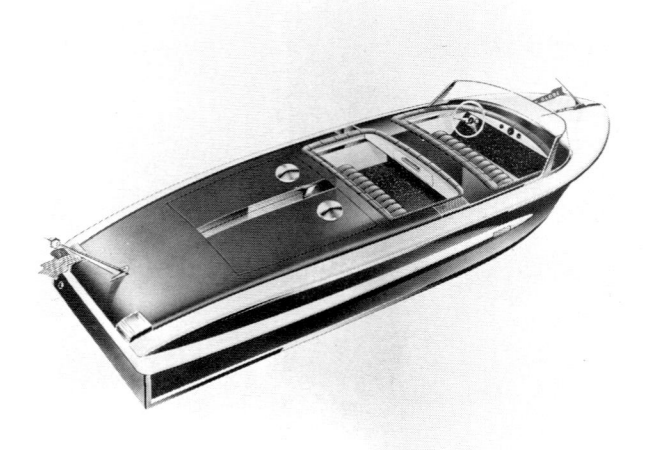

The sleek, new 1950 Globe 22' runabout

1950 14' Globe outboard powered by 22 h.p. Johnson—same hull as 14' inboard model.

ECKFIELD BOAT COMPANY—THE SENSATION OF THE SEASON

Mention the city Algonac, Michigan to any antique boat fan and his or her eyes will light up and immediately thoughts of Chris-Craft Boat Company come to mind. I must admit this was my experience until several months ago. . . .

Late last fall, I received a letter from a woman whose husband had been a marine engineer for 45 years with Chris-Craft Boat Company. That in itself was certainly an accomplishment; however, upon further correspondence with the woman and with her brother-in-law, the following story surfaced.

It seems that Algonac was not only the home of the mighty Chris-Craft Corporation, but also the Eckfield Boat Company. You say, "Eckfield Boat Company?—never heard of them". . . .Well, neither had I until recently. What follows is an interesting review of a little-known builder who went on to play a major role in power boat design through the early 1970's.

In 1925, Dr. C. C. Eckfield founded the Eckfield Boat Company on land next to the Chris-Craft Boat Company for the manufacture and sale of all types of power boats. Young Gene Eckfield, upon graduating from the University of Michigan in marine engineering, took over operation of the firm through 1929 when the depression caused its closing. In those few years many innovations were introduced by young Eckfield. Here are a few of the more important ones. Unlike Chris-Craft, Eckfield sold both outboard- and inboard-powered craft. They were an authorized Johnson Sea Horse motor dealer and Mr. Eckfield was credited with being the first to use the step on an outboard hydroplane bottom. In fact, numerous outboard racing shells in various classes were sold nationwide during the late 1920's. Another "first" offered by Eckfield occurred in 1928 when a pert little 18' outboard-powered cabin cruiser was made available and the boat received great reviews.[13]

Since this is a book on THE REAL RUNABOUTS, we must include a sample of the boats Gene and his firm turned out. The first was a 21' three-cockpit model called the "Escapade". This boat was designed by Gene himself and was powered by a Gray six-cylinder 90 h.p. engine. Top speed was estimated to be 33 m.p.h. Another boat designed by Mr. Eckfield was a larger 24' sedan or open runabout with the name "Parrot". She looked similar to boats offered by other builders in the late 1920's and early '30's. I understand this boat was not built at the plant, but the design was sold to other boat builders who in turn built boats from the plans.

By 1929, the depression brought boat sales to a screeching halt, so young Gene went across the street and took a job with the engineering department of Chris-Craft which would last for forty-five years.[14] In that period of time, Mr. Eckfield played a major role in designing many of both the large and small Chris-Craft boats we have taken for granted all these years. This brief account is a credit to a man who, though behind the scenes, played a major role in the design and styling of the antique and classic speedboats and cruisers we now hold so important in these days when mass production and fiberglass have taken their toll. Well done, Gene! Your designs will live on in the fine wooden boats that are preserved, as well as used, by thousands all over this country.

Eckfield trademark

Early 1920's Eckfield magazine ad

[13] *POWER BOATING*, (May '28).

[14] "Letter", K. C. Eckfield, (Feb. '78).

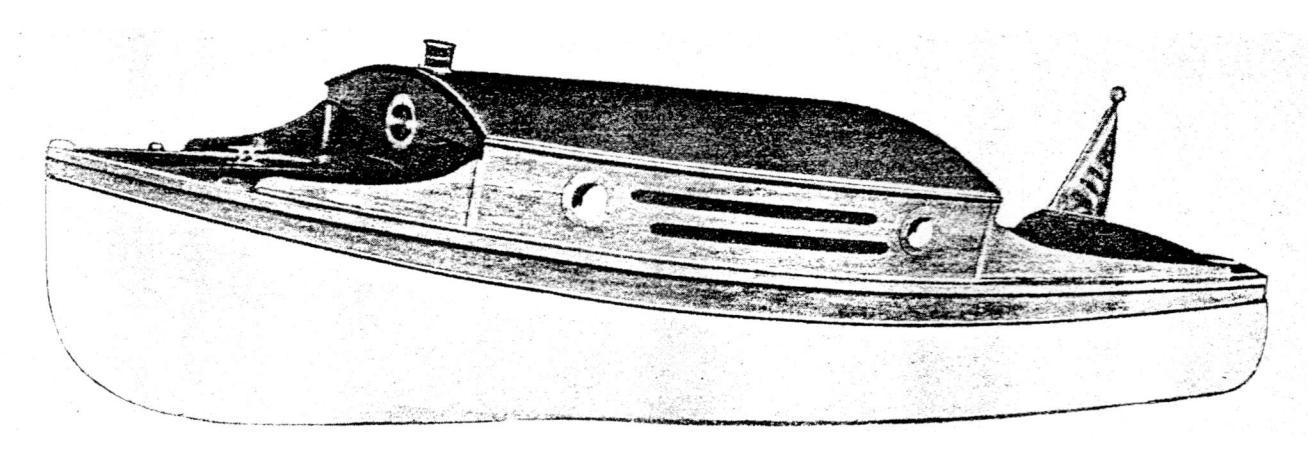

1928 18' Eckfield outboard cruiser

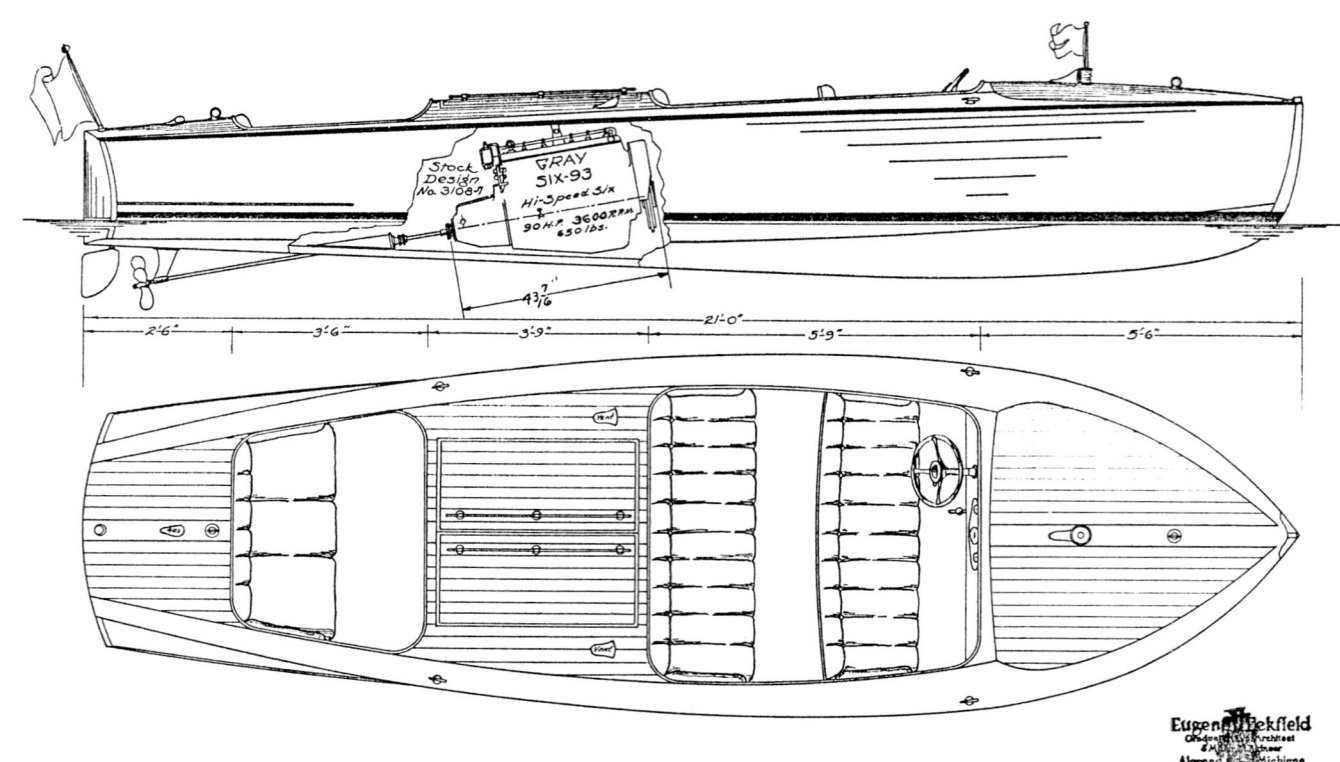

Escapade

Length — 21'-0"
Beam - deck — 6'-5½"
" - chine — 5'-7"
Freeboard - For'd — 2'-2"
" Aft — 1'-5"
Passengers — Eight
Draft with 12" propeller — 1'-7"
Speed — 35 M.P.H.

Design No. 3108-7
Eugene L. Eckfield
Naval Architect
Algonac, Michigan

Complete Building Plans
for Professional & Amateur Builders

Concave Vee-bottom Construction
Sawn Frames - Battened Seams
Single Planked Sides
Single or double Planked Bottom
Designed Power:
  Gray Six-93 High Speed Six
Clearance for 13" dia. propeller
Shaft Angle — 10°

1930 21' Eckfield runabout

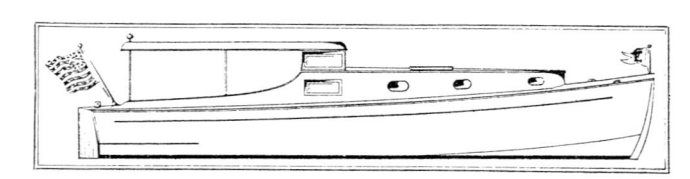

32' Eckfield cabin cruiser

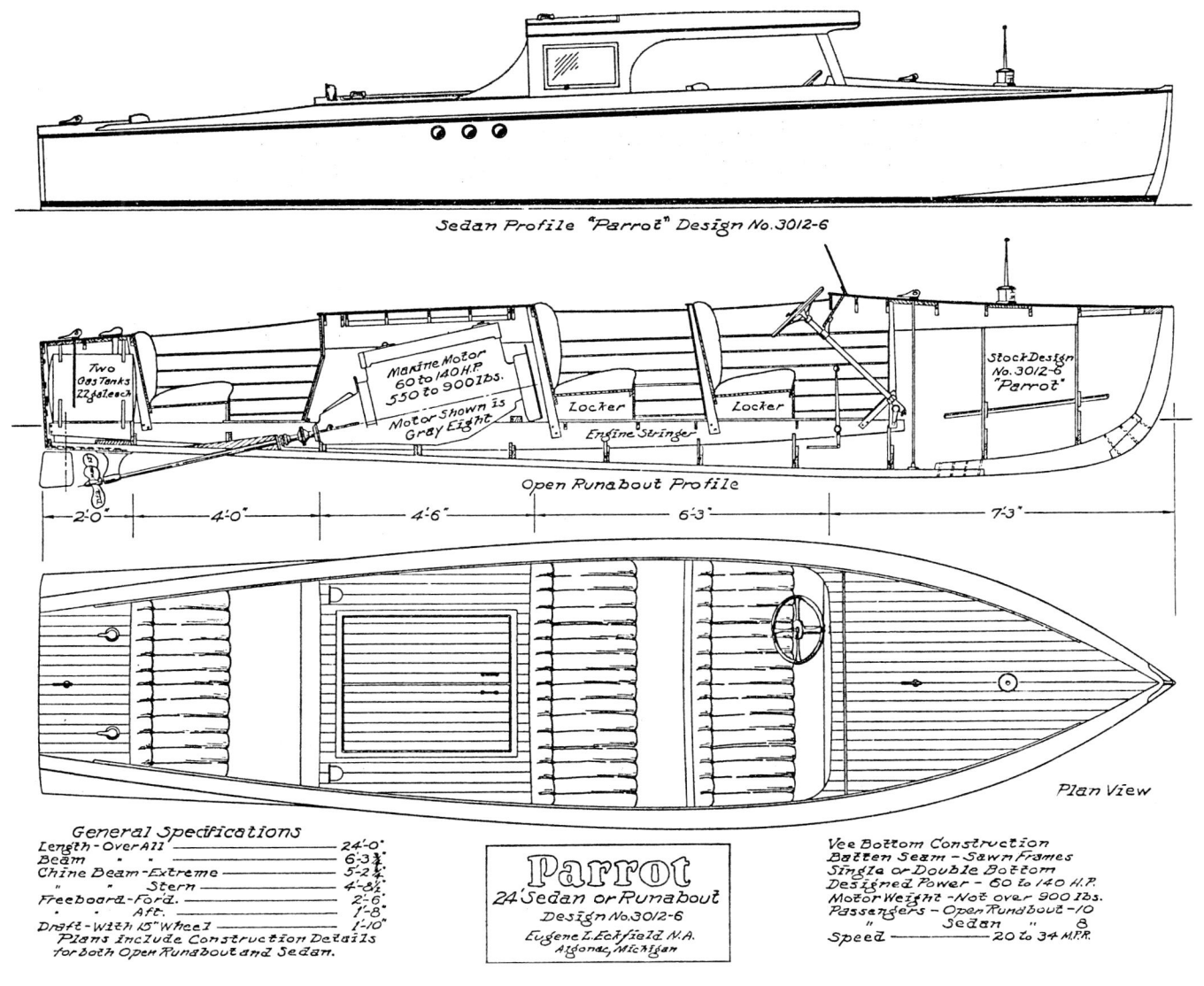

Sleek 24' Eckfield sedan

Meteor Boat Company of Piqua, Ohio shall be our next stop. This firm sold factory-direct for several years in the mid-1930's and also manufactured such varied items as funeral coaches, record players and other items.

METEOR—GREATEST VALUE IN THE HISTORY OF MOTOR BOATING

There once was a firm which built speedboats as well as hearses and ambulances. That firm is still very much in business today although they have not built power boats since 1932. The Meteor Motor Car Company was founded by the late Maurice Wolfe who died in 1935. It seems young Maurice was interested in mechanical things of all kinds and during his lifetime built cars, ambulances, hearses, phonographs, motor boats and radios. You must admit, anyone who had done all that in one lifetime must have been quite a man.

When I decided I would include Meteor boats in this book I quickly wrote the Chamber of Commerce in Piqua, Ohio, inquiring about the former Meteor Boat Company. Some days later I received a post card stating that the firm was still in business in the town and I should contact them directly. I hurried off a note telling them what I wanted to know and before very long a big, thick manila envelope arrived at my home. Boy, I was really excited! I thought I really was going to strike it rich! All that material about Meteor Boats! What a find!

Upon opening the package, I was surprised to find complete color photos of all the 1978 Miller-Meteor ambulances. After the surprise of seeing the contents of the envelope, the nice letter included told me "Yes, they once built speedboats" and "No, they had no material about them."

I did find out that the first boats were built in 1928 and were 27' long. They came equipped with or without convertible roof and were powered by Red Seal Continental engines, the same ones used in their hearses of the same year. Mr. Wolfe decided that he wanted to build and sell motor boats along with hearses and ambulances, so he built a small plant on the banks of the Miami River at Piqua. His idea was to build the boats there and sell them factory-direct rather than through dealers to cut down costs. Enclosed are ads from 1929 and 1930. Only one 27' three-cockpit model was ever offered and Wolfe said his boats compared with any offered by others whose boats sold for twice the money. The style was much like those offered by Dart, Chris-Craft, Gar Wood or others of that time.

1929 saw the Meteor on display at the New York Boat Show. Sales response to Wolfe's idea was very good. Meteors began to appear not just in the Ohio area but scattered all over the country. 1931 was the last year of offering the 27' speedboat. It seemed that the Depression had all but destroyed Wolfe's potential buyers so he quit building boats and went back to funeral cars and the like. Thus a very unusual situation came to an end, and the idea of selling mahogany inboard speedboats to the public in that way did also. I have just recently become aware of a man in Ohio who is trying to restore a Meteor speedboat. Let's hope he is successful. Probably no more than two or three Meteors still exist in this whole country. I hope that others do surface and that they too are preserved.

Mr. Wolfe was successful with his boat works and had it not been for the Depression, may have built boats for a much longer time.

1929 Meteor ad—27' runabout

27' 1930 Meteor runabout—only one model offered

FALLS FLYER—UNIQUENESS IN MOTOR BOATS

LARSON BOAT COMPANY

One of the most unique styles of inboard runabout ever built would have to be a masterpiece turned out by the Larson Boat Works located in Little Falls, Minnesota. I am quite sure most readers have never heard of, or seen a "Flyer" in their life. Take it from me, they are really something!

Through the kindness of Glen Kraywinkle, manager of the Little Falls Chamber of Commerce and Paul Larson, founder and former owner of Larson Boat Company, I am able to share the following limited material on these excellent boats. I can remember seeing a Falls Flyer back about 1953 that was being used for speed boat rides up in northern Minnesota. Their design was very unusual—in fact, to the point that Mr. Larson obtained a design patent on his prize runabout. First of all, the two photos showing the 19' Falls Flyer with the famous midget, Johnny of Phillip Morris, were loaned to me by Paul for use in this book. In both views you can see the extremely curved hull design somewhat on the order of the Canadian Greavette inboards mentioned in *Volume I*. I

Falls Flyer at rest behind Larson factory in northern Minnesota, about 1950.

Paul Larson and "Johnny" in Falls Flyer inboard

can personally assure you that the Falls Flyer is an extremely smooth-riding craft, even in heavy waves. All boats were styled along similar lines—very curved hull sides, semi-flat bottom and sloping rear deck. The rear deck, sloping as it did, also acted as a built-in set of trim tabs keeping the stern from sinking in upon take-off at high speeds.

The very first Falls Flyers were built in both outboard as well as inboard styles. The wooden-hulled models were made of cedar strips, covered with muslin cloth and painted to a point where barely a board showed through. In fact, to all but the most trained eye, the boats resembled fiberglass in their smoothness of finish. I have seen only one 14' Flyer wooden outboard and it was not restored. I have become aware of another, which is said to be in perfect condition. My first antique, or perhaps classic, boat was a 1955 14' Falls Flyer outboard. This boat was patterned exactly after the wooden model, except it was built of fiberglass. The hull bottom and deck and sides were made in two separate molds and then joined together as one complete unit. Hardware on all Falls Flyers was special-designed and custom-built. My outboard had a most unusual bow handle flowing into a cut water which was like a duck with outspread wings. We all must admit, that's a pretty rare type of bow handle. Another feature on the outboard included steering wheel mounted either forward or aft, depending on the owner's preference. It just so happened mine had steering and engine controls in the front seat. Any Falls Flyer seemed to be a very safe-riding boat. Though their bottom was flat, three heavy keels helped hold them under control in sharp corners, etc. Although they do lean extensively on the corners, they never show a tendency to flip.

To get back to the inboard versions once more, all were painted in the same basic colors. The main portion of the deck and hull sides above the spray rails was cream colored while the bottom, in most cases, was bright red. Black enamel was used on the nose as well as around the edges of the cockpits and down the center of the back deck. Fine pinstripes in contrasting colors separated the cream from the black as well as from the red on all boats.

From 1940 through 1957, Falls Flyer boats were built in goodly numbers at Little Falls. Following a major fire that destroyed all of the Larson plant in 1949, no new wooden boats were ever built again. All the firm's records were lost, thus making it difficult to obtain more facts on these interesting boats.

To show you the timeless interest shown in the inboard Falls Flyer, one belonging to F. Todd Warner was displayed at the Minneapolis Boat Show with four other finely done boats, yet the Flyer received the most attention from visitors, media, etc. Some may call it an "ugly duckling", but all must admit it is unusual in its design. Warner's boat is a 19' version built in 1937. Her

Mint, 1937 Falls Flyer runabout

Marge and Chuck Steel with "Boondoggle", a 1939 Falls Flyer

power source is a 95 h.p. Gray engine. When he bought her, she was still in remarkable shape, still equipped with the original upholstery, pennants, etc. All the boat needed was a refinishing, which it received. It seems others found it a fascinating boat too, as Todd sold it after the show. He is glad the boat will operate on his home lake.

Other models of the Falls Flyer were of a shorter 14' variety where the engine was mounted forward and the driver sat aft. Please notice the photo of this style boat in this section. I am only aware of the boat shown here, as Mr. Larson said only 40 were ever built of wood. The 14' version was powered by a 45 h.p. Gray engine.

The owner of the 14' Falls Flyer purchased it at a local marina for $100 and proceeded to spend countless hours restoring the boat to its original condition. He later found out the boat had first belonged to a millionaire and was built in 1939, just before all production came to an end on the wooden Flyers.

About 1949 saw the end of building the wooden Falls Flyer boats. It seems the fire of that year, plus the increased cost of labor and materials, caused Larson to give up ever building another wooden hull. From research I have found Larson Boat Works also built approximately 15 all-mahogany 21' utility inboards. Mr. Larson had no remaining material about the boats other than he remembers the firm building them. They also built some small 16' or 17' all-mahogany utilities.

Recently, one of these boats appeared for sale in a newspaper and I was fortunate enough to obtain a rather dark polaroid photo of the same. She appears to be in good condition and was also built about 1936. I only hope someone buys the boat, refinishes it and keeps it so we will have at least one example of the great boat building genius of the "Wizard of the North Woods". So. . . if you ever see a very curved-style runabout scoot across the lake or river where you are, chances are it's a Falls Flyer from far-off northern Minnesota.

From Falls Flyers let's now move on to a review of some custom speedboat builders too. Most of the following firms built fewer boats but most were "one of a kind," constructed to specific sets of plans as well as owner's own desires, etc. The first and one of the most famous of all the companies we shall look at will be Robinson Marine Construction Company of Benton Harbor, Michigan—builder of the famous Seagull cruisers.

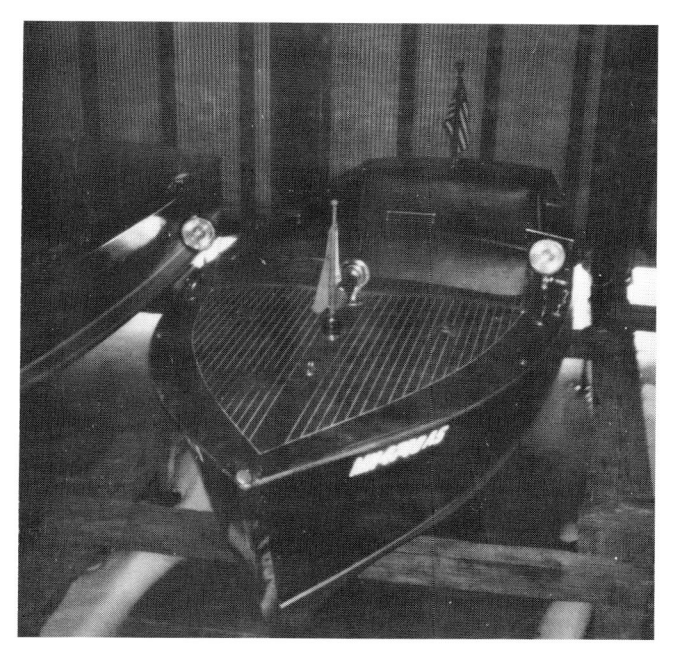

1936 Larson all-mahogany utility

95

CHAPTER III
MORE CUSTOM BUILDERS

ROBINSON—SEAGULL
OFTEN SEEN—RARELY PASSED

One of my very favorite large boat builders would have to be the Robinson Marine Construction Company of Benton Harbor, Michigan. I had a most difficult time obtaining much history of this builder but did have some luck.

City officials advised me that the firm dated back to 1926 when they first began operation. It seems they did commercial as well as recreational boat building, repairs, etc. By the late 1920's Mr. Robinson was already beginning to specialize in the building of sleek, fast, all-varnished commuter-type cruisers which were very, very popular in those days. Robinson "Seagulls", as they were called, came in all sizes from 30' sedan runabouts up through 50' custom beasts that would "boggle" the mind.

I was fortunate last summer to receive photos of a rare Seagull sedan runabout still in use on the Great Lakes. The boat looks much like a Hacker Commuter of the same period and for good reason—John Hacker designed the boat. It was built so that passengers could walk between the twin engines just as on the Hacker Craft commuter. The hardtop roof was covered with a coarse, black leather; large cane-woven seats were located in the back area under the hardtop roof. The hull sides were varnished while king plank and covering boards were finished black like the Hacker Crafts of the era. The firm also built a few open speedboats but mostly the more famous all-varnished cruisers. Their final boats appeared in about 1948. After that, no more Seagulls were built—especially the varnished types. The last of them were completed prior to World War II. Today a few Robinson Seagull all-varnished commuters are still around, but not many. Many of them were destroyed over the years or had their hulls painted over rather than varnished to cut down on maintenance costs, etc. The era of the Seagull was from about 1930 through 1935. After that time both costs and lack of skilled craftsmen brought about the final end of nearly all varnished cruisers.

The rest of this section, though very short on written history, will tell the Robinson story in photos. I hope you enjoy it and if you have ever seen a true Robinson Seagull, you may consider yourself very lucky. They truly were, and are, exceptional boats in every way!

1930 45' Robinson Commuter

1930 38' Robinson Commuter with 300 h.p. Scripps V-12. Sleeps 4, 35 m.p.h.

Robinson Seagull sedan runabout

1930 Seagull sedan runabout

Robinson-Hacker display at 1930 Los Angeles Boat Show

1930 39' Sport Sedan by Robinson

97

Often Seen
BUT SELDOM PASSED
At Yachting's Smartest Rendezvous

Robinson Cruisers and Commuters have become the focal point of dramatic enthusiasm for those yachtsmen who demand a fast hull distinguished by those rare attributes of sparkling beauty and jaunty sophistication. Robinson Seagulls are built with long sweeping lines and lithe free riding grace that bespeak a smartness of contour and a telling superiority of underbottom design—the product of accumulated experience and fine hand-wrought details of construction. Heavily ribbed and framed in oak, planked throughout in African mahogany, single and twin screw powered, built in three splendid sizes—39, 40 and 45 foot lengths—your Robinson Seagull will ride out the roughest weather with perfect ease because of its buoyant lift and vigorous speeds. Descriptive catalog, fully illustrated with genuine action pictures, will be mailed on request.

PACIFIC COAST DISTRIBUTOR
S. CLYDE KYLE, 102 New Montgomery St., San Francisco

ROBINSON Seagull CRUISERS

The 45-foot Seagull Custom-Commuter with bridge deck controls is available in single and double cabin design. Speeds, twin-screw powered, up to 40 miles per hour.

ROBINSON MARINE CONSTRUCTION CO. — BENTON HARBOR, MICHIGAN

1930 Robinson Seagull ad

The Seagull 39-foot Sedan Cruiser is a deluxe model with galley, toilet, lockers and four pullman berths, including spacious after cockpit.

1931 39-foot Robinson Seagull Sport Sedan with forward open riding cockpit and bridge deck controls. Complete cruising accommodations for four.

1931—The 40-foot Robinson Seagull Speed Cruiser is available with both single- and twin-screw power. Speeds up to 35 miles per hour.

1932 45' Seagull Commuter with twin Hall-Scott engines

50' Custom Commuter by Robinson with two Hall-Scott Invaders. Sleeps 9.

1933 50' Robinson deluxe cruiser—a real one-of-a-kind!

"Yap Yap"— 1934 45-foot Robinson Express Cruiser

98

1934 Robinson Seagull owned by Roger Firestone, using Twin Scripps engines

1935—Custom-built 45' mail boat for Mackinac Island

Seagull Commuters under construction at Benton Harbor, Michigan —1935.

Future Robinson Seagulls under construction—1936

Although We Are Now Engaged in the
DEFENSE BUILDING PROGRAM
We Are Looking Forward to the
Peacetime Fleet of Tomorrow

★

Beyond the immediate present, we foresee the greatest pleasure fleet America has ever known. We have not forgotten the many friends who are now enjoying our fine craft in all parts of the country and when these yachtsmen are ready to re-order we, too, will be ready to serve. The policy of the best in materials and workmanship, engineering and design, will always guide our efforts.

★

ROBINSON MARINE CONSTRUCTION CO.
INCORPORATED
BENTON HARBOR ★ MICHIGAN

One of the final Robinson cruisers ever built—1941

PHILBRICK BOAT COMPANY
CUSTOM AND STOCK RUNABOUTS
SINCE 1934

As we saw in *Volume I*, fine wooden mahogany speedboats are still being manufactured on a custom basis here and there. I have recently become acquainted with a firm which has been quietly building great inboard runabouts since 1934 out in sunny California. In visiting with the firm's congenial owner, Don Philbrick, I soon became aware of Don's keen interest in building only the finest inboards possible.

I was approached by Bob McBride of Campbell, California at the 1977 Antique Boat Show at Lake Minnetonka and he asked what I knew about Philbrick boats. I told him I was very sorry but I had never heard of them. He went on to tell me a little about what they built, etc., and I was anxious to get more material on the firm so that it could be included in this new book. Bob was kind enough to interview Don Philbrick for me and the following material is included here because of the kindness of Bob McBride.

It seems Don Philbrick graduated from high school in 1934 and almost immediately went into boat building. Over the years he built mostly inboards in all sizes from 16' through 20' in length. Don feels anything under 19' a poor excuse for a speedboat. The only reason he ever did build any small boats such as 16-footers, was the idea some years ago in California, that boats should be "garage-size" so owners could trail them and keep them at home. Today there are more and larger marinas so most owners keep their boats on the water rather than trail them around. Bob McBride described the Philbrick runabout as somewhat along the lines of a Chris-Craft "Capri" and I guess he is pretty close.

The conclusion of this section will describe the current offering by Philbrick, a sleek 20½' twin-cockpit-forward speedster that any of us would love to own. According to John B. Beckett, Philbrick Boat Works sales manager, the following information describes the new Philbrick speedboat perfectly.[1]

The new 20½' model is virtually unchanged from the Philbrick inboards built in the 1930's and 1940's except for some minor changes in technology over the years. The hulls as we mentioned are 20½' long with a beam of 6' 10". The bottoms of each boat are of double layers of plywood for less shrinking, swelling, etc., and covered with fiberglass. The hull sides and decks are planked with solid mahogany—the finest Honduras mahogany available. All boats are powered with a 250 h.p. Chrysler marine engine using a "V" drive to keep the shaft angle as low as possible. A thirty-gallon gas tank and fuel gauge is also standard equipment. All boats are varnished with numerous coats and hand rubbed between applications. Production figures were not available but I

Sleek 20½' Philbrick runabout

Overall view taken at Philbrick factory

Front cockpit of sleek Philbrick runabout

---
[1] "Letter", John B. Beckett, (Jan. 12, '78).

am sure only a dozen or so are built each year. Price runs somewhere over $25,000 per boat. You may contact the builder directly by letter or phone as their address and phone number are listed in the back part of this book. Boats are sold factory direct, helping to keep prices lower, which is especially important when you are dealing with a more expensive boat as this one definitely is.

I feel fortunate in having three good photos of the most recent runabout offered by Philbrick, the 20½' twin-cockpit-forward model. This boat at first reminded me of the small Riva runabouts built in the early 1960's. The only real equipment that is not of the old design on the Philbrick is the modern wraparound windshield. However, the new style looks very nice and does not distract from the boat. Chris-Craft air vents are used on the rear deck and a built-in ski tow bar is located just aft of the second seat. Exhaust pipes are neatly constructed into a spray rail which sweeps across the transom. My own favorite feature found on the Philbrick is the bright red bottom paint which gives each boat the look of speedboats built years ago. All in all, I am sure every reader will enjoy a brief "preview" of a boat from the far west that many of us may never have heard of before this time.

GAGE-HACKER—FOR BOATING AT ITS FINEST

Gage-Hacker insignia—a familiar sight on Lake Geneva, Wisconsin!

Back in 1965, while on a college field trip, my brother Art and I stopped at Gage Marine in Williams Bay, Wisconsin around the first of April. We walked down near the firm's massive docks and viewed a number of wooden and steel-hulled excursion boats owned by Gage which were all covered with huge tarps but remained afloat with the assistance of a "bubbler" system, which at that time was still quite novel here in the Midwest. For you readers who are not familiar with such a system, it works on the principle of pumping warm water up from the bottom of the lake to the top, as well as causing the water to constantly be moving, thus making it almost impossible for ice to form around boats, docks or whatever else a person wants to save. Anyhow, that was not our main reason for stopping. When we walked into the building a number of men were hovering over a bare skeleton of a runabout. While conversing with several of the men we found out that Gage Marine was building custom mahogany inboards still in 1965, and that sales of them were brisk on Lake Geneva. To this day I have my copy of the two-page brochure the firm put out concerning those sleek-looking craft. When I decided to do a second book I wanted to include a section on those fine craft. After numerous phone calls and letters back and forth between Bill Gage and me, suitable material was gathered to do this report. I think you are going to find the Gage-Hacker a rather remarkable craft in many ways.

If you are not familiar with Lake Geneva, Wisconsin, it is a long, rather narrow lake which can become very rough when the wind blows down the lake from west to east or vice versa. Geneva for years and years has been a tourist mecca for southeast Wisconsin and the Chicago, Illinois area. Fine old mansions dot the lake with all other types and sizes of homes, cabins, etc. surrounding its beautiful shoreline. The water there is crystal clear, thanks to stringent laws concerning marine heads, holding tanks, etc. The lake has always been a mecca for inboard power boats of all sizes as they are best suited to the lake's changeable conditions. Mr. Gage felt that when firms such as Chris-Craft, Hacker and others stopped building wooden inboards that there still was a market on his lake for such craft. Upon looking over several late 1940's era Hacker Craft speedboats his firm had owned, he wondered why the boats had lasted so long in excellent condition while being operated in all types of weather.

It was finally decided that the Hacker Craft boats possessed certain bottom qualities not offered by other builders. For some reason the Hacker rode the sometimes rough Lake Geneva water with little or no bottom problems that often plagued other boats. Upon further

Photo of 22' Gage-Hacker utility—1963

investigation, Gage decided that the bottom design offered by John Hacker was the reason his older boats rode so well. In other words, Hacker designed his boats with not just a flat bottom as most others, but what you would call a moderate "V" bottom running all the way back to the transom. Perhaps not as fast as a totally flat-bottom speedboat, the Hacker did allow a much softer, more stable ride. Photo #3 shows a Gage-Hacker being planked and you can see the amount of "V" in the bottom running fore to aft. Bill Gage has told me that most of the approximately 25 runabouts the firm built from 1961 through 1967 are as good as new and none have suffered from split planking, leaks, etc. Two other reasons mentioned by Gage for the success of his boats are that all frames, keels, chine areas, etc. were carefully secured by the firm's own methods, not just relying on a few screws here and there. Also, proper bedding and sealing of all wood helped the Gage-Hacker boats to hold up so well over the years. As Bill said, workmen hated to take time to do things like bed or seal end grain of wood, but attention to these little chores has helped to keep all the Gage-Hacker boats still in excellent condition; they should go on providing excellent service for years to come.

Diagonal planking double layer and deep "V" hull—Early 1960's model.

Now that we have reviewed a little history and philosophy of Gage Marine, let's move on to a more detailed look at those great boats.

As I mentioned before, the notion of a Gage-Hacker inboard came from older Hacker Crafts which had worked so well and had been in use for many years. Gage contacted John Hacker who eventually came up with a design suitable for Lake Geneva and finally two models were decided on. Boats 22' and 26' were built, about 25 in six years or so.[2] I am very indebted to Bill Gage for providing the excellent photos that accompany this section.

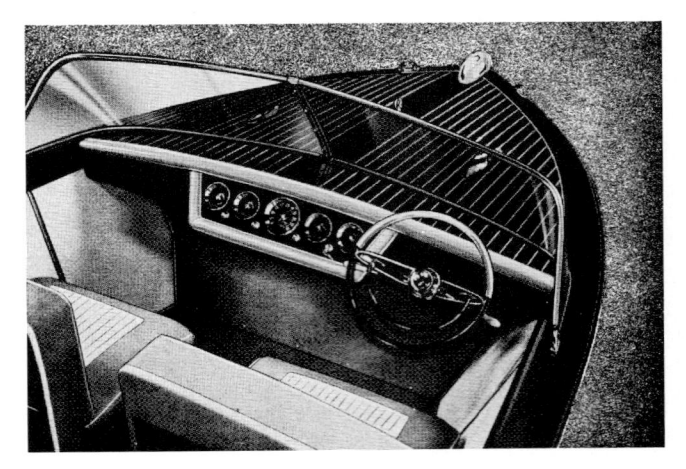

---
[2]"Gage Marine Corp.", *ANTIQUE BOATING*, (Summer '76), 14.

Luxurious Gage-Hacker dashboard of the mid-1960's

As I mentioned before, the smallest Gage-Hacker was a 22' utility which came powered with a 240 h.p. V-8 engine. The larger 26' version came with either single or twin engines up to 600 h.p. Gage Marine never was guilty of underpowering their craft to meet competition. There is nothing worse than a large speedboat that is underpowered.

The first Gage-Hackers built were finished with the attractive white "spear" running down each side. Later boats were sometimes done completely in varnish with no such trim, causing them to closely resemble a Chris-Craft, Century, etc. The equipment list on every Gage-Hacker was very complete. The only options not included as standard equipment were convertible top and side curtains, mooring cover, electric bilge pump and spotlight.

1964—22' Gage-Hacker utility

22' Gage-Hacker utility at cruising speed

102

The two photos shown at this point are of the 22' utility which was built about 1964. Both views were taken at less than wide open speeds for the benefit of the photographer. The base price for a standard 22' utility was right around $5,000 according to Gage. All Gage-Hacker speedboats maintained an excellent planing angle. Even at slower speeds, the driver had excellent visibility at all times, with no "blind spots" arising. The next photo also shows another 22' Gage-Hacker runabout on display at the First National Bank in Lake Geneva, Wisconsin. Because of a narrow doorway the boat had to be tilted on its side to enter the building. Quite a striking display to have in any lobby.

Gage-Hacker in Lake Geneva, Wisconsin bank, 1964

1963 26' custom Gage-Hacker runabout

The "queen" of all Gage-Hacker runabouts must be the big 26' twin-cockpit-forward model shown tied to a dock on Lake Geneva. You will note behind the engine hatch is another flush-mounted hatch which covers a huge storage compartment for gear, etc. The big runabout was the only one of its type ever built and was powered by a 280 h.p. V-8 Chrysler engine. Mr. Gage informed me the boat performed just beautifully. Three other 26' hulls were built with two single-engine models while the other had twin engines. Gage Marine preferred Chrysler engines but also used 215 or 225 h.p. Grays on occasion. You will also note that Gage Marine ran both the outside as well as inside planking diagonally and in opposite directions. It seems this was a favorite method of construction with John Hacker, and Bill Gage found it worked perfectly for them also. Another feature of diagonal planking was that construction time and labor costs could be lowered greatly. In closing, I asked Bill if the 26' runabout was still there and he said, "No". The owner, it seems, was taken ill and the boat ended up in Sturgeon Bay, Wisconsin where it was finally sold. He does not know for sure where it is today. All the other 24 or so boats still are used every season at Lake Geneva, most still in the hands of original owners even after 17 years—which is a real recommendation for any boat.

Thus we have been able to study another custom builder of a more modern period. Bill Gage and his Gage Marine maintain, store and "pamper" the remaining fleet of fine Gage-Hacker masterpieces over at Lake Geneva. If ever you get over in Bill's area, try and stop by his beautiful operation. You will be hard put to find another dealership anywhere that is any more complete and in better condition.

The "proud home" of Gage Marine Corporation, Williams Bay, Wisconsin.

Now we shall "skip" across the broad Atlantic Ocean and view another firm who, differing from Gage Marine, is currently "gearing up" to build fine wooden speedboats like those built in the past. Their story and ideas for the future are exciting and I hope their plans meet with all kinds of success.

LEATHER RUNABOUTS OF ENGLAND

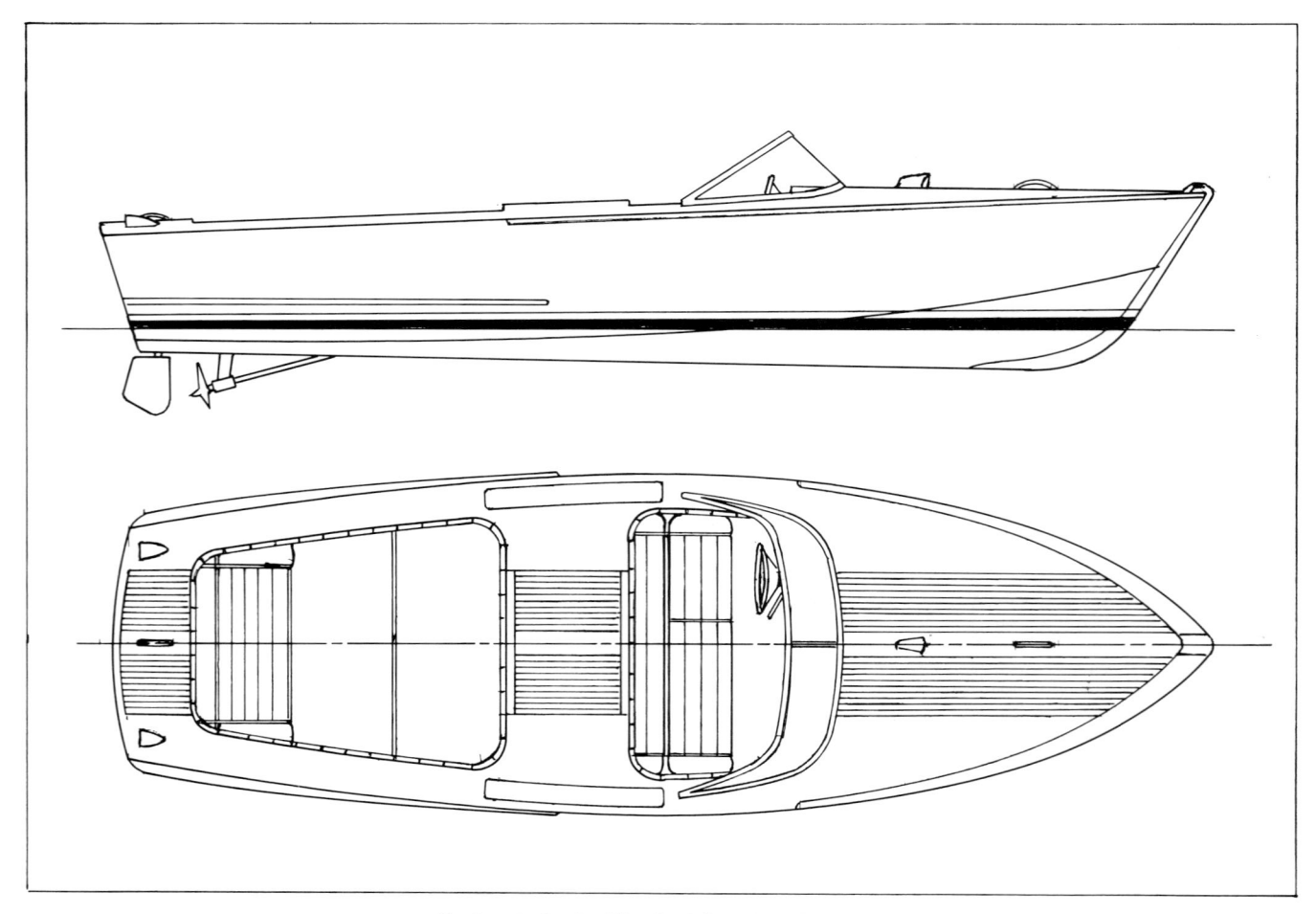

Engineer's sketch of Leather inboard runabout

One day last winter I received a rather detailed letter from a Mr. John Leather of Cowes, Isle of Wight, England, concerning his plans to begin building true all-mahogany speedboats for export to the United States. Mr. Leather, a qualified naval architect, worked for the Brooke Boat Company of England that is reviewed elsewhere in this book. Mr. Leather worked over 34 years building and designing all types of cruisers and runabouts in England.

His current plans are to build four inboard runabouts a year in England and export the boats here to the United States to be sold. At this time I do not have any photos to show you exactly what the boats will look like. Anyway, Mr. Leather and his son plan to form a team and build about four runabouts, as I mentioned before, and the following will describe in more detail just what they will be offering.

First of all the boat will be 21' 6" long with an all-mahogany planked hull styled along classic runabout lines. Hull planking will consist of Central American mahogany planking on stout oak frames. Clamp and deck frames will be spruce, and engine girders of oak. Deck planking will be all mahogany with all fastenings bronze and copper; propeller shaft of monel metal and an American-brand gasoline engine for power. Exact horsepower selections have not been made as yet, but most likely a Chrysler power plant will be selected. All deck hardware, etc., will be bronze and each hull will be given nine coats of hand-applied varnish, carefully rubbed down between each coat. I am really excited about these boats and look forward to seeing material on the first when it is completed. Mr. Leather assures me his boats will be competitive in price with any others currently available here in this country built to the same specifications. The runabout will have two seats in the forward cockpit with a large sunbathing cockpit aft like many other European-built craft such as Boesch, Riva, etc.

All in all, this venture sounds as if it does have merit, and Mr. Leather and his son are very earnest in their desire to build and sell such boats. Though they only plan to build four boats the first year, production could be increased if demand for the boat warrants it. I, for one, wish Mr. Leather and his son all the best with this new project. For you readers who might like more details concerning the Leather runabouts, I am listing Mr. Leather's complete address at this point. It is hoped the boats will be sold in this country by dealers interested in the sale of such craft, but that has not been totally decided at this time.

Mr. John Leather
"Stanwood"
118 Baring Road
Cowes, Isle of Wight, England

Although the next firm we shall review did not build true all-mahogany inboards, their sleek "Aquilifer" runabouts and others were a last ditch effort by an American firm to offer luxury wooden speedboats in the late 1950's and early 1960's. You may be very surprised when you see just what Ancarrow Marine built at a time when only a handful of firms still offered wooden boats at all.

ANCARROW MARINE—SPEED AND PERFORMANCE SPEAK FOR THEMSELVES

The mid-1950's saw a firm begin building luxury runabouts that were among the finest ever made. Ancarrow Marine, Inc. of Richmond, Virginia was founded in 1956 by Mr. Newton H. Ancarrow and his dream was to build the ultimate inboard-powered runabout. Arnold Apel who had operated Ventnor Boat Company in the past was hired to act as production manager and he would play a major role in the design and construction of each boat. Originally, Ancarrow was seeking to purchase an inboard that builders would guarantee him would reach an honest 60 m.p.h., yet allow its owner a comfortable ride under all weather conditions. Since he could find no boat or builder to offer him such a product, Mr. Ancarrow took on the task himself.

The ultimate in U.S. speedboats, 1957 style!

In August of 1957 reports became available concerning the all-new Ancarrow Marine's first runabout, the Aquilifer. This all-new boat was tank tested by the Stevens Institute of Technology and was said to be patterned along the lines of racing boats to offer ultimate speed as well as safety to its new owner.[3] The boat was a sleek, 24' twin-cockpit-forward model. Every Aquilifer built was water tested at the factory for several hours before shipping, and each was guaranteed to reach 60 m.p.h. Power source for the boat consisted of two 300 h.p. Cadillac Crusader engines plus all the latest instrumentation as well as the Kiddie fire extinguisher system installed in the engine compartments. Chris-o-matic controls were used on the big runabout also. We can see that Ancarrow Marine was striving to offer a truly luxury runabout in a time when wooden boat sales were really in a slump. The Aquilifer was designed to rival even the Riva, the all-time champ in luxury-class speedboats. Many may not feel that the Ancarrow boats were a threat to Riva's crown since they were constructed of Dutch-African mahogany plywood, not true mahogany planking as were Riva and others still building at that time.

Regardless of your own personal feeling, we all must admit that the Aquilifer was, at the time, the most luxurious inboard being built here in the United States for the consumer market. The first 1957 model Aquilifer came equipped with two huge fiberglass tail fins which were the rage in those years. Although mainly for looks, the fins were so constructed as to act as air vents for the engine compartment and a large chrome and fiberglass air scoop ahead of the windshield also helped cool and ventilate the area beneath the front deck and passenger compartment. When you were ready to have your boat refinished or to do it yourself, all you had to do was reach under the rear deck and remove two wing nuts on each fin and simply lift them off. Pretty neat trick if you ask me.... The 24' Aquilifer sold for $19,450.00 in 1957 with the twin 300 h.p. Cadillac engines. Four other engine options were also offered, the smallest of which consisted of twin 125 h.p. Dearborn Interceptors which would move the boat along at up to 43 m.p.h. and sold for $16,130.00. You can see from these prices that the

[3]"The Ancarrow Aquilfer", YACHTING, (Feb. '58), 55.

Aquilifier runabouts being built late in 1957

Front driver's seat of luxury Aquilifier custom runabout

Aquilifer was solely designed for the luxury market. Even today, prices like $19,000.00 for strictly a runabout are considered to be in the luxury class by most people. The original boats were finished in the following manner: hull sides and tail fins were a pale blue, the bottom red, the waterline black and decks and transom were varnished bright. Interior upholstery was bright blue with white trim.[4]

In reviewing the photos of the first Aquilifer, you will have to agree with me the boat is striking in design and

---

[4]"Aquilifer", *MOTOR BOATING*, (Aug. '57), 32.

was definitely an eye-catcher wherever it appeared. Having found success with his first model, Mr. Ancarrow offered four new models for 1958. All were unusual in their own right and all deserve to be mentioned one at a time here. The most unique of the four models for 1958

1958 19' single cockpit Ancarrow Praetorian runabout. Powered by 300 h.p. Cadillac Crusader engine.

would have to be the 19' Praetorian. She was a sleek, single-cockpit model seating two, which came equipped with a 300 h.p. Cadillac engine. There were six other engine options offered but most buyers preferred the largest one. The high rear tail fins on this boat were its trademark and also acted as deck vents for the engine compartment. The boat was an ultimate two-seater, and was designed strictly for high-speed running.

The boat came painted in the following colors: hull sides and fins were a bright orange while the bottom was white and the waterline was black. The deck and transom of each model was varnished. Many said this boat was to replace Chris-Craft's past offering, the

106

Cobra, another single-seated, finned runabout. This theory was not shared by the author, but the two boats did have similar features, etc.

Dashboard and front cockpit of 1958 Praetorian 19' runabout

If you needed a boat less racy and with additional seating, Ancarrow offered another 19' runabout called the Patrician. This boat also came with the big Cadillac 300 h.p., but smaller engines were also available. The tail fins on this boat were probably the biggest on any of the 1958 Ancarrow fleet. Their use back in 1958 were very popular style-wise, but by today's standards almost look hideous. The Patrician was painted in a rather dark shade of blue with red and white upholstery and all-varnished decks and transom.

The least deluxe of all Ancarrow boats would have to have been the Gladiator. She was a simply designed and furnished 20' open utility, a boat which did not appear to have much in common with the builder's other more deluxe offerings. Anyhow, this boat was designed with the fisherman in mind. Two large seats ahead of the engine box, along with plenty of open space behind the engine box, allowed for the use of fishing chairs, camp gear, etc., for the owner. The Gladiator was painted dark green on its hull sides with red bottom paint and all-white upholstery. It had an unusual green tinted wrap-around windshield up front.

The "queen" of the 1958's, the Aquilifer II, now was lengthened to 25 feet and a super deluxe model was being offered which came with a sleek fiberglass hardtop, electric windows and other "goodies", just to mention a few. You will note the new 25-foot version has its tail fins completely redesigned and moved to the far edges of the rear deck on both sides. This allowed for easier access into the engine compartment over the 1957 model. The new fins also looked to be more a part of the rear deck and did not look like an afterthought, something bolted on just for looks. The 1958 paint scheme on the Aquilifer II remained the same as in 1957.[5]

Least spectacular of the 1958 Ancarrow fleet—the 20' utility Gladiator

Queen of the fleet—Anacarrow's Aquilifer II, luxury runabout, 1958. Note tail fins...

---

[5]"Ancarrow Builds for Speed", *MOTOR BOATING*, (June '58), 91.

Complete 1958 Ancarrow marine fleet out for a cruise

Sleek single-seat speedster, Praetorian, flat-out

Twin-cockpit Patrician at rest—1959 version

Racy, new Consul operating at high speed

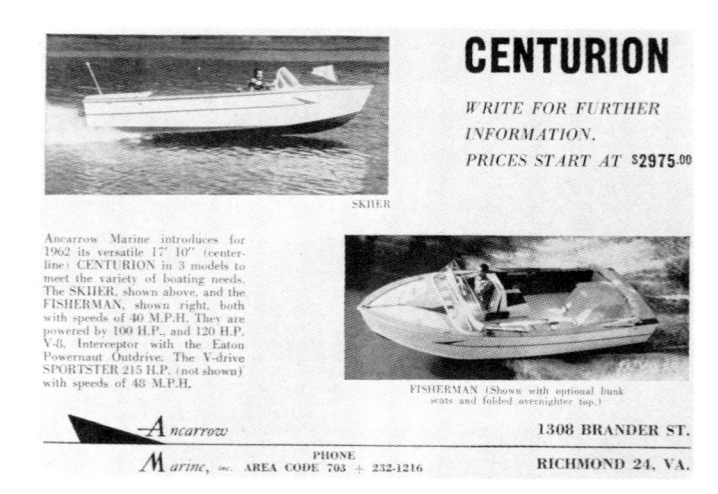

Ultimate luxury Aquilifier Mark I with hardtop for 1960

CENTURION

WRITE FOR FURTHER INFORMATION.
PRICES START AT $2975.00

SKIER

Ancarrow Marine introduces for 1962 its versatile 17' 10" (centerline) CENTURION in 3 models to meet the variety of boating needs. The SKIER, shown above, and the FISHERMAN, shown right, both with speeds of 40 M.P.H. They are powered by 100 H.P., or 120 H.P. V-8, Interceptor with the Eaton Powernaut Outdrive. The V-drive SPORTSTER 215 H.P. (not shown) with speeds of 48 M.P.H.

FISHERMAN (Shown with optional bunk seats and folded overnighter top.)

Ancarrow Marine, inc.   PHONE AREA CODE 703 + 232-1216   1308 BRANDER ST. RICHMOND 24, VA.

1962 Ancarrow magazine ad

In the years after 1959 Ancarrow ceased to build the big Aquilifer but slowly changed over to all-fiberglass runabouts, fishing boats and even a cruiser or two. There are some photos here showing some of their more deluxe inboards. You will note the almost total absence of tail fins which dominated the line some years before. By the mid-1960's, the firm completely stopped boat building, a number of things causing its demise. The lack of a luxury wood speedboat market along with the rise of fiberglass boats, popularity of outboard motors and the recession of the period all contributed to the closing of this firm. Although never building a true all-mahogany speedboat, Ancarrow did make a "last ditch" effort to capture the fleeting luxury speedboat business here in this country. I have no idea how many ANCARROW inboards still are in use today, but I hope those still around will be saved and preserved for future generations to see and enjoy. There will probably never be another boat built like them in this country with the price of materials, labor, etc. these days, so let's enjoy the few that I am sure are still in use, most likely on our Eastern coast.

COMMUTER CRUISERS—THE ULTIMATE REAL RUNABOUT

14-passenger 34' Chris-Craft Commuter. Twin 200 h.p. engines—1930 style

Back in the late 1920's somebody got the bright idea to take a large speedboat hull, add sleeping and eating facilities, etc., and *voila!*—the Commuter-cruiser was born. At one time the ownership of an all-varnished, sleek Commuter was the ultimate nautical status symbol. Prior to 1932 it appeared that a continual contest was on to see who could built the longest, most deluxe Commuter of all. In researching this portion I could not fail to marvel at the numerous firms who were very much into this type of boat. Names like Chris-Craft, Hacker Craft and many more come to mind as leaders in this field. Chris-Craft in 1931 offered a rather large selection of all-varnished Commuters in sizes from 34' through 48' in length. Hacker Craft, on the other hand, built its boats without the typical flying bridge control stations that most other boats came equipped with. We shall review closely the boats built by both these builders farther into this portion.

1931 34' Custom Commuter by Chris-Craft

69' all-mahogany Wheeler Commuter with two 800 h.p. Packard engines—artist's drawing.

In my review of Commuter boats I have found material concerning a very large all-mahogany Commuter built in late 1934. It seemed an eastern buyer had the Wheeler Shipyards, Inc. of Brooklyn, New York build a massive 69' Vee-drive twin-engine cruiser for his personal use. This boat was powered by two 800 h.p. Packard engines and top speed was to be more than 25 m.p.h.[6] Note the open front seat behind the streamlined windshield on the front deck. Controls were located high atop the flying bridge with owner's and guests' cabins located forward as well as aft. The Wheeler design featured the unique "Torpedo" stern that others like Dee Wite, Hacker, etc. put to good use at the time. I have been unable to find out the history of this boat; hopefully it was saved from destruction and may be in use this very day.

The Robinson Marine Construction Company of Benton Harbor, Michigan also did much to perfect the concept of an inboard all-mahogany high-speed cruiser. We shall review the Robinson "Seagulls", as they were known, elsewhere in this book. It will suffice here to show one photo of the classic Seagull to whet the interest of you readers. . . . As you will see in the photo, Robinson also preferred the flying bridge control station on their high-speed Commuters. In many cases, the Seagull had another complete set of engine and steering controls mounted up forward where the paid captain or pilot could run the boat if the owner wanted to carry on a business or social get-together in the aft seating area. Around Detroit, Michigan and Chicago, Illinois quite a few fast Commuters were used to "speed" businessmen to and from their waterfront offices. In fact, the Mercury Boat Lines of Chicago used to operate some older Robinson Seagulls which had their cabin facilities removed and extra seating added both inside the cabin as well as outside on the deck areas. The Seagulls worked out very

---

[6]"New Wheeler Commuter", *POWER BOATING*, (Dec. '34), 40.

1931 40' twin-engine Robinson Commuter. Top speed, 40 m.p.h.

nicely for "taxi" or "speed boat ride" operations as most were built with twin engines for a good high speed ride and looked very exciting with their shiny all-varnished hulls.

Announcing A New 42 Ft. Commuter

A NEW era in commuter design is inaugurated by the 1929 Robinson Seagull Commuter, a forty-two-foot V-bottom mahogany craft of exceptional speed and accommodations.... Twin powered with Sterling engines.... Dual controls operating either from forward cockpit or bridge.... In refinement and equipment it leaves nothing to be desired.... Your request for details will bring prompt response.

ROBINSON MARINE CONSTRUCTION CO.
202 West Main Street
BENTON HARBOR, MICHIGAN

Robinson Seagull

Magazine ad in 1929

With the stock market "crash" of late 1929, those who one moment "had the world by the tail", in many cases lost millions of dollars in wealth in just days. One of the first trappings of wealth to disappear were the high-speed Commuter boats. Firms built very few after 1933 or so, except for Robinson who hung on somewhat longer but who also gave up about 1935. Never again would economics allow for the building of such deluxe all-mahogany cruiser-speedboats at prices anyone other than Howard Hughes or the like could own. A lot of the old Seagulls and other Commuters were put into storage or left out uncovered, and with the passage of time soon were only fit for firewood. I am familiar with a handful of nicely maintained Commuters here in the Midwest as well as on eastern coasts. Some that remained were

1931 45' Robinson custom Commuter

1931 40' Robinson Seagull speed cruiser

110

Very sleek double-ended mahogany Cruiser—about 1936

Chris-Craft 1931 38' Commuting Cruiser

Chris-Craft 1931 48' custom yacht

Large 48' Chris-Craft yacht—1930's era

Posh, 1931 35' Hacker-Craft Commuter

painted white, thus loosing one of their most interesting features—an all-varnished, gleaming hull. Costs of commercial refinishing and materials precluded the practice of keeping most of these big "beasts" varnished in the 1970's.

Now let's look in detail at a typical Hacker Craft Commuter as compared to the deluxe 40' Gar Wood model. As I already mentioned, Hacker Craft did not offer a flying bridge model as did most builders. 1930 saw Hacker offering two Commuters in 35' and 38' lengths. In reviewing the photo of the 35' Hacker Commuter, you will notice it very closely resembles speedboat hulls of the same size. Hacker designed and built cruisers with living facilities located under the sedan hardtop amidships. The following accommodations were standard on the 35' model. The longitudinal seats on both sides converted into comfortable beds for two people and a galley, ice box, sink and toilet were also included inside the cabin area. Aft, a full-size rear cockpit allowed passengers to enjoy an open-air ride much as any other smaller speedboats would offer. The engines were mounted in the open area behind the cabin but ahead of the rear seat. Each motor compartment had an upholstered top and served as additional seating. The engines were also so mounted that you could pass from the rear seat forward through a walkway running between both engines. This feature was unique basically with Hacker but it also appeared on a few other John Hacker-designed Commuters.

The 1932 Gar Wood 40' Commuter was more typical in her design. That particular boat had a large open rear deck seating area with controls located on the flying bridge. Inside the cabin area sleeping facilities for five adults were contained as well as galley, head, radio, writing desk and folding dining room table. The front open cockpit could be equipped with steering and throttle controls. Power options ranged from a single, large 12-cylinder, 425 h.p. Gar Wood engine with Vee-drive, or else two 200 h.p., six-cylinder Gar Wood straight inboards. All Commuters came fully equipped right down to linens, silverware, etc. Yes, the true, all-varnished type Commuter was a real beauty and it is a pity more of these "giants" were not saved. At the conclusion of this section I will list a sampling of firms who built Commuter-cruisers over the years. I am sure there were many others, but this will give you an idea.

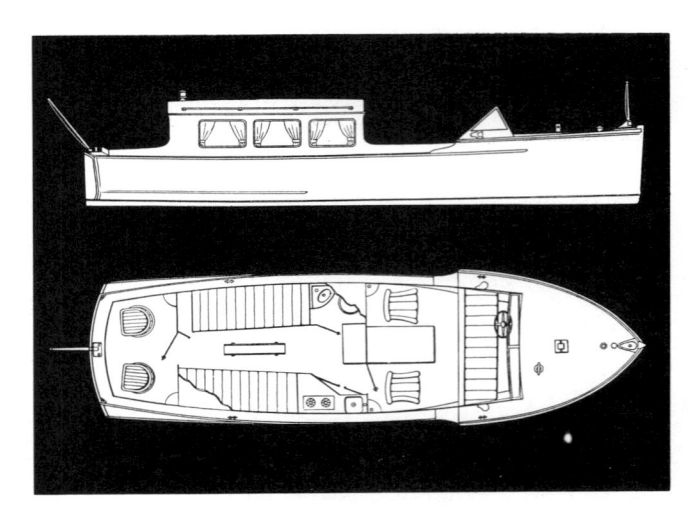

1932 40' Gar Wood cruiser

Cabin facilities on 1932 40' Gar Wood cruiser

Control station on 1932 40' Gar Wood cruiser

1931 30' A.C.F. runabout Commuter

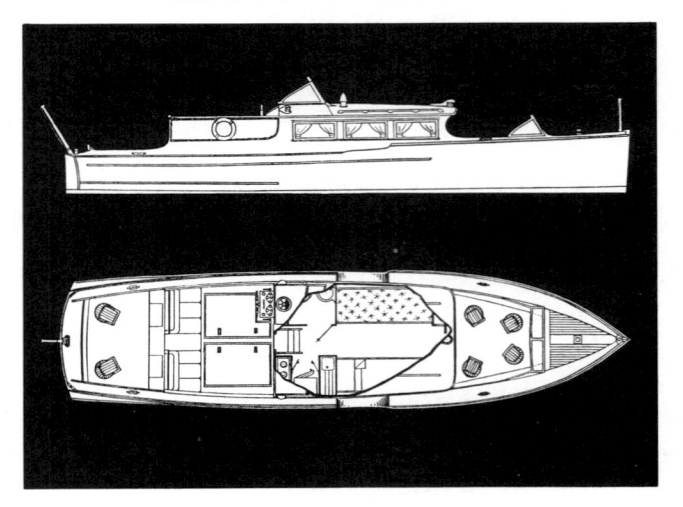

1931 38' twin screw A.C.F. Commuter

112

Beautiful custom-built Consolidated Commuter—1939

Posh, 1936 Huskins 52' Commuter designed by John Hacker

New, 1928 Sea-Lyon Commuter—42' model

Very sleek 52' Commuter Hacker Craft

Framing of a 43' Custom Commuter by Hacker Craft

A sample of firms who built commuter-type cruisers in the 1920's and 1930's:

A.C.F.—New York City, New York
Chris-Craft, Inc.—Algonac, Michigan
Consolidated Shipyards—Morris Heights, New York
Gar Wood Industries—Marysville, Michigan
Hacker Craft—Mt. Clemens, Michigan
Huskins Shipyard—Bay City, Michigan
Lauders Marine Construction Company—Stanford, Connecticut
Richardson Boat Company—Tonawanda, New York
Robinson Marine Construction Company—Benton Harbor, Michigan
Sea-Lyon—Lyon-Tuttle Shipyard—City Island, New York
Stephens Marine, Inc.—Stockton, California
Tonka Craft—Minnetonka Boat Works—Wayzata, Minnesota
Wheeler Shipyards—New York City, New York

CHAPTER IV
MORE EUROPEAN AND CANADIAN BUILDERS

TARONI OF ITALY—MASTER OF THE OCEAN ALL OVER THE WORLD

1961 Taroni Explorer runabout

While I was in high school I received a bright orange envelope with strange foreign addresses on it. Upon opening it I found literature on two mahogany runabouts built by Cantiere Nautico Taroni of Italy. Of course all technical material on both boats—the Mistral and the Explorer—was in metric terms.

To this day I have been able to find little information about this firm except that they still built fiberglass boats some years ago. I wrote them months ago when I began to do preliminary research on this book, but no answer to date has been received from Italy.

The smaller runabout called the Explorer was 5.35 meters long and came with either a 110 or 145 h.p. engine. Photos show the boats slightly resemble a small Riva; also note the water ski tow bar mounted on the stern deck with a boarding ladder hanging on the transom itself. It appears the engine box is quite slanted in design and was so made to be raised up, covering the rear seat, making a roomy sun deck in the rear area of the craft. There is also a closeup of the driver's seat which shows steering wheel mounted on the left, with a folding roof hidden under cockpit padding on the top of the front seat back. I have never seen a Taroni inboard personally and am quite sure most were sold only in Europe. If you have information you can share with me concerning these or other mahogany inboards like them, contact me by phone, mail, etc.

1961 Explorer side view by Taroni of Italy

Explorer driver's seat

The other Taroni was called the Mistral and it was 5.90 meters in length. It could be ordered with either 155 or 180 h.p. power plant. This boat was designed for the water skier who needed more power and speed for good skiing. Though the boat was slightly longer, its basic style was like the Explorer.

Although I do not have much on this particular firm to share with you, I felt justified to show you examples of other runabouts built overseas, lest we forget runabouts were built in almost every nation—as you will see by the time you finish reading this book.

1961 Mistral on water, by Taroni of Italy

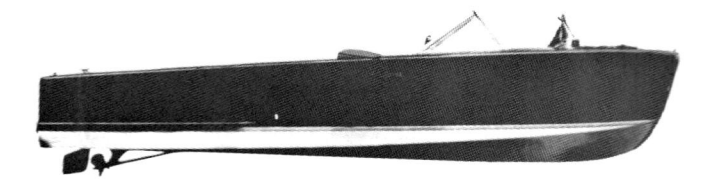

Mistral driver's cockpit, 1961

From Italy we shall now cross back over the Atlantic to the Province of Ontario in Canada and take a good look at the old Duke Boats. Duke Boats of Port Carling, Ontario operated for years, building fine launches for use all over Canada. Although no longer building boats, the firm is very much alive and well with new owners who are immersed in the care of antique and classic boats.

Side view of 1961 Mistral, an Italian runabout

DUKE BOATS OF CANADA—BUILDERS OF FINE LAUNCHES

A firm I very much wanted to cover in *Volume I* but was unable to because of space was the famous Duke Boats of Port Carling, Ontario, Canada. I am glad to report that Mr. Audrey Duke, a former partner in the firm, provided me with a fine history of the firm as well as photos to illustrate this section.

Duke Boats of Port Carling had its beginning back in the years following the end of World War I when the late Charles Duke went to work for the Ditchburn Boat Company of Gravenhurst, Ontario. As we saw in *Volume I*, Ditchburn was one of the major launch builders in all of Canada. Charles remained in the employment of Ditchburn for only a short time when he moved back home to Port Carling and joined the Disappearing Propeller Company, a famous Canadian boat builder who made small launches whose props could be raised up into the hull for shallow water use as well as for beaching, etc. In the summer of 1924 Claude Duke, son of Charles, worked for the new Greavette Boat Company which was owned and operated by Ernest Greavette. The Greavette plant was then located on the site of the former Matheson Boat Works which would later become the location for the Duke Boats operation.

A short-lived partnership was formed in late 1924 between Charles Duke and Ernest Greavette. Ernest Greavette was a brother of Tom Greavette, founder of the famous Greavette Boat Company located in Gravenhurst. The partnership was dissolved in 1926 with young Charles Duke acquiring the whole operation and changing the firm's name to Duke Motor Service. In the first years of operation Duke Motor Service occupied a two-story building with one slip on the water but this soon proved to be too small for the firm. The former warehouse of the Disappearing Propeller Company was then used but it burned completely on December 8, 1930 destroying over $100,000 worth of boats and equipment. A second fire in 1931 destroyed another building occupied by Duke but this time it was possible to launch a number of boats out of the building from winter storage before it too was destroyed.

One of many storage sheds of former Duke Boats

Aud Duke aboard a Duke utility. (Photo by *The Muskoka Sun* newspaper.)

The Duke that started it all! The Playmate. . . .

Overall view of 1941 Duke custom runabout

Things looked a little bleak for the Duke Motor Service after the fire but it did rebuild as did most of the other businesses lost in the fire of October 28, 1931. The new Duke plant was designed much like the earlier ones. The upstairs was used for new boat construction while the lower floor was for service. About this time the name Duke Boats was also adopted since most of the time was now spent building and not just servicing boats. An all-new storage building was also built on the site of the original one as storage of boats was becoming a bigger part of the firm's business every year. As time went on both the factory and warehouse buildings were enlarged as needs arose.

In 1927 Duke Boats built its first boats which consisted of about 25 rowboats and one launch. As the years went by, fewer and fewer rowboats were built and more and more inboard launches. Most launches, as the Canadians call them—or speedboats, as we would more likely call them—were in sizes from 18' to 30' in length. Nearly all were custom-built to the owner's specifications too. In 1933 Duke began to build an all-new type boat called the Playmate. This particular boat started out as a custom fishing boat for a customer who wanted a small, light launch with a wide transom and a big fishing seat across the back. Various models were built and sales

1941 19' deluxe Duke runabout

1940's era 24' Duke custom runabout

19' 1941 Duke standard lapstrake utility

Another 3-cockpit Duke masterpiece! Early 1950's.

became larger than production could keep up with. In those early years of the 1930's, over 30 were built and sold each winter; the Playmate eventually evolved into more of an inboard runabout.

Most of the Duke Boats models were sold factory-direct as Aud and his brother would take boats around throughout the Muskoka area and demonstrate them to various people. Over the years management felt direct selling was one reason Duke boats were and still are very popular in Canadian waters. There are some photos of Duke runabouts and fishing boats shown here that were built about 1941. Note the graceful lines of the speed-boats and the very barrel back styled transoms. Upon first looking, I thought the Duke runabouts looked much like the Greavette inboards built prior to about 1933 (when Greavette began using their famous rounded hulls).

Just prior to the start of World War II, Duke Boats was prospering but as time passed nearly all needed supplies for boat building and repairing were no longer available so the firm was afraid it might have to close down. In late 1941 Duke was given a contract to build rowboats for the use of the government in the war effort. Shortly after that Duke built the first 26' craft powered by two-cylinder diesel engines which were to act as tenders to government mine sweepers. The company was able to build one of these crafts to strict government specifications every two weeks.

With the eventual end of the war Duke Boats got right back into pleasure boat building and it seemed it would never get caught up with orders that poured in from all over the area. However, by about 1955 new boat building began to taper off and only two stock models still remained in the firm's lineup. Charles Duke died in September, 1954 and the firm incorporated the next year with Mr. Duke's daughter, Alva Wilson receiving some of the shares of the firm along with her brothers. The firm was given a new name—Duke Boats, Limited—with Audrey Duke as president and Claude Duke as vice-president. Mrs. Wilson was appointed secretary-treasurer.

22' 1955 Duke Classic launch

Mid-50's era Duke three-seat utility

As mentioned, since 1955 new boat building has given way mostly to restoration, repair and storage of older wooden boats. Today, Duke Marine Services (as it is now called) is operated by two young men—Rick Terry and Ed Skinner—who are interested in keeping the tradition of fine wooden boats alive and well in the Ontario lake

Aboard the Margie III, Claude and Aud Duke (with hats) welcome new owners, Ed Skinner and Rick Terry. With the sale of Duke Boats, a long tradition ends in Port Carling, one spanning many, many years. (Photo by *The Muskoka Sun* **newspaper.)**

country. In visiting with Mr. Skinner recently, I was advised the firm is so busy with restoration, storage and repair work on "golden oldies" that they have no time to sell new modern boats which they thought they might have to get into. Many people have told me the Duke plant turns out some of the finest restoration and refinishing work done anywhere—bar none. The firm has a larger set of buildings on the river at Port Carling where boats are worked on year around. If you ever are able to get to the Port Carling area, look up these two young men, Terry and Ed, and look over their operation.

It is very refreshing to see young people still interested enough to want to learn and continue the tradition of fine wood boat care and building that would be lost completely if no one took the time to study and to find out how to carry on for future generations.

In conclusion, there are some photos shown here of various Duke runabouts (or launches as the British and Canadians call them). Duke appears to have adopted the more modern semi-curved or wraparound windshield back in the mid-1950's. Their later boats do not appear to be quite as streamlined as those of the 1940's, with less-curved transoms, a more basic style with higher freeboard, and fewer gimmicks. I for one find them very attractive and since most were built along the same basic lines, one year looked much like any other with only minimal changes in all boats. Some day I would love to visit Duke Marine Services and see just what is being done there as well as look in the storage buildings and peer at some of the old beauties that spend their winters there being pampered by the fellows.

Duke Boats, for some 50-odd years, played an important role in Canadian boat building and the tradition goes on today with new faces and new plans but the same old caring for wood boats that few people or firms still offer.

BOESCH BOATS—HORIZON GLIDING

One firm I was determined to include in *Volume II* was Boesch Motorboote Company of Zurich, Switzerland. However, repeated letters to the firm's home office yielded absolutely nothing. It got to the point where I decided to leave the firm out, when suddenly a big, thick packet of old photos, brochures and historical pamphlets "appeared" at my door recently. I am now proud to say there will be a nice selection of material on the fine Boesch speedboats in this book.

Most of us, Americans in particular, are not familiar with the name Boesch because all or most of their boats are sold only in Europe. A few are in use along our East Coast but most are sold in Switzerland, Germany, France, Spain, Denmark, Belgium, Luxembourg, Portugal, Czecheslovakia and Yugoslavia.

In the early days it seems that a man who owned a laundry along the shores of Zurich Lake in Switzerland needed a boat to haul his employees to and from work across the lake. This all took place in 1859. That man—Heinrich Treichler—went on to form his own shipyard on the lake. By 1896 his son Frity had taken over operation of the family-run business. The shipyard was moved to Kilchberg, a suburb of Zurich, at about that same time; then Frity's brother Alfred took over the "reins" of control. The shipyard had its name changed to "Frity Treichler and Cie" and became a major boat builder in the country. An example of the firm's international clientele would include the Graf Zeppelin as well as other princely houses of European royalty.[7]

The largest yacht built by the firm in those days was a 12-ton yacht for the royal Court of Wittenberg. In fact, fully two-thirds of all boats built by the firm in the early days were exported all over Europe, quite unusual for a boatyard located on an inland lake.

The two brothers, Alfred and Frity, did not get along well and Alfred built his own shipyard in Wollishafer and prospered while by 1929 Frity closed his old location down for good. 1920 saw the name "Boesch" appear for the first time. In that year, Mr. Jacob Boesch, father of the current head of the firm, took over as president of the shipyard at Kilchberg. Mr. Boesch had worked for the Triechler Boat Company for twenty-five years before he assumed the position of president at the yard.

Boats built by Boesch Boats of Zurich under Jacob's direction were the mahogany planked variety much like those built by others worldwide. There are two photos at this point showing a "torpedo style" Boesch runabout as well as a sleek two-cockpit model from the mid-1930's. In 1938, at the age of 68, Jacob Boesch finally retired and turned over operation of the family shipyard to his son Walter. It was Walter's dream to build and sell the

1930's 22' Boesch "Torpedo" runabout

1950's era Boesch custom-built runabout

optimum-performing inboard speedboat.[8] A term which describes what Walter eventually did was called "Boesch Horizon Gliding", which translated means the boat must plane along at a level angle, making the driver and the passengers feel like they are gliding through the air on a cloud.

With the start of World War II, in 1939 Boesch Boats no longer could build motorboats so the firm built engines for war use. Young Walter and his employees did a good job at that too, and after the war's end the firm again returned to pleasure boat building. The boat that really helped the Boesch reputation in the late 1940's was a sleek Star-class sailboat; the firm used a new synthetic glue Boesch had developed which allowed the boats to be built from plywood rather than the old planked methods. These new Stars, though built to rigid class specifications, weighed about fifty percent less than older boats that were being sailed at the time. Orders for the newly constructed Stars came in from all over the world. When gas was no longer rationed, motorboats were again added to the line and the wealthy from Europe flooded the firm with orders for new, sleek mahogany speedboats.

---

[7] "Boesch Information #2", (Oct. '70), 3.

[8] "Boesch Information #2", (Oct. '70), 5.

By the mid-1950's all Boesch boats were being built of plywood, molded to the hull shape much like that used by Riva.

In 1957 Walter Boesch decided to build motor boats only. Amateur water skiers in Europe and elsewhere were demanding fast inboards that could safely and easily tow a group of skiers. Most inboards built by Boesch prior to that time were about 24' in length and of the three-cockpit variety. There is a photo shown at this point of one such runabout with three seats and twin windshields.

Late 1930's era Boesch runabout

1957 Boesch runabout

The first "new look" Boesch runabout was 16' long and called a "Type 500". It was an open utility type inboard with seating for five and equipped for water skiing. Its hull was also of a molded plywood design rather than the former solid planked variety. Weight was effectively reduced while the hull remained stiffer with fewer frames, braces, etc. In 1957 when the first Boesch 500 came out, twenty of the runabouts were sold in Geneva, Switzerland alone. Three requirements of all Boesch runabouts built by Walter and his crew in the 1950's were the following: the boat must plane properly; it should have a good, constant rate of speed; and it must develop the proper wake for water skiing.

Since the 1960's, Boesch inboards (now made of fiberglass) are used for all the national and regional ski tournaments across Europe. In fact, water ski clubs from all over Europe own one or more Boesch inboards for their own use. Boesch inboards were used exclusively as tow boats at the World Waterskiing Championships at Vichy in 1963, and in Copenhagen in 1969. 1971 found Boesch boats chosen the official and exclusive ski boats at the world ski events held at Bandos.

The rest of this report shall deal with the wooden Boesch speedboats that were built in the 1950's and 1960's. Boesch in those days offered three series of boats in the following sizes: 5.10 meters, 5.80 meters, 6.40 meters. Translated into feet the boats were 16' 7", 19', and 21' long. It seems the firm offered several models in each length. For example, in the 16' 7" or smallest length, Boesch offered both a deluxe as well as a standard model. The standard models all had plywood decks and less deluxe appointments, hardware, etc.

Saint Tropez deLuxe 16' utility, 1955

1955 19' Acapulco deLuxe runabout by Boesch

My own preference was for the deluxe models with their all-mahogany planked, striped decks and nicer windshields and hardware. Four 19' versions were also offered. The least deluxe one was an open utility called the "Water Ski Special". It had two seats ahead of the

121

engine box and an open area behind that. The next model was called the "Acapulco de Luxe" and was a twin-cockpit-forward version with a large padded engine compartment aft. These boats were very similar to those built by other European builders of that era. The Europeans built many of their inboards with either the rear deck all padded, or if it was an open utility inboard the area behind the engine box formed a padded sun deck also. Another sleek 19' Boesch was called the "Cabrio-Sport de Luxe" and though it looked much like the Acapulco de Luxe, this other boat had its second seats behind the driver facing each other. This was a rather novel idea for seating. All Boesch inboards used basically American engines and the throttle and shift controls were mounted together as one unit on the dashboard. You pushed the handle in for forward, pulled it way back for reverse, and turned it left or right for faster or slower. If you preferred your 19' as a sedan model, that was available also. The "Lemania de Luxe" was built so that the top could be removed but the side windows and frames remained always in place. On many lakes in Europe the short, cool summers called for some type of shelter on a fast-moving boat, and this is how Boesch solved the problem. If you preferred the big 21' inboards you could choose from one sedan, one runabout and one utility. The runabout was called the "Runabout de Luxe 640" and it had two big roomy cockpits forward and a small seat concealed under the rear deck with its own hatch covering. This boat was called the queen of all Boesch speedboats and is my own favorite too. The "Costa Brava de Luxe" was another 21' boat with front bucket seats, a full bench seat ahead of the engine and a big padded area aft, atop the engine compartment. These boats were popular along the sea coasts of Europe and Africa where customers ventured out in rough, open seas to fish, ski, etc. The other 21' Boesch was another sedan model called the "Portofino 640 Type". She was identical to the smaller 19' model already mentioned.

1955 19' Lemania deLuxe sedan by Boesch

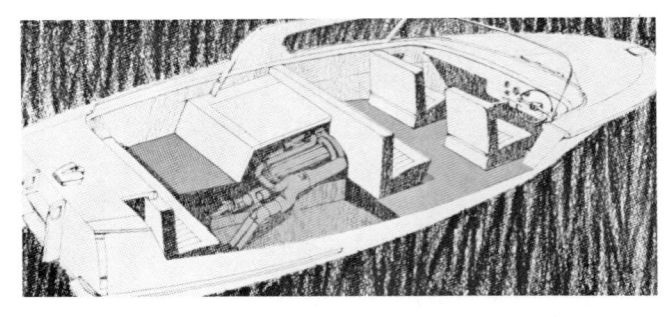

Interior view of Boesch Lemania deLuxe 580 sedan

1955 21' runabout deLuxe 640 by Boesch

19' Cabrio Sport deLuxe runabout

21' Boesch Costa Brava deLuxe runabout

I hope that you enjoy seeing material on Boesch boats. I myself really found them to be quite fascinating. The Boesch firm used several novel features on its wooden inboards. One was the unique spotlight built right into the nose and controlled remotely from the dashboard. Another was the way their exhaust pipes were designed to shoot the exhaust, water and noise downward into the wake behind the boat, greatly reducing these problems.

Boesch Motorboote Company also maintains a chain of fine marinas and storage sheds all over Europe where owners of Boesch boats can take their craft for repairs, storage, etc. All in all, it followed in the tradition of other fine European builders offering wooden speedboats to customers who could afford the best and who demanded the best also. I think it is really fun to read about such firms who are not building just to sell boats but to sell quality boats to those who want the finest.

Now we shall move northward to England and review a firm who led that nation in the construction and sale of mahogany speedboats in the 1920's and 1930's—Brooke Boat Company of England.

3 views of various Boesch service centers in Europe

BROOKE OF ENGLAND—BUILT LIKE SHIPS. . . .DRIVE LIKE CARS

I was unaware that overseas—England, in particular—was a real "hot bed" of inboard speedboat building which climaxed in the mid-1930's. There were a handful of firms in those years who turned out a varied selection of "gems" looking almost identical to anything built here in the United States at the same time. We shall review two firms who built all-mahogany runabouts in England in the 1930's with the most concentration on Brooke Marine Construction Company, Ltd. of Lowestoft. First, though, we shall briefly look at the British Power Boat Company of Hythe, England. The firm was founded by Mr. Scott Paine and from a start of only five employees,

British Power Boat Company in 1930 with 23' speedboats under construction.

1930 17' "Dolphin" runabout with 40 h.p. Lycoming engine

Completed British Power Boat Company launches—1930

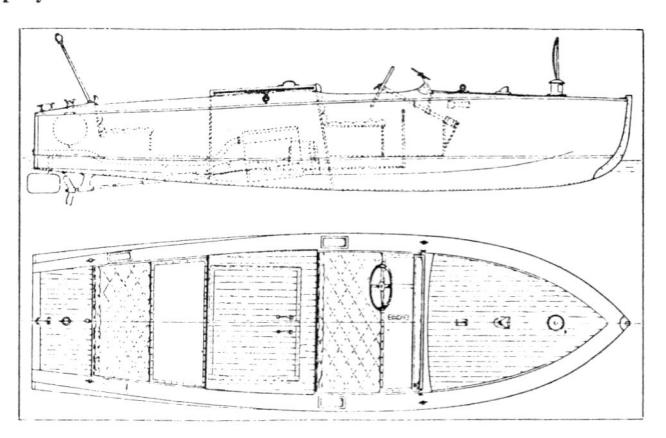

1931 Dolphin 17' runabout

1930 23' "Sea King" runabout built by British Power Boat Company

1931 dashboard view of the Dolphin by British Motor Boat Company

the firm mushroomed to employ over 150 full-time people building and maintaining speedboats and launches.[9] British Power Boat Company built 23' inboard runabouts as well as 35' cruisers and smaller outboard hulls. The all-new mechanized plant opened in March, 1930 and was one of the finest in all Europe. Mr. Pane spent a long while here in the states visiting other boat builders, obtaining new types of hardware, accessories, etc. Paine offered complete refinishing, storage, gasoline and dockage right next door to the factory. Photos in this portion show examples of Mr. Paine's

---
[9]"A Modern Speedboat Factory", *THE MOTOR BOAT*, (Mar. '30), 294.

124

excellent boats. Models did not change greatly from year to year and sizes ranged from small 17' split-cockpit versions that were powered by a 40 h.p. Lycoming, up to 23' three-cockpit speedsters with 125 h.p. Chrysler engines. There are two things that caught my eye concerning most British-built inboards. First of all, the English inboards had very squared-off transoms, unlike boats built in this country that often had exaggerated amounts of tumblehome in their transoms. Such things as deck hardware, windshields, etc. were almost identical to what we Americans have on our own boats. Always being faced with the high cost of gasoline, the British powered their speedboats with smaller engines to conserve energy and keep operating costs low. There are several other photos shown here of British Power Boat Company products. It is hoped that the varied views help illustrate the rather complete selection of models over the years. I could not find out whether the firm is still in business, but chances are it closed during the great world Depression of the 1930's, or else the destruction wrought by World War II in England probably ended its operation. Anyhow, I hope you found the above of interest.

Brooke Boats of Lowestoft, England was a very large and diverse firm in Europe building all sizes of boats from small 12' dinghys through large ocean-going steel hulled ships. I am very indebted to Mr. John Leather of England who provided me much of the material from his own collection concerning Brooke runabouts as well as other brands. First of all, I have copies of two different 1914 era folders showing both light, fast launches as well as racing and semi-racing launches. It seems the Brooke racing launches were famous in Europe and in 1913 their boats won the following numbers of awards, trophies, etc.: 9 gold medals, 14 silver medals, 7 bronze medals, 127 cups and trophies, and 245 first prizes.[10] We all must admit, that is some record! Racing launches ranged in size from 21' through 40' "beasts" which sped along over 32 m.p.h. That was a fast pace in 1914. The fastest 1914 model was called the "Crusader" and looked slightly like an old Gar Wood Miss America type boat with a long front deck and engines mounted amidships with the driver and mechanic riding aft. A large 300 h.p. "V" type engine was used that pushed the boat at speeds near 42 m.p.h. Two passengers besides the crew could squeeze into the Crusader but the quarters were really cramped. On the less racy side, Brooke had a nice selection of smaller, slower pleasure craft ranging in size from 21' to 35' in length. All 21' Brooke launches had their engines mounted forward with seating for from two to four passengers aft. As I mentioned earlier, the British used smaller engines in most of their power boats. In the 21' models, the buyer could choose engines ranging in size from a 14 h.p. four-cylinder Brooke up to a 40 h.p. model that sped the boat at about 22 knots. There was a nifty two-seater offered in 1914 by Brooke and it had a sort of early "torpedo" stern and its little engine mounted towards the bow of the craft. All these early Brooke models resembled greatly the "tooth-pick" styled boats we viewed in the first chapter of *Volume I*. As years went by, Brooke boats changed in design, closely resembling models built in this country by builders like Chris-Craft, Hacker and others. Brooke Boat Company reached its zenith about 1935 as far as runabouts were concerned. I am fortunate to have a photo of a 1929 18' Brooke "Empire" runabout which was taken in 1965 in an antique boat show parade held in England. Though the hull is painted white, the boat is almost a dead ringer for a small Chris-Craft built at the same time.

1929 18' Brooke "Empire" runabout

The firm built basically the same boats every year from 1930 through about 1935. To start with, I will review models from that period as well as several from the late 1920's. The first boat was built starting in 1928 by Brooke and was called "An 18' Standardized Runabout".[11] That little "cutie" was a split-cockpit model with a nice "V" windshield and a well-styled hull and deck. Power was supplied by a 10 h.p., four-cylinder Brooke engine. The throttle control on this boat consisted of a floor-mounted footfeed as well as a push-rod mounted on the dashboard. A very complete instrument panel was standard equipment consisting of a tachometer, oil pressure gauge and battery gauge. Top speed for the 18' runabout was 16 m.p.h., not very fast by American standards, but favorable to the British for their type of boating. The hull was built totally of mahogany with oak framing and was varnished completely except for a red bottom and white waterline. Another interesting feature was Brooke's use of an outboard-mounted rudder on that boat controlled by steering cables which ran across the aft deck and down under the side decks up to the wheel. Mr. Leather tells me only about 30 of these boats were built in the years from 1927 through 1930.[12] Nearly all boats were sold in England; however, one went to Canada, another to Singapore, and the last to Amsterdam.

[10] "1914 Brooke Racing Launch Catalog", *1914 Catalog*, p. 2.
[11] "An 18-Foot Standardized Runabout", *THE MOTOR BOAT*, (Aug. '27), 168.
[12] "A Letter", from John Leather, (April '78).

A large Brooke runabout that was always popular was the large 24' three-cockpit model which first was built in 1929 and 1930. Only 17 were ever built and again, most of those remained in England while others went to Bermuda, Buenos Aires and Turkey. In contrast to the smaller Brooke boats the 24' had a 100 h.p. engine which was really very large for an English boat.

The 24' runabout had a beam of 6' and drew 2' of water while at rest.[13] Planking was the carvel variety all of Honduras mahogany. Five adults could ride in the front two seats of the Brooke 24' while two others could ride aft in the rumble seat. The 24' runabout eventually would be called the Brooke "Seacar". I am fortunate to have a good photo of a 24' Seacar. Although the hull was painted, you can get a good idea just what one looked like. I shall now review for you a selection of Brooke runabouts built from about 1930 through 1938. There were others but I have tried to pick some of the more interesting ones. The following is a model listing of some of the more popular Brooke inboards.

MODEL	LENGTH	ENGINE SIZE	SPEED
Sport runabout	16'	10 h.p. Brooke	11 m.p.h.
Empire runabout	18'	10 h.p. Brooke	11 m.p.h.
Standard runabout	20'	10 h.p. Brooke	11 m.p.h.
Seacar	24'	100 h.p. Brooke	30 m.p.h.

1930 24' Brooke Seacar runabout

1930 19' Brooke Seacar runabout

[13] "A High-Speed Brooke Runabout", THE MOTOR BOAT, (June '28), 518.

We shall now look at some of the above models in more detail. First comes the 18' Empire runabout. The photo of the 18' Empire shows a neat little four-seater with engine mounted amidships. The hull was built completely of Honduras mahogany with American elm covering boards. Power was by a 10 h.p. Brooke and top speed was estimated to be 16 m.p.h., a very nice craft for traveling up and down the miles of winding canals all over England. The next larger model was called the 19' Seacar runabout. Records show only six were ever built and again I am fortunate to have an excellent closeup of one of the remaining models taken in 1965 at an antique boat rally. This boat resembles greatly the Empire 18' except it had a Hacker Craft type windshield as well as a larger 40 h.p. Brooke engine. Planking on the newer Brooke boats was double, the inner layer being laid diagonally with the outside layer running fore to aft. The rear cockpit was designed to allow extra leg room for passengers. Often the complaint was that only children could ever ride aft as most rear seats were too cramped for adult comfort. Fuel tanks were mounted under the front deck rather than the stern deck as was done in this country. This practice moved needed weight forward, helping that rather small engine to plane the boat at speeds near 25 m.p.h.[14]

For those customers wishing a slower type launch, Brooke built their popular 20' runabout. This boat had seating for four aft with the small four-cylinder Brooke engine mounted beneath the long front deck. Speed was only 12 m.p.h. but again speed was not the reason this boat was built. Its major uses were for fishing and hunting trips, or to act as a tender to a large yacht. The boat only needed 1' 6" of water for safe operation so it soon became very popular with the fishermen who could

1930 18' Brooke "Empire" runabout

[14] "A 19-Foot Standardized Runabout", THE MOTOR BOAT, (June '30), 528.

126

1930 19' Brooke Seacar runabout

1931 19' Brooke inboard

1931 Brooke 19' Seacar runabout with 40 h.p. Brooke engine

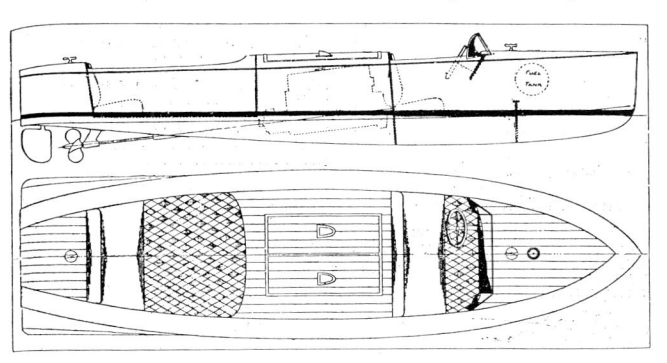

1930 18' Brooke standard runabout

poke into shallow bays and streams looking for the elusive fish which had been off limits to power boats in earlier times.

The final Brooke we shall look at was the big 24' Seacar. She was as close to anything built here in the U.S. as I have ever seen. She was advertised as a boat which British businessmen could use to speed to and from their offices, avoiding traffic, pollution and other inconveniences. As I mentioned at the very start of this section, most British inboards were a little more slab-sided than were American boats and their transoms were more squared-off and less curved than, for example, a Chris-Craft from the same period. Most of the larger Brooke speedboats were equipped with a second rub-rail mounted about six inches below the edge of the deck along each hull side for added protection along docks and walls.

One final boat I must mention, though I have no photo of it, was made in 1933 and was called The Mermaid. This boat was a super deluxe slow launch with a sloping rear deck, two wicker chairs for the driver and passenger up front and a full padded seat behind that. Engines ranged from 5 to 30 h.p. and were mounted forward. This boat was strictly for cruising inland rivers and streams in comfort. Folding convertible tops were also available. Few of these boats were ever built as they were quite expensive and the demand for such craft was low. Brooke Boats turned out various runabouts until World War II when war contracts took up all their time. Following the war the firm switched mainly to large steel ship building and repairs, and never entered the wood speedboat field again. I am grateful to John Leather and Jack Mitchey, Port of Lowestoft Research Society of England, for providing many of the photos and historical material used in this section. I hope the readers of this book found English speedboats as interesting as I did.

The final firm we shall review in this chapter of the book will be a Canadian one—Minett-Shields of Bracebridge, Ontario. Minett-Shields built probably some of the finest power launches in all of North America through about 1948 or so. I am sure you will like what you see photo-wise of Minett. These boats belong in a class all by themselves.

MINETT-SHIELDS OF CANADA—FOR THOSE NOT SATISFIED WITH NORMAL STANDARDS

A boat builder only briefly mentioned in *Volume I*—Minett-Shields—turned out some of the finest launches in all the world. Located close to Ditchburn Boat Works, there was a friendly rivalry between the two firms over the years.

I wish to thank Mr. Les Tennant of Bracebridge, Ontario who related to me an interesting account of the "rise and fall" of Minett Boat Company. It seems young Les' dad had a small sawmill two miles north of Bracebridge which he moved in 1907; the old building was up for rent. Young H. C. (Bert) Minett, who lived about 30 miles from the town, came in and rented the place for the building of wooden boats. He decided on the Bracebridge location because it was on the water and also had access to the railroad for shipping. Mr. Minett rented the old factory from 1911 until about 1923 or so. In those short years, Minett quickly gained a reputation as a fine boat builder and boats were sold all over that area. Many are still in daily use today. The only bad thing with Minett's location was that the plant sat just above the Bracebridge Falls. Therefore, boats had to be loaded on horse-drawn wagons and taken down along a gravel road to the water below. One of the largest boats ever built at the first Minett plant was the large 55' cruiser, Rita, which was custom-built for an American owner who had to have the boat loaded on a railroad flat

Beautiful 1917 28' Minett launch. 120 h.p. Chrysler six-cylinder engine.

car and moved ten miles to Gravenhurst where the boat was launched right under the noses of the Greavette and Ditchburn Boat Companies.

As was the case with many boat builders, their real talent lay in construction and design and not business management. This was the case for Minett also. In 1923

"Norwood" II Vintage Minett-Shields launch. (Photo by *CANADIAN BOATING* magazine.)

1929 Minett-Shields launch at full speed

1936 Minett-Shields racing boat. (Photo by *CANADIAN BOATING* magazine.)

the Minett Boat Company bought better land below the falls which allowed for easier launching and access to railroad tracks closeby. At that time Minett had taken on the building of two mammoth 55' cruisers and several launches and it seems this was more than he could afford. A young man, the late Bryson Shields, whose family had lived in that area during the summer for years, started a new firm in 1927 called "Minett-Shields Limited". In the new firm Minett was designer-builder and Shields in charge of finance and promotion. After the new firm got into full swing the two 55' cruisers were completed and sold. The building of runabouts and launches continued until 1948 when all building ceased.

In researching material concerning the Ventnor Boat Company, I discovered that Minett-Shields was the Canadian builder for Ventnor and the photo in this section of the 1936 race boat, Delta, resembles greatly the design of American-made Ventnors though she was built in Bracebridge. I only wish I had more photos to illustrate this section, but from what boats are shown the reader can gain some idea of why Minett-Shields boats are so highly prized in these days of mass production.

The next portion of this book, though mainly photos, is material gathered since the first book was published. I have laid it out in the same order as it appeared in *Volume I*, starting with Chris-Craft and going right on to the end. I want to thank my many readers who made much of the following material available to me for use in this second book. There are short introductions to each section, telling about specific things to look at or bits of information gathered since *Volume I* was released.

CHAPTER V
MATERIAL APPLYING TO VOLUME I

Since the publication of my first book, *THE REAL RUNABOUTS, Volume I*, a tremendous amount of photos, bits and pieces of information has come flooding in to me and at this time I want to share it with you, my readers. I suggest that if you have Volume I that you get it out, as it will help to fill in on some of the material that was mentioned there which may be illustrated in this book. For example, to make this as easy as possible to read, I am following the same sequence in this chapter as was followed in *Volume I*. We shall start with Chris-Craft and go on down the line, ending up with Riva from Italy.

CHRIS-CRAFT
Algonac, Michigan

A lot of people have sent me Chris-Craft photos, etc., and to settle the old argument, "Who was the first franchised Chris-Craft dealer," I would like to thank Jim Mertaugh of Hessel, Michigan for sending old photos of their boat works from the early 1930's as well as a copy of their Chris-Craft franchise signed in February, 1926. Note at the top the "No. 1" notation, as well as the boats ordered on the original order at the bottom of the page. I think this pretty well answers the question, "Who was really the first Chris-Craft dealer in the U.S.?" there is

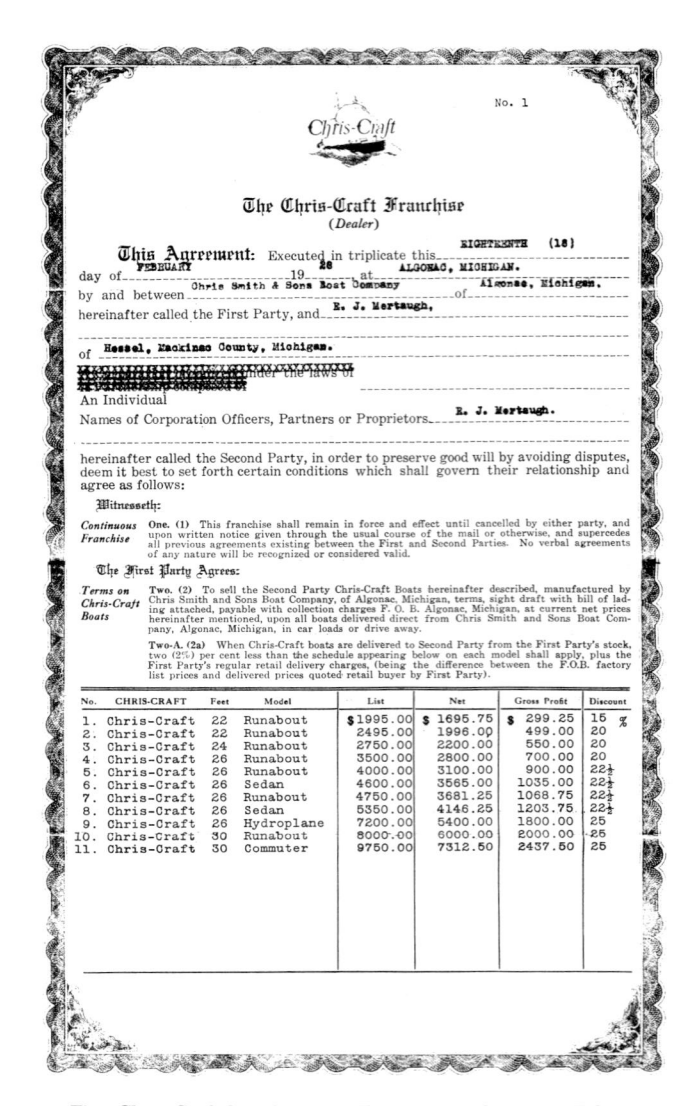

First Chris-Craft franchise with E. J. Mertaugh, signed February 18, 1926. Note original order of boats listed below franchise.

Early views of E. J. Mertaugh Boat Works in Hessel, Michigan

1920's style boat hauling equipment!

First U.S. franchised Chris-Craft dealer in 1926

130

1911 Chris-Craft 12 h.p. speeds to 16 m.p.h.!

1928 38' Chris-Craft cruiser

1930 26' Chris-Craft with 225 Scripps engine

Model 122 38' Commuter Cruiser in 1930

1930 48' Chris-Craft yacht

An early 1929 C.C. Commuter with Flying Bridge

Late 1920's Chris-Craft yacht tender

1931 20' Chris-Craft runabout

1931 22' Chris-Craft runabout with folding roof

1931 24' Chris-Craft runabout

1931 24' Chris-Craft hardtop

1931 24' Chris-Craft runabout, Model 203

1931 Chris-Craft 26' standard convertible sedan

1931 28' Chris-Craft sedan

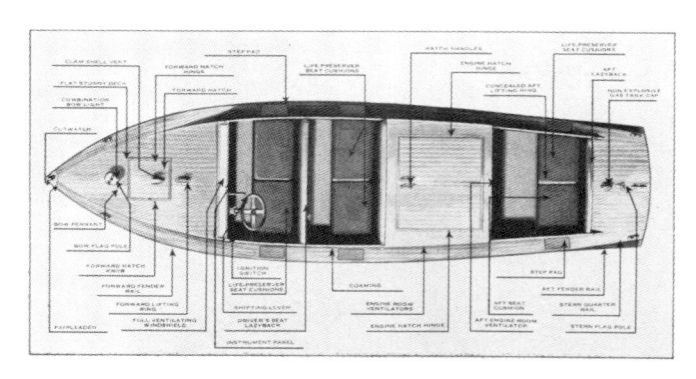

Typical 1931 Chris-Craft runabout illustration

also an assortment of photos showing Chris-Craft commuters, runabouts, etc. from the late 1920's up to about 1930 or so. 1931 was a big year at Chris-Craft, and I was fortunate in obtaining photos of many of the models offered in that year from the 20' runabout up through the big 28' custom convertible sedan. Other readers requested another old list of Chris-Craft dealers, so you will find a 1932 listing at this point. Quite a number of these firms are still in operation, so good luck in your search for old parts, old boats, brochures, etc.

THESE AUTHORIZED DEALERS DISPLAY 1932 LEVEL RIDING *Chris-Craft*

CALIFORNIA
WILMINGTON
  Harry C. Wilson & Co. Ltd.
  Foot of Avalon Blvd.
CONNECTICUT
DANBURY
  Alfred H. Higson
  125 White Street
HARTFORD
  Weston M. Jenks
  8 Ford Street
STAMFORD
  Connecticut Yacht Service
  Southfield Avenue, Waterside
WEST HAVEN
  Shutter Radio & Marine Co.
  529 Campbell Avenue.
DISTRICT OF COLUMBIA
WASHINGTON, D. C.
  Flood Gate Motor Boat Sales
  14th & Water Street
GEORGIA
MACON
  Macon Motor Boat & Supply Co.
  561 Mulberry Street
ILLINOIS
McHENRY
  Hunter Boat Company
INDIANA
ANGOLA
  Meyer Boat Livery
KANSAS
KANSAS CITY
  Simmons Sporting Goods Co.
  507 Minnesota Avenue
KENTUCKY
LOUISVILLE
  Falls City Boat Works
  132 North Fourth Street
MAINE
BAR HARBOR
  F. B. Hayes
  9 West Street
BOOTHBAY HARBOR
  R. A. Scott
PORTLAND
  Albert G. Frost
  24 Forest Avenue
MARYLAND
BALTIMORE
  Raymond W. Thompson
  1400 N. Charles Street
MASSACHUSETTS
FAIR HAVEN
  Casey Boat Building Co.
  Union Wharf
BOSTON
  Walter H. Moreton Corp.
  1045 Commonwealth Avenue
MICHIGAN
DETROIT
  Motor Boat Sales & Service Co.
  Foot of Alter Road
LELAND
  Stander Motor Company
PETOSKEY
  Petoskey Boat Works
SPRING LAKE
  E. J. Bauman Marine Corp.
MINNESOTA
WAYZATA
  Minnetonka Boat Works, Inc.
MISSOURI
BAGNELL
  Franklin & Miles Boat Service
  Osage Beach, Lake of the Ozarks
ST. LOUIS
  Schneider Nash Sales & Service
  4919 South Kingshighway Blvd.
NEW HAMPSHIRE
WOLFEBORO
  Goodhue & Hawkins
  Lake Winnipesaukee
SUNAPEE
  Smith Machine Co.
THE WEIRS
  Irwin Corporation
  Lake Winnipesaukee
NEW JERSEY
BRIELLE
  Feuerbach & Hansen, Inc.
LAKE HOPATCONG
  Hockenjos Boat Co.
  Great Cove
LAKE MOHAWK
  Stickle Bros., Inc.
NEWARK
  Carl W. Bush Co.
  518 Broad Street
PATERSON
  Coleman Halloran Inc.
  Market at 35th Street
SEABRIGHT
  H. L. Zobel
  Ocean Avenue
STONE HARBOR
  J. Salveson & Son
NEW YORK
ARVERNE
  Cohrone Boat Co., Inc.
  Foot of Elizabeth Street
BAY SHORE, L. I.
  Roy M. Brewster
  193 W. Main Street
BAYVILLE
  Seawanhaka Garage
BEMUS POINT
  L. S. Aero Marine, Inc.
BUFFALO
  Swan Marine Sales Company
  38 Swan Street
CARTHAGE
  D. F. Gettings
  320 State Street
CLAYTON
  George Mercier
  Riverside Drive
EAST SETAUKET, L. I.
  Lyon Bros. Cont. Co.
FREEPORT, L. I.
  Chatfield Marine Sales &
  Service Inc., Hudson Point
GLOVERSVILLE
  I. Heiman
  188 S. Main Street
LAKE GEORGE
  E. N. Lamb & Sons
  Bolton Landing
LAKE MAHOPAC
  C. J. Benjamin
LAKE PLACID
  George & Bliss
LOCKPORT
  Arthur Lerch
  38 Spaulding Street
LONG BEACH, L. I.
  Ace Speedboat Lines
  N. End Long Beach Bridge
MAMARONECK, L. I.
  Orienta Boat Works
  Orienta Point
NEW ROCHELLE
  Charles F. Weller
  400 Main Street
NEW YORK
  Chris-Craft Corporation
  1 West 52nd Street
  Armstrong & Galbraith
  79 Barclay
NIAGARA FALLS
  Pierce Smale Motor Corp.
  213 Tenth Street
NORTHPORT
  Conklin & Stiles Boat Co.
  260 Main Street
NORTH TROY
  Harry H. Henry
  655 Second Avenue
OGDENSBURG
  Ward's Sporting Goods Store
  321 Isabella Street
PORT WASHINGTON, L. I.
  Manhasset Bay Boat Corp.
ROCHESTER
  Howe & Rogers Co.
  89 Clinton St.
  Rochester Marine Co., Inc.
  115 North Street
SYRACUSE
  Syracuse Motor Marine Corp.
  344 West Genesee Street
UTICA
  Utica Auto Electric Service
  404 Seneca Street
OHIO
BUCKEYE LAKE
  Sayre Brothers
CLEVELAND
  Cleveland Yacht & Supply Co.
  2909 Detroit Avenue
LAKESIDE
  Worthy R. Brown & Son, Inc.
  Erie Beach Boat House
PORTSMOUTH
  Glockner Hdwe. Company
  2nd & Chillicothe
ZANESVILLE
  Triangle Motor Sales
PENNSYLVANIA
BEAVER FALLS
  G. H. Hamilton Mfg. Co.
  5th Street & 7th Avenue
ESSINGTON
  Yacht Repair & Storage Co.
KENNETT SQUARE
  A. T. Conord
LANCASTER
  Darmstaetter's
  35 N. Queen Street
PAUPACK
  A. Josco
PHILADELPHIA
  Essington Yacht Yards
  1415 North Broad Street
PITTSBURGH
  Chris-Craft Pittsburgh Co.
  2743 Liberty Avenue
YORK
  Byron H. Resh
  125 South Duke Street
  H. O. Young
SOUTH CAROLINA
COLUMBIA
  Oliver Motor Company
  2007 Main Street
TEXAS
FORT WORTH
  Marion E. Herring Boat Works
  Nine Mile Bridge, Lake Worth
VERMONT
BURLINGTON
  Champlain Marine & Realty Co.
VIRGINIA
HAMPTON
  The Sportsman Shop
  123 E. Queen Street
WASHINGTON
WENATCHEE
  Warren Motor Co.
WISCONSIN
DELAVAN
  Delavan Lake Boat Company
FONTANA
  Palmer Boat Company
  Lake Geneva
GREEN LAKE
  Brooks Garage & Boat Co.
MADISON
  Tracy Boat Company
  412 North Franklin Street
OSHKOSH
  Clark & Lund

Partial list of 1932 Chris-Craft dealers

1932 Chris-Craft runabouts on parade!

The mid-1930's from 1934 on were the years when Chris-Craft and other speedboat builders put on elaborate displays at the national boat shows. There is a nice grouping of boat show photos at this point which make interesting viewing. I always wondered what a Chris-Craft showroom looked like as few pictures were ever shown of the operations. Well, thanks to Bud Sayre,

Partial view of Chris-Craft speedboat display at the 1934 New York Boat Show.

133

1934 Chris-Craft display at Chicago Motor Boat Show

First showing of a C.C. utility at the 1934 New York City Boat Show!

First 1934 Chris-Craft utility. Note steering tiller over stern.

Checking things over at Chris-Craft in 1934

Dashboard of 1934 18' Chris-Craft runabout

1935 Chris-Craft 18' DeLuxe Runabout, Models 24, 25

1934 18' Chris-Craft at rest.

1935 Chris-Craft 19' Double-Cockpit-Forward, Models 26, 27

1935 Chris-Craft 16' DeLuxe Runabout, Models 20, 22

1935 Chris-Craft 16' Double-Cockpit-Forward, Model 21

1935 Chris-Craft 16' Standard Utility, Model 10

1935 Chris-Craft 18' DeLuxe Utility, Models 12, 14

1935 Chris-Craft 21' DeLuxe Utility, Models 16, 17, 18

long-time Chris-Craft dealer in Buckeye Lake, Ohio, we are privileged to have an excellent view of the show room which was located at the factory at Algonac. I was really excited to be able to obtain a photo of that store as many customers never got a chance to get to Michigan to see just where their boats came from.

In *Volume I,* page 14, I mentioned a custom-built 1936 28' Chris-Craft fishing boat. I am fortunate in now having a photo taken of it while at rest. The boat was a

Chris-Craft display at the 1935 New York Boat Show

Mr. and Mrs. Chris Smith after Chris' 75th birthday in 1936

Chris-Craft Showroom at Algonac, Michigan—1935

1936 red, white and blue racers ready to have hardware and trim installed.

A new 1936 racing runabout just launched for the first time

Custom-built 1936 28' Chris-Craft fishing boat

137

The 1936 18' Chris-Craft racing runabout—hit of the Paris Boat Show.

true "one of a kind" and would be a rare find today. Several times on pages 14 and 15 the topic of the then popular Racing Runabouts by Chris-Craft came up. I now have good photos of several of these craft, one of which shows an 18' Racing Runabout on display at the 1936 Paris, France Boat Show. The rest of the late 1930's were also big years at Chris-Craft. There are more photos of boats built during that period shown at this point.

1940 and 1941 were described in some detail starting on page 19 of *Volume I*. I now have gathered some good photos of the 1940 Chris-Craft fleet, starting with a red, white and blue 16' Racing runabout, followed by the stylish 1940 17' Deluxe runabout as well as the rare 23' Custom runabout. The ultimate 1940 Chris runabout was the big 27' Custom runabout with jade green upholstery and the new two-piece folding windshields. 1941

CHRIS-CRAFT for 1937

3 new 1937 Chris-Crafts at rest

Custom 1938 24' Sportsman Chris-Craft with convertible top extension

1938 Chris-Craft display at New York Boat Show

1940 16' Chris-Craft racing runabout with red, white and blue color scheme.

1938 19' custom runabout by Chris-Craft

1940 17' Chris-Craft deluxe runabout

Custom-built 31' Chris-Craft runabout—twin engines, 1938

1940 23' Chris-Craft custom runabout

1940 27' Chris-Craft custom runabout

1941 16' Chris-Craft Hydroplane

1941 17' special runabout

1941 16' deluxe utility by Chris-Craft

1941 17' deluxe runabout

1941 16' Chris-Craft Hydroplane

1941 19' custom runabout

140

1941 22' Chris-Craft utility, built just before start of World War II

1941 23' custom runabout

1942 17' Chris-Craft runabout with 60 h.p. engine. Boat owned by customer from Brazil.

Grand opening of new Chris-Craft dealer in March of 1947 at Seattle, Washington.

saw some more changes at Chris-Craft. Small utility type inboards from 16' and up were offered as well as a "super neat" 16' Hydroplane, seating two and designed strictly for racing. There was no seat behind the engine in this boat as there was in the old 16' Racing runabouts. Even the literature said the boat was strictly for racing and not pleasure. I am sure not too many of these boats were ever built and to date have seen photos of only one; it had been modified from its original condition. More conventional speedboats for 1941 would have to include the little 17' Special runabout with red bottom and upholstery. Note the old round style bow light still used on that particular boat. The 17' Deluxe runabout for 1941 was the same as 1940 except it now had turquoise rather than gold upholstery as before. The Chris-Craft shown on the bottom of page 13, *Volume I*, is really a 1941 17' Deluxe runabout, rather than a 1935 18' runabout as it was listed. The ever popular 19' Custom runabout was unchanged in 1941 also. It had been restyled in 1940 when new deck lines and windshield were added. The biggest Chris-Craft runabout in 1941 was a new 23'

1950 17' Chris-Craft Sportsman

1950 19' racing runabout

Aerial view of Holland, Michigan Chris-Craft factory in 1941

1950 20' Riviera runabout

Neat little 16' Riviera runabout—1950

Custom model. You could not buy the 27' three-seater after 1940.

The years following 1947 found Chris-Craft greatly expanding its offerings. By 1950, the speedboat selection ranged from a nice 16' Riviera runabout up through the 20' Racing runabout. As we saw in *Volume I*, Chris-Craft offered various wooden speedboats through the early 1960's when finally all-wooden boat building came to an end. To see how much prices have changed, look over closely the page of 1935 prices, specifications,

Chris-Craft

Runabout Prices Effective April 1, 1935

All Prices F.O.B. at Factory—Subject to Change Without Notice

Model No.	Length	Type	Seating Capacity	Speed	Motor	Price at Factory
20	16′	De Luxe Runabout—	6 Passenger	Up to 32 M.P.H.	55 H.P.	$ 895
*21	16′	De Luxe Runabout—	6 Passenger	Up to 32 M.P.H.	55 H.P.	945
22	16′	De Luxe Runabout—	6 Passenger	Up to 35 M.P.H.	73 H.P.	1,045
*23	18′	De Luxe Runabout—	6 Passenger	Up to 31 M.P.H.	55 H.P.	1,145
24	18′	De Luxe Runabout—	6 Passenger	Up to 33 M.P.H.	73 H.P.	1,245
25	18′	De Luxe Runabout—	6 Passenger	Up to 36 M.P.H.	92 H.P.	1,445
*26	19′	De Luxe Runabout—	6 Passenger	Up to 33 M.P.H.	73 H.P.	1,345
*27	19′	De Luxe Runabout—	6 Passenger	Up to 36 M.P.H.	92 H.P.	1,545
28	22′	Custom Runabout—	9 Passenger	Up to 32 M.P.H.	92 H.P.	1,995
29	22′	Custom Runabout—	9 Passenger	Up to 35 M.P.H.	125 H.P.	2,295
30	22′	Custom Runabout—	9 Passenger	Up to 40 M.P.H.	152 H.P.	2,595
31	25′	Custom Runabout—	12 Passenger	Up to 38 M.P.H.	152 H.P.	3,450
32	27′	Custom Runabout—	12 Passenger	Up to 45 M.P.H.	250 H.P.	4,950

All Models Have Rounded Padded Cockpits of Airplane Type and Box Springs.
*Stern Motor Installation—Direct Drive—Two Cockpits Forward.

Chris-Craft

1935

Utility Prices Effective April 1, 1935

All Prices F.O.B. at Factory—Subject to Change Without Notice

Model No.	Length	Type	Speed M.P.H.	Motor	Price at Factory
10	16′	Standard Utility	3 to 26	45 H.P.	$ 660
11	18′	Standard Utility	3 to 29	55 H.P.	845
12	18′	De Luxe Utility	3 to 29	55 H.P.	995
13	18′	Standard Utility	3 to 32	73 H.P.	995
14	18′	De Luxe Utility	3 to 32	73 H.P.	1,145
15	21′	Standard Utility	3 to 26	55 H.P.	995
16	21′	De Luxe Utility	3 to 26	55 H.P.	1,145
17	21′	De Luxe Utility	3 to 29	73 H.P.	1,295
18	21′	De Luxe Utility	3 to 32	92 H.P.	1,495

All Motors Rubber Mounted

Condensed Runabout Specifications

CONSTRUCTION

MODEL NUMBERS	20	21	22	23	24	25
Frames and Spacing — Main	7/8"x2 1/2" 12" & 24"	7/8"x2 1/2" 12" & 24"	7/8"x2 1/2" 12" & 24"	7/8"x2 1/2" 16"	7/8"x2 1/2" 16"	7/8"x2 1/2" 16"
Frames and Spacing — Intermediate	5/8"x1" 6"	5/8"x1" 6"	5/8"x1" 6"	5/8"x1" 8"	5/8"x1" 8"	5/8"x1" 8"
Bottom—Double Planked	9/16"	9/16"	9/16"	5/8"	5/8"	5/8"
Sides—Batten Seam	3/8"	3/8"	3/8"	3/8"	3/8"	3/8"
Keel	1 1/2"x3 3/4"	1 1/2"x3 3/4"	1 1/2"x3 3/4"	1 3/4"x3 3/4"	1 3/4"x3 3/4"	1 3/4"x3 3/4"
Keelson (Bilge Stringers)	LENGTH OF BOAT					
Fastenings	BRASS SCREWS AND BOLTS					
Trim	CHROME PLATED HARDWARE, ALL MODELS					
Rudder	MANGANESE BRONZE, ALL MODELS					
Strut	MANGANESE BRONZE, ALL MODELS					
Strut Bushing	CHRIS-CRAFT BRONZE, ALL MODELS					
Shaft Material	BRONZE, ALL MODELS					
Shaft Diameter	1"	1"	1"	1"	1"	1"

ALL MODELS: Salt water equipment furnished as standard—Mahogany wood—Natural varnish finish.
All Chris-Craft Runabouts embody the new revolutionary LEVEL RIDING PRINCIPLE.

(OVER)

Condensed Runabout Specifications

CONSTRUCTION

MODEL NUMBERS	26	27	28	29	30	31	32
Frames and Spacings — Main	7/8"x2 3/4" 12" & 24"	7/8"x2 3/4" 12" & 24"	7/8"x3" 12" & 24"	7/8"x3" 12" & 24"	7/8"x3" 12" & 24"	7/8"x3" 24"	7/8"x3" 24"
Frames and Spacings — Intermediate	5/8"x1" 6"	5/8"x1" 6"	5/8"x1" 6"	5/8"x1" 6"	5/8"x1" 6"	5/8"x1" 8"	7/8"x1" 8"
Bottom—Double Planked	5/8"	5/8"	5/8"	5/8"	5/8"	5/8"	5/8"
Sides—Batten Seam	3/8"	3/8"	1/2"	1/2"	1/2"	1/2"	1/2"
Keel	1 3/4"x3 3/4"	1 3/4"x3 3/4"	1 3/4"x3 3/4"	1 3/4"x3 3/4"	1 3/4"x3 3/4"	1 3/4"x3 3/4"	1 3/4"x3 3/4"
Keelson (Bilge Stringers)	LENGTH OF BOAT						
Fastenings	BRASS SCREWS AND BOLTS						
Trim	CHROME PLATED HARDWARE, ALL MODELS						
Rudder	MANGANESE BRONZE, ALL MODELS						
Strut	MANGANESE BRONZE, ALL MODELS						
Strut Bushing	CHRIS-CRAFT BRONZE, ALL MODELS						
Shaft Material	BRONZE, ALL MODELS						
Shaft Diameter	1"	1"	1"	1 1/4"	1 1/4"	1 1/4"	1 1/4"

ALL MODELS: Salt water equipment furnished as standard—Mahogany wood—Natural varnish finish.
All Chris-Craft Runabouts embody the new revolutionary LEVEL RIDING PRINCIPLE.

Condensed Utility Specifications

CONSTRUCTION

MODEL NUMBERS	10	11	12	13	14
Frames and Spacings — Main	7/8"x2 1/2" 24"	7/8"x2 1/2" 22"	7/8"x2 1/2" 22"	7/8"x2 1/2" 22"	7/8"x2 1/2" 22"
Frames and Spacings — Intermediate	5/8"x1" 6"	5/8"x1" 6"	5/8"x1" 6"	5/8"x1" 6"	5/8"x1" 6"
Bottom-Double Planked	9/16"	5/8"	5/8"	5/8"	5/8"
Sides—Batten Seam	3/8"	3/8"	3/8"	3/8"	3/8"
Keel	1 1/2"x3 3/4"	1 3/4"x3 3/4"	1 3/4"x3 3/4"	1 3/4"x3 3/4"	1 3/4"x3 3/4"
Keelson (Bilge Stringers)	LENGTH OF BOAT				
Fastenings	BRASS SCREWS AND BOLTS				
Trim	CHROME PLATED, ALL MODELS				
Rudder	MANGANESE BRONZE, ALL MODELS				
Strut and Skeg	MANGANESE BRONZE, ALL MODELS				
Strut Bushing	CHRIS-CRAFT BRONZE, ALL MODELS				
Shaft Material	BRONZE, ALL MODELS				
Shaft Diameter	1"	1"	1"	1"	1"

ALL MODELS: Salt water equipment furnished as standard—Mahogany wood—Natural varnish finish.

(OVER)

Lifting Ring Dimensions

A—Overall Dimension
B—Stern to Aft Lifting Ring
C—Distance Between Lifting Rings
D—Forward Lifting Ring to Bow

Size Boat	A	B	C	D
16′ Runabout	16′	2 1/2″	13′8 1/2″	2′1″
16′ Utility	16′	2 1/2″	13′8 1/2″	2′1″
18′ Runabout	18′	2 1/2″	15′7 3/4″	2′1 3/4″
18′ Utility	18′	2 1/2″	15′8 1/2″	2′1″
19′ Runabout	19′	2 1/2″	16′11 1/2″	1′10″
21′ Utility	21′	2 1/2″	19′1 1/2″	1′8″
22′ Runabout	22′	1′6 5/8″	18′7 1/2″	1′9 7/8″
25′ Runabout	25′	2′	17′6″	5′6″
25′ Utility Cruiser	25′	5″	22′4″	2′3″
27′ Runabout	27′	2′8 3/4″	18′6 1/4″	5′9″

etc., and see what your money would buy you 43 years ago. . . .

Although I have not described every photo in this section, I hope you enjoy all of them; I hope they tend to expand for you material about Chris-Craft covered in *Volume I*. We shall now move on to another firm we covered, namely Hacker Craft Boat Company of Mount Clemens, Michigan.

HACKER CRAFT BOAT COMPANY
Mount Clemens, Michigan

Since *Volume I* came out, probably more material was collected concerning Hacker Craft than about any other boat builder. We start off with an old 1921 Hacker ad showing the record breaker, Nick-Nack, in use. I was very lucky to also obtain a mint copy of a 1927 Hacker Craft catalog in excellent condition. There was so much great material in that booklet I am afraid I may have gone a little overboard, but I think all that is shown here will be of special interest to us, the Hacker buffs everywhere. In 1927 Hacker Craft issued a 24-page catalog with an

1924 split-cockpit Hacker Craft runabout

1925 Hacker 26' Dolphin runabout

1921 Hacker Craft ad

Showing the dryness of the ride offered by Hacker Craft's 24' Dolphin

Smaller Dolphin on St. Clair River in 1927

Closeups of Dolphin cockpits and motor room

Views illustrating the extreme roominess of the Dolphin-De Luxe

145

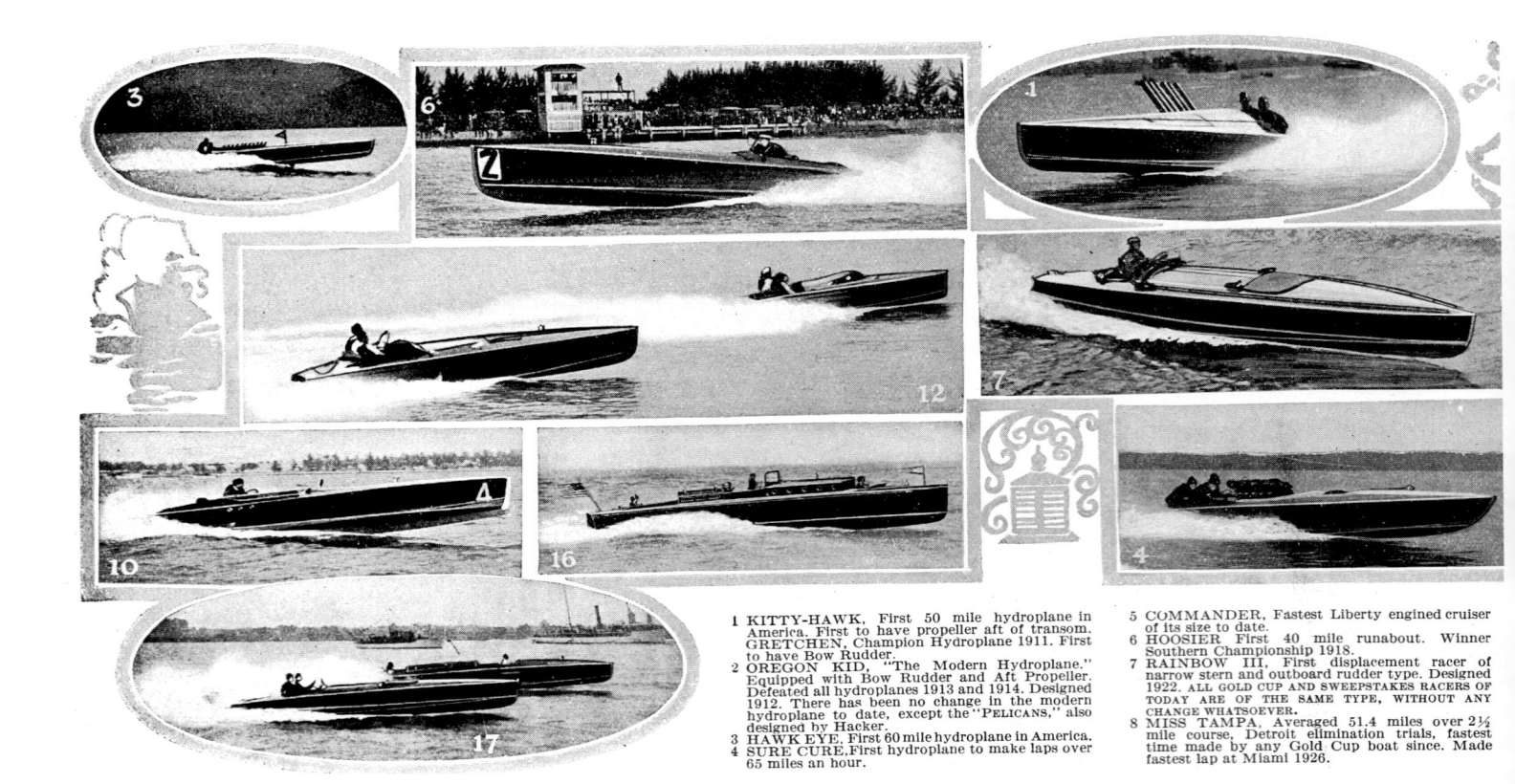

1 KITTY-HAWK, First 50 mile hydroplane in America. First to have propeller aft of transom. GRETCHEN, Champion Hydroplane 1911. First to have Bow Rudder.
2 OREGON KID, "The Modern Hydroplane." Equipped with Bow Rudder and Aft Propeller. Defeated all hydroplanes 1913 and 1914. Designed 1912. There has been no change in the modern hydroplane to date, except the "PELICANS," also designed by Hacker.
3 HAWK EYE, First 60 mile hydroplane in America.
4 SURE CURE, First hydroplane to make laps over 65 miles an hour.
5 COMMANDER, Fastest Liberty engined cruiser of its size to date.
6 HOOSIER First 40 mile runabout. Winner Southern Championship 1918.
7 RAINBOW III, First displacement racer of narrow stern and outboard rudder type. Designed 1922. ALL GOLD CUP AND SWEEPSTAKES RACERS OF TODAY ARE OF THE SAME TYPE, WITHOUT ANY CHANGE WHATSOEVER.
8 MISS TAMPA, Averaged 51.4 miles over 2½ mile course, Detroit elimination trials, fastest time made by any Gold Cup boat since. Made fastest lap at Miami 1926.

Photo display from 1927 Hacker catalog

HULL and DECK CONSTRUCTION
Dolphin-De Luxe

Showing High-Class, Clean-Cut Construction

1 Deck Beams
2 Walnut Instrument Board
3 Paneled Bulkhead with Lockers
4 Watertight Bulkhead
5 Intermediate Frames
6 Main Frames, Bent Rib Between, Spaced every Six Inches
7 Bulkhead Seat Back
8 Close Framed Hatch
9 Bulkhead End of Motor Room
10 Engine Stringers from Stern to Bulkhead through bolted to Frames
11 Cockpit Lining
12 Cockpit End Arranged with Removable Back
13 Aft Beams
14 Center Plank
15 Gas Tank
16 Mahogany Transom

Drawing of Dolphin-De Luxe construction features

9 999 First 60 mile runabout in America. Made 61.4 miles in December, 1923. Owned by Edsel Ford.
10 ADIEU, First of its type built. Winner Fisher Trophy 1922-1924.
11 NICK NACK. Same type as "ADIEU." Winner same trophy 1923.
12 LADY HELENS. Champion Junior Gold Cup Boats. "HELEN I" won in 1924, "HELEN II," 1926. "HELEN I" was second.
13 SPITFIRES, Latest development in hydroplanes. Champions of 151 class, breaking all records and winning Elgin Trophy.
14 CALIFORNIA, Winner Southern Championship and holder of World's Record in competition of 51.2 miles.
   ANGELES. Same type Hacker-built. Fastest 151 hydroplane in the world. Speed 60.11 miles.
15 YANKEE DOODLE, Said to have made the greatest speed of any watercraft.
16 VIAWATER, Fastest twin Liberty engined cruiser of its size to date.
17 RAINBOW III and WOODFISH in a brush.
18 A Hacker Runabout in open sea in Italy.

1927—views inside Hacker shops at Mt Clemens, Michigan

147

The fine handling of the 24' Dolphin under power!

Another view of a Dolphin by Hacker Craft—1927

Larger 1927 deluxe Dolphin does her thing.

unusual green, white and purple colored cover. Only two models were offered at that time. The smaller runabout, known as the Dolphin was just under 24' in length. This boat was a three-cockpit model and had a split front seat so passengers could move from the driver's seat to the second seat without crawling over the back rests, etc. To show customers all the "firsts" that Hackers enjoyed in the 1920's, a two-page spread of photos and descriptions was inserted in the 1927 catalog. They are reproduced here in toto for your enjoyment. If you preferred a larger, more deluxe runabout by Hacker, your boat was the Dolphin De Luxe. This boat was 28' long and had for power a 150 h.p. Scripps model "G" which pushed the boat close to 40 m.p.h. Already in '27, Hacker Craft had adopted the practice of painting their bottoms marblehead green. The chart that shows the arrangement of the Dolphin De Luxe was so interesting that it is shown at this time also.

Probably the rarest photo in this whole book appears next, thanks to Tom Flood and his dad, Leo. This is an actual photo taken near the Hacker Craft plant in 1929 during tests of the King of Siam's new 40' custom Limo. I was really excited to have access to such a photo for this book, and I hope you enjoy it also.

It was a Hacker Craft practice to put out many of its catalogs without a year printed on the cover. Many of the photos were used year in and year out without change. For example, the 38' Commuter cruiser was the same in the early 1930's as it was in the 1940 publication.

SHOWING THE ARRANGEMENT OF DOLPHIN-DE LUXE
The Incomparable Runabout

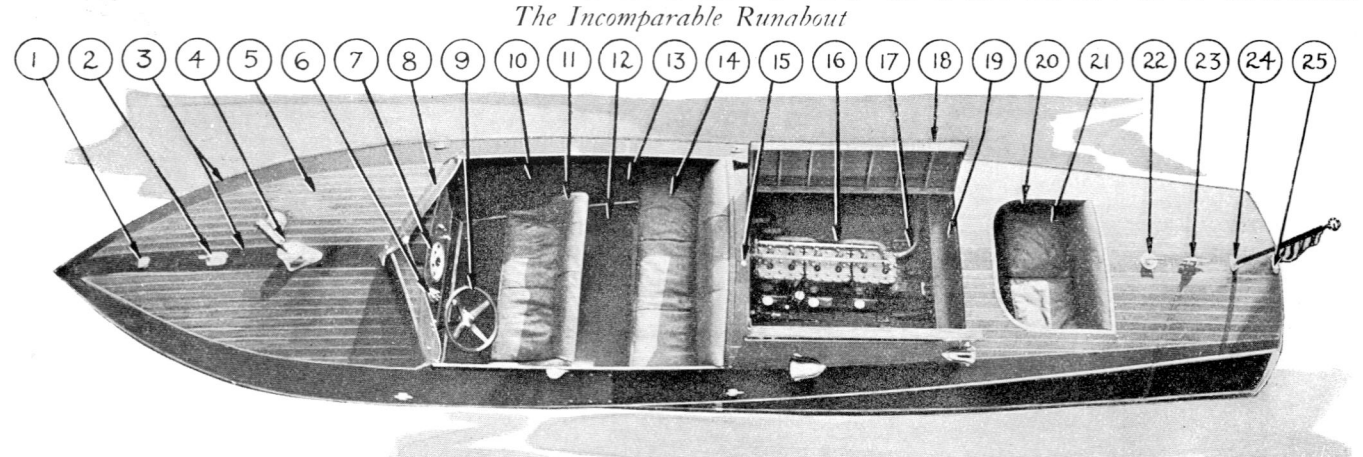

1. Vent for Watertight Bulkhead
2. Lifting Ring and Cleat.
3. Walnut Stained Center plank and Covering Boards
4. Stream Line Vent and Light
5. Mahogany Stripped Deck
6. Pierce Arrow Switch with Lock
7. Full Elgin Panel
8. Angled Windshield ... Metal Stiles ... Indestructo Glass
9. Auto Steerer
10. Passageway
11. Three Passenger Forward Seat. Spring Seat-back
12. Floor Linoleum Covered
13. Extra Large Space
14. Four Passenger Aft Seat. Genuine Leather Upholstery ... Deep Spring Seat and Back ... Meritas lined sides.
15. Yale Hatch Lock
16. Showing Motor Installation
17. One Piece Copper Exhaust Pipe
18. Hatch Cover
19. Shelf For Tools
20. Two to Three Passenger Aft Cockpit
21. Kapoc Filled Leather Cushions and Back. Cable Lifts Under Seat
22. Gas Tank Filler
23. Cleat
24. Electric Flag Pole Light
25. Chuck

Detailed drawing of 28' Dolphin-De Luxe

Actual view of King of Siam's custom Hacker-Limo.—1929

1929 Hacker Craft magazine ad

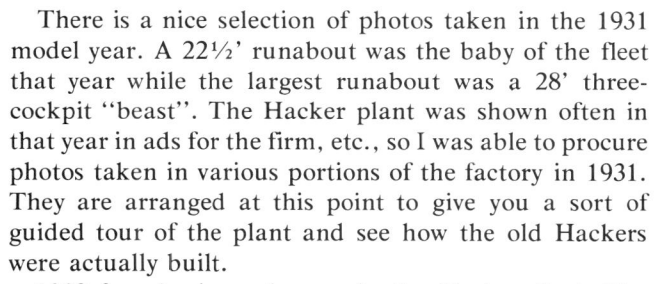

1931 22½' Hacker Craft runabout

There is a nice selection of photos taken in the 1931 model year. A 22½' runabout was the baby of the fleet that year while the largest runabout was a 28' three-cockpit "beast". The Hacker plant was shown often in that year in ads for the firm, etc., so I was able to procure photos taken in various portions of the factory in 1931. They are arranged at this point to give you a sort of guided tour of the plant and see how the old Hackers were actually built.

1932 found minor changes in the Hacker fleet. The then smallest boat had been lengthened to an even 23' and was also then powered by a Chrysler Crown engine. The biggest Hacker runabout in 1932 was a massive 32' streamliner that carried a 450 h.p. Kermath Sea Raider engine. That boat had a newer, more racy "V" windshield too, and seating for over 10 passengers. On page 28 of *Volume I* we discussed the big 60' mahogany Hacker cruiser designed and built to compete and break the world's record crossing the Atlantic. The boat was built and tests were run off the coast of Bermuda, proving the boat to be seaworthy. The photo shown here will give you a better idea just what that wild craft looked like. I was unable to find whether the boat ever did make the run or not. My own guess is it was never attempted as the Depression and general world conditions did not warrant such undertakings.

It was in 1934 that Hacker built its first three-cockpit 20' runabout. This boat also had a new "V" windshield which made the boat look much sleeker. A lot of inquiries and material came in about the good ol' El Lagarto which we discussed on pages 28 and 29 of *Volume I*. There is a photo on page 28 showing the El

Four 1931 Hacker Craft running flat out

Every detail reveals rare qualities in this smart, small ship. Passenger cockpits are unusually large and roomy, seating a fair sized crowd with comfort.

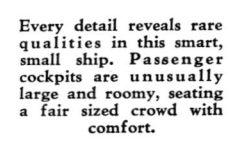

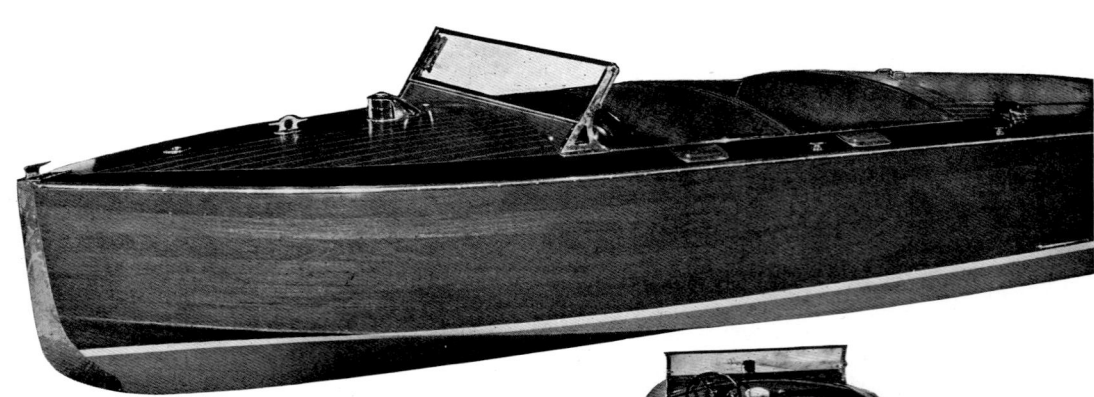

The 22½ Footer
From Every Perspective, Well-Planned *and* Proportioned

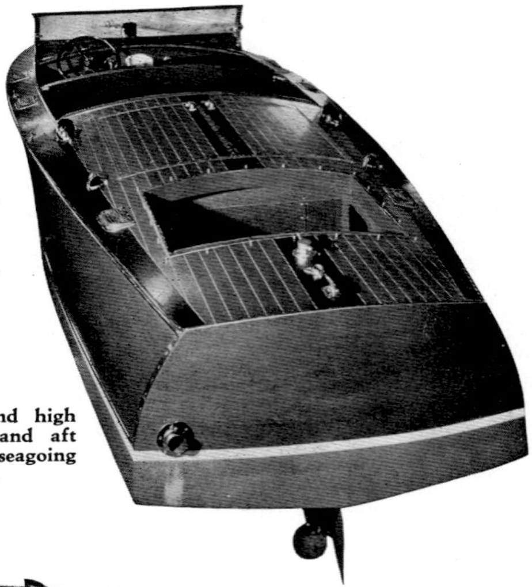

A modern, easy handling steering gear, conveniently located reverse gear control, fully fitted instrument board, full vision, adjustable windshield, all contribute to ease in handling.

Liberal beam and high freeboard fore and aft insure unusual seagoing qualities.

The upholstering is all genuine leather with springs sufficiently deep to guarantee absolute riding comfort.

1931 views of Hacker Craft 22½' runabout

1931 28' Hacker Craft runabout

1931 38' Hacker Craft commuter

1931 35' Hacker Craft commuter

Large 1931 38' Hacker Craft cruiser commuter

Deluxe wood shop at Hacker Craft Boat Company in 1931

A framed-up hull about to be turned over for planking.

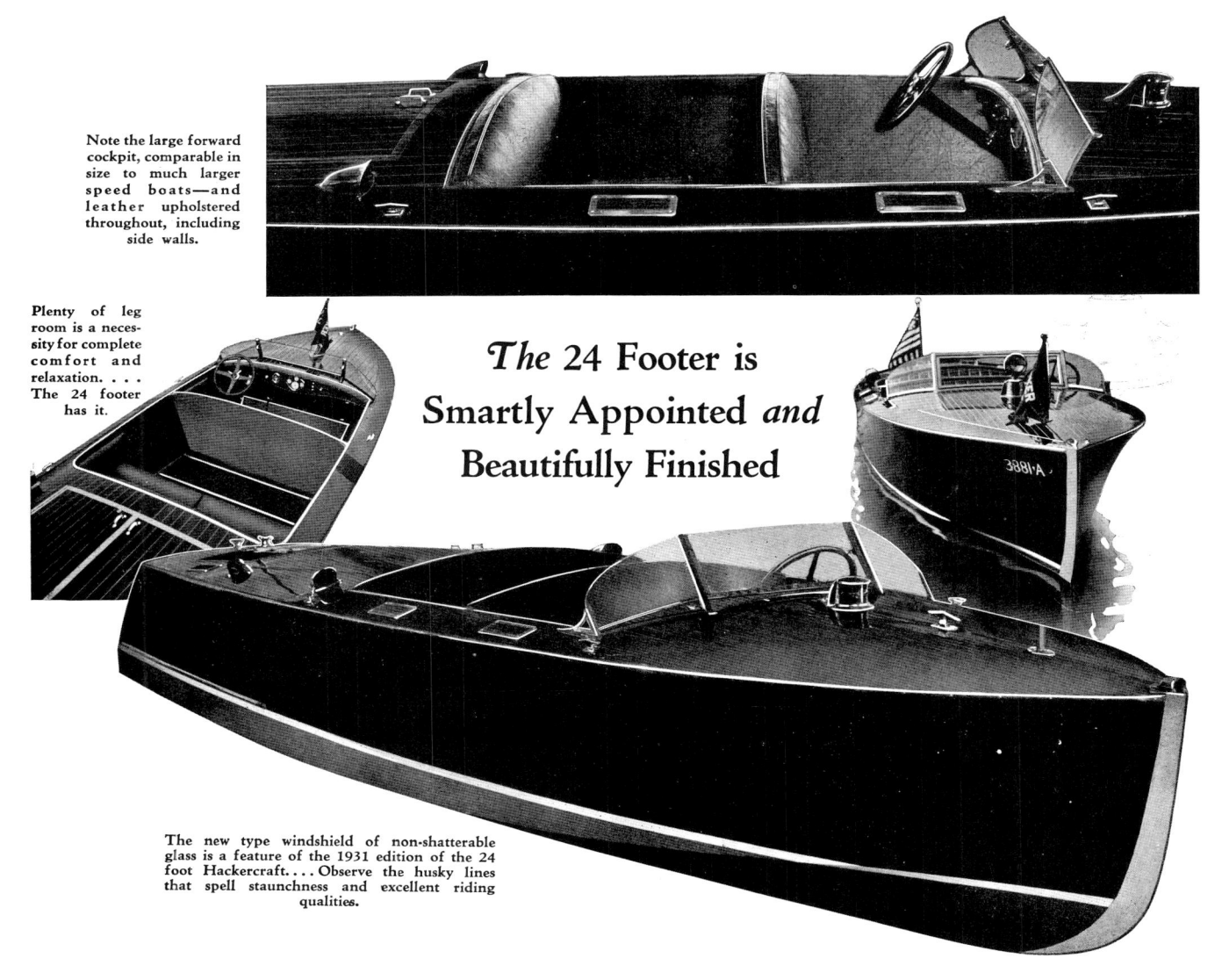

Note the large forward cockpit, comparable in size to much larger speed boats—and leather upholstered throughout, including side walls.

Plenty of leg room is a necessity for complete comfort and relaxation. . . . The 24 footer has it.

The 24 Footer is Smartly Appointed *and* Beautifully Finished

The new type windshield of non-shatterable glass is a feature of the 1931 edition of the 24 foot Hackercraft. . . . Observe the husky lines that spell staunchness and excellent riding qualities.

Good detailed views of the 24' 1931 Hacker Craft runabout

Another view of planking Hacker Craft runabouts in 1931.

Hackercraft ready for the finishing touches of the hardware—1931 view.

Hacker Craft speedboats being framed and planked in 1930's.

Engines being installed at Mt. Clemens, Michigan plant of Hacker Craft Boat Company.

Completed Hacker hulls being sanded prior to finishing.

23' 1932 Hacker runabout speeds to 37 m.p.h. with Chrysler Crown —$2,495.00.

32' 1932 Hacker Craft runabout with 450 h.p. Kermath Sea Raider, 53 m.p.h.—$11,500.

Another Hacker Craft completed and ready to be lowered into the water for the first time.

Drawing of 1934 Hacker Craft Trans-Atlantic racer

152

1930 view of Hacker runabout before she was converted to famous racing craft El Lagarto

Sleek, 1934 20' Hacker Craft runabout

New 1937 21' Hacker Craft painted utility with cabin

1934 32' Hacker Craft deluxe runabout

Typical 1937 Hacker Craft showroom view

Hacker 19' runabout captures second place in Albany to New York City race in 1937.

The 26' deluxe runabout with seating capacity for 11 adults. It will step along at 52 m.p.h. with cushioned ease. Genuine mahogany planking. 1938.

153

Custom 1937 28' Hacker Limousine powered by Scripps V-12 300 h.p. engine

Lagarto (she was known originally as the Miss Mary). Well, I now have a photo of her between the time she was the Miss Mary and the El Lagarto. The view was taken in 1930 and shows the hull while it was being used as a family runabout and not a racing boat as it would be several years later.

In the late 1930's Hacker expanded a lot, adding new dealers all over this country and also building some nice smaller runabouts and utilities in the 16' through 22' size. A few custom sedan runabouts were still turned out in the late 1930's. One was a sleek 28' model with a 300 h.p. V-12 Scripps engine. All Hackers had the new "V" windshields by 1940 with the old three-piece model being replaced for good.

The biggest of all Hackers was built in late 1939 for Mr. George Whittell who wanted built the "ultimate Hacker Craft of all times". I think he got his wish as no

Beautiful 28' 1938 streamlined Hacker Craft runabout

Sleek Thunder Bird 55' Hacker Craft on Lake Tahoe, California

Thunder Bird at rest—a deluxe Hacker Craft sedan

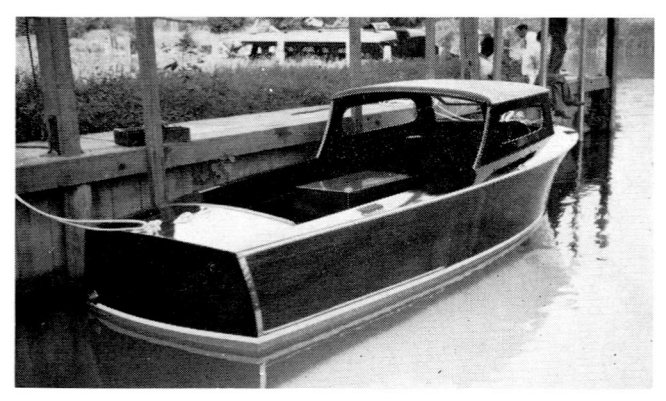

The 19' Cabin utility boat—ideal for hunting, fishing and general camp and summer cottage use. Plenty of room for sporting equipment and luggage. Speeds up to 35 m.p.h. 1938.

Stock 1937 Hacker 19' sport speedster

other craft was ever built by the firm to such dimensions.*
The boat was 55' long and weighed over 15 tons. It was not a cruiser at first but strictly a king-size runabout with hardtop roof. The boat was first powered by two 550 h.p Kermath engines. Bill Harrah, local Casino and museum magnate purchased the boat in the early 1960's from Mr. Whittell and has changed the boat to some degree. He first of all repowered the boat with twin 1,000 h.p. Allison V-12 aircraft engines; the boat's interior was redesigned by the installation of an all-stainless steel galley, plush seating and eating facilities and by adding a sort of

---

*The craft was designed by John Hacker but built at Bay City, Michigan by Huskins Boat Company.

154

Splendid custom 28' 1938 Hacker Craft powered by Scripps V-12 325 h.p. engine. Top speed, 55 m.p.h.

Custom 1940 Hacker-designed Super runabout on Lake Tahoe, California. Thunder Bird has two 500 h.p. Kermath engines.

1942 34' Hacker Craft target boat ready for delivery

1942 34' Hacker Craft Target boat leaving the plant

1948 19' Hacker Craft runabout with 115 h.p. Chrysler engine

"flying bridge" control center towards the aft area of the craft. Top speed is almost 70 m.p.h. as was attested to by a reader who wrote and told me he raced alongside the craft one day with his big "California type" jet boat and got left in the Thunderbird's wake. The first photo of the Thunderbird was taken by the Kermath Engine Company to use in one of the firm's magazine ads while the other two were taken by one of my readers several years ago when the boat happened to be in the water. The complete hardtop cabin area is built totally of stainless steel which really added to the great looks of the big "giant". If ever you get out to Lake Tahoe you should try and see the Thunderbird. I have been told, even a glance at the craft racing down the lake will send shivers up any antique boat buff's spine whether he likes speedboats or not. During World War II Hacker turned out various types of naval craft. One variety was a 34' Target boat built by the firm for use by the Army-Air Force. Again thanks to Leo Flood who helped build many of these craft. I got a kick out of the photo showing one all loaded on a semi leaving the plant for delivery to the government.

Following the end of the war, new management took over the firm and production returned to smaller runabouts and utilities along with a custom model or two every so often. The 30' Comanche, a custom Hacker sedan, is still very much in use out at Lake Tahoe. The boat had a Scripps V-12 power plant when new; the present owner was pleased to be able to obtain copies of the two photos shown here of his boat when it was still new at Mount Clemens.

1948 Hacker Boat Company ad

1948 19' Hacker Craft cabin utility

1948 22' Hacker Craft sedan

1950 custom Hacker sedan, 30'

22' 1949 Hacker Craft utility in power slide full bore

Factory view of a 1950 Hacker Craft sedan with V-12 Scripps engine for power.

I mentioned on page 34 of *Volume I* about the low priced, painted Hacker utility, the Sports Dolphin, which was introduced in 1950. There is a good photo of one of those boats shown here and you can judge for yourself whether or not it did anything for Hacker's business about that time. The final years at Hacker found fewer and fewer boats being built. The last big

156

The fateful 22' Sport Dolphin which eventually helped lead to the downfall of Hacker Craft.

Nice riding 24' 1950 Hacker Craft runabout

Charlie Ward's new 1953 Hacker Craft 30' twin-engine runabout

runabout came on the scene about 1953 when Charles Ward of Minneapolis had a twin-engine 30' runabout built for his private use. This boat, to me, had more of the classic Hacker looks and style and was a fitting climax to the end of an era that went way back to about 1910 when John Hacker built his first power boats. I still think Hacker is my favorite brand of inboard; yours might be another—even so, you will have to agree Hacker Craft were very unique boats always, and were (and still are) very collectable boats nationwide.

The next company we discussed in *Volume I* was Century, thoroughbred of boats, a firm located in Manistee, Michigan, which dates back to the early 1920's and is still in business to this day.

CENTURY BOAT COMPANY
Manistee, Michigan

Of all the boat builders covered in *Volume I* there seems to be considerable interest growing about Century speedboats. Century was a smaller firm until about the late 1930's when they began to sell nationally and advertise more in boating magazines, etc. There are several photos shown at this point of various Century models from 1937 through about 1941.

Wise Men Don't Hesitate
They Buy Century

They know that Century boats are good boats... designed right... built right... beautiful boats that perform right under every circumstance. You can have lazy speed... or tremendous power. You can idle along or be out in front. There are boats for every purpose in the small boat field... rowboats... outboard runabouts... outboard utility boats... outboard racing hydroplanes... inboard runabouts and inboard utility boats... also high-power racing craft... there are two great sailboats Snipes and Comets.

Get a catalog today... get a demonstration as soon as possible... and then become a Century owner and find true water enjoyment.

CENTURY BOAT COMPANY
MANISTEE   DEPT. M   MICHIGAN

1937 Century magazine ad

1937 Century 17' utility

1937 18' deluxe Sea Maid runabout

1941 Century 20' sedan runabout

CENTURY NEW DAY CRUISER

A number of new boats appear in the Century Fleet this year... among them the Century Day Cruiser series... built for heavy offshore fishing, day cruising... for the rougher water of the ocean coasts—and for the days on the large inland lakes when an open cockpit boat would be uncomfortable.

Some of these models may be fitted with sleeping accommodations.

TWO NEW CATALOGS

Century has issued two new catalogs this year... one illustrating and describing the entire inboard line and sailboats... the other covering the outboard line—which shows for the first time the new "Sportsman" series... something new in fine boat building.

Ask for either... or both catalogs

**CENTURY BOAT
• COMPANY •**
DEPARTMENT J
MANISTEE, MICHIGAN

1939 Century Day Cruiser inboard sedan

1949 19' Century Sea Maid speeds to 43 m.p.h.

1953 16' Century Resorter utility with 130 h.p.

158

1953 18' Century utility speeds to 42 m.p.h.

With the end of World War II Century came out with some beautiful hulls which were among the best ever built. From 1948 through 1953 Century built basically the same model lineup each year. There are some good photos of the 1953 Century boats at this point. The Resorters and Sea Maids are both very popular boats with the collectors right now. Century still carries a considerable quantity of parts for their older boats at the Manistee plant. In the technical section of this book in Chapter VI, there is a name, address and phone number

First Century lapstrake utility—1953—Viking, 19'

1953 20' Century Resorter with convertible top

159

Racy, 1953 Century Sea Maid 18' runabout

for the person to contact at Manistee, Michigan for possible help. To help you owners, fans and others with Century boats built after 1953, there is a complete section in Chapter VI called "Collector's Guide to Modern Century Inboards". I think this section will be very popular with all Century fans, dealers, etc. so be sure to check it out. As I said at the start, Century boats are now beginning to become popular with the collectors so we will see more and more of these fine craft at antique boat shows and in use by people who prefer a "Thoroughbred of Boats"!

DEE WITE BOATS
Detroit, Michigan

Dee Wite boats are another favorite of mine, and are still popular with some collectors. However, useable boats are hard to find, and hardware for them even harder. Starting back in 1929 Dee Wite offered a 17' twin-cockpit runabout which had its power source consisting of an outboard motor mounted behind the second seat under a motor hatch. An electric starting outboard motor was a rarity in 1929 but a breakthrough for power boats. I also obtained a good closeup photo of a 1931 Dee Wite which was used in a long distance run from Detroit to St. Louis via the Atlantic Coast. The three-cockpit runabout had a Lodge engine and was 22' long.

1929 17' inboard-outboard by Dee Wite—a first of its kind!

1932 was a big year at Dee Wite and I am glad to now have good photos of a twin-cockpit-forward runabout, 19' long, as well as another two-seater with the 100 h.p. Lodge engine. In 1932 it seems Dee Wite really put the name on in big letters so all could see it, even at a distance. We talked a lot about the most famous Dee Wite Torpedos and I have since obtained good photos of both a 1932 28-footer and a 1932 32' model. These boats were among the most elegant of all runabouts, especially the 32-foot versions. A 40-foot Torpedo is shown on page 44

The New DEE WITE

See It At The New York Boat Show

THE NEWEST AND FINEST RUNABOUT AFLOAT

Totally new standards of beauty, performance, sea-worthiness and value have been established in this new Dee Wite All-Mahogany Runabout! At a price but little more than that of an ordinary outboard, this boat gives you the roominess, and stability of an expensive runabout. Every inch a thoroughbred! Genuine African mahogany and sturdy oak combine to make its construction perfect. It has a double-planked bottom, windshield, autotype steering wheel, double cockpits, upholstered seats, AND A UNIQUE INBOARD MOTOR FEATURE FOUND IN NO OTHER BOAT OF ITS TYPE! Dry, safe, easily controlled and fast enough to thrill the young folks. As easy to drive as an automobile. Delivered completely equipped—ready to use except motor. Send for descriptive literature.

Boat Division   DWIGHT LUMBER COMPANY   Dept. 122   Detroit, Michigan

Dee Wite 1929 small 17' inboard-outboard

1931 22' Dee Wite runabout

160

Sleek, 1932 19' Dee Wite runabout with 100 h.p. Lodge engine, $1,445.

1932 22' deluxe runabout—32 m.p.h. with 100 h.p. Lodge engine—$2,395.

1932 Lodge 28' custom runabout designed and built by Dee Wite, Inc., Detroit.

of *Volume I*. Very few of these boats were built as they cost around $15,000 each back in 1932, the market being rather limited for such a priced boat at that time. I would love to see a fully restored Dee Wite Torpedo in any size. I am sure there must be several still in existence somewhere in this country. If you have one or know of one, please contact me with information, photos, etc., as I would love to use them in a future book on speedboats.

GAR WOOD BOAT COMPANY
Marysville, Michigan

A very nice assortment of Gar Wood material has also come in to me since last August. First of all I am fortunate to have two great photos of Mr. Ben B. Bryan's sleek 1928 28' Gar Wood Limo. runabout. The boat's name was Rub-A-Dub-Dub II and was powered by a 185 h.p. Kermath engine. In reminiscing with the author, Ben (who is now retired) said his biggest thrill was winning the Chicago Tribune Regatta in 1931 against 16 other speedboats. Nearly 20,000 fans watched the races along Chicago's lakefront area. That would be a thrill to any of us speedboat buffs, I am quite sure. Ben also owned a Sunflower craft which we shall look at in a later section.

In *Volume I* there was little concerning Gar Wood boats for 1931. It was in that year that Gar added his first stock cruiser, an all-new 40' Commuter type which was powered by a big 425 h.p., or twin 200 h.p. Scripps engines if you preferred dual power. The first photo shows the prototype hull alongside the Gar Wood docks at Marysville with engine in place before cabin and decks were installed. The second photo shows the completed boat under power. Though the Gar Wood cruiser styles would change, this first boat set a precedent for cruisers built by Gar Wood up through the late 1940's.

1932 was another big model year at Gar Wood. I have been able to dig up a good selection of 1932 Gar Wood

Very distinctive 1932 32' Dee Wite Torpedo. 225 h.p. Kermath, 42 m.p.h.

Sleek 28' Gar Wood Limousine at rest

1928 28' Gar Wood Limousine Rub-A-Dub-Dub II, 185 Kermath engine

Trial run of new 1931 Gar Wood cabin cruiser

1931 40' Gar Wood cruiser

1932 18' Gar Wood runabout

1932 22' Gar Wood runabout

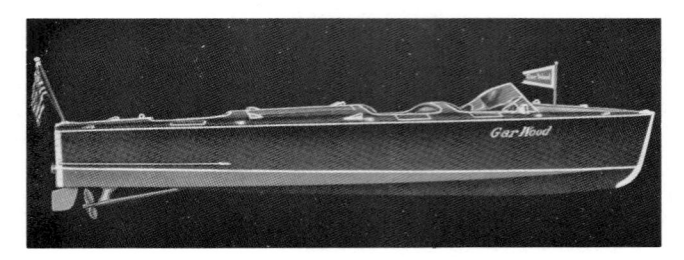

1932 25' Gar Wood runabout

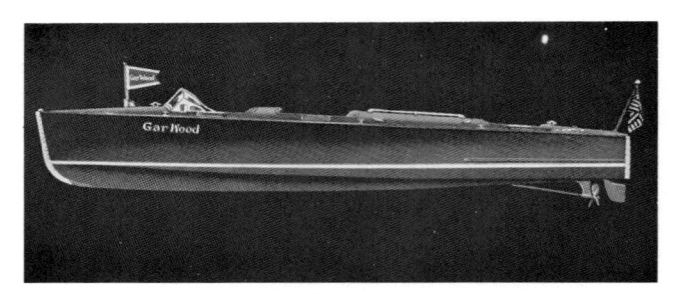

1932 Gar Wood 28' runabout

1932 Gar Wood 33' runabout

1932 view of Gar Wood plant at Marysville on the banks of St. Clair River

Final finishing section at Gar Wood in 1932

Decking of 1932 Gar Woods in factory

photos showing many of the then popular models. By 1932 you could buy small Gar Woods like an 18' split-cockpit; others included a 22' three-cockpit, a 25', a 28', and the "queen"—a massive twin-windshield 33' 50 m.p.h. speedboat. The 33-footer came equipped with a Gar Wood 12-cylinder 525 h.p. gas guzzler. She was my favorite Gar Wood in that year, I guess mostly since she was such a large boat. Always interesting are views taken in the various factories where the boats were built. In 1932 Gar Wood included views of boats under construction as well as a good outside view of the plant. They are all shown at this point. Gar Wood, like Chris-Craft and others, had beautiful displays at the major boat shows held each winter. 1934 was no exception—at least four new 1934 models are visible in the photo here. The 16' Sport Speedster brought a lot of comments from readers.

Sleek 1932 Gar Woods on display in downtown New York City

1935 16' Gar Wood speedster with 93 h.p. Chrysler engine

Excellent view of the 1934 Gar Wood display at the New York Boat Show.

1935 28' Gar Wood Landau runabout owned by William K. Vanderbilt—210 h.p. Scripps engine

I, too, think she was a real "cutie" and wonder how many, if any, are still in use. I have obtained another factory photo taken in October, 1934 just before the boat went on the market. Factory officials are seated in the stern seat after just returning from a preview ride. That first boat came with a standard 93 h.p. Chrysler six-cylinder engine and moved out at 40 m.p.h. It appears this first windshield was larger and more curved than those shown on later model speedsters. Do you think so too?

1935 through 1937 were big years at Gar Wood. Perhaps some of their most streamlined boats came out at that time. 1937 models are well covered on pages 49 and 50 in *Volume I*. However, I now have good photos of other Gar Woods from 1935 to 1937. One of the most popular twin-cockpit Gar Woods in 1937 was the 19' model. There is an excellent factory view shown here that reveals how the twin "V" windshield could be folded down and locked onto the deck when it was not wanted.

Custom Gar Woods were built quite regularly during the late 1930's. Another excellent example was built in 1937 for a customer on Lake Tahoe, California. The boat was a 26-footer with extra-fancy landau hardtop forward. I am quite sure our old friend Dick Clarke at Sierra Boat Company knows where this boat is or he even possibly cares for it at his huge marina. 1938 saw the addition of a totally new Gar Wood—a three-cockpit 22' runabout with "V" drive attached to a 117 h.p. Chrysler

Custom 25' 1936 Gar Wood split-cockpit runabout for South American customer

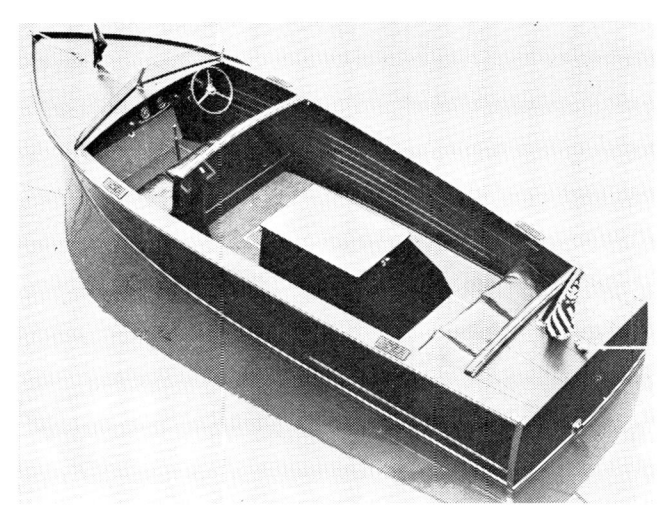

18' deluxe 1936 Gar Wood utility

1937 Gar Wood 24' streamline cabin utility

1936 20' Gar Wood leaving Marysville, Michigan for Yakima, Washington. Note semi-trailer rig.

1938 Gar Wood boat display at the New York City Boat Show

Excellent view of 1937 Gar Wood 19' custom runabout with folding windshield.

engine. If you will look at the drawing of the 22' Streamline runabout on the bottom of page 61 in *Volume I*, you will see the front deck does not have the unusual fin running down the king plank as is shown on the two actual photos taken in 1938 that appear here. I must say, I do not care for the deck design on the '38 model, and

1937 19' Gar Wood runabout with "V" windshield

166

others must not have either, as in 1939 it was completely changed as you shall see in the very next photo. I wonder just how many of those three-cockpit runabouts are still in use. I have heard that the "V" drives were some trouble as they were quite new at that time and maybe not all the "bugs" were out of them. . . .

By 1940 Gar Wood was offering many models, most quite unchanged from years before. The old factory remained about the same but I did get several more views of it taken about 1940 or so. Prior to 1941 Gar Wood was building an assortment of sedans, express cruisers, etc. Some of these boats were of the varnished type while others were painted. The largest 1941 model was an all-varnished 30' overnighter cruiser with twin engines. Gar Wood kept their famous "barrel-bow and stern" right up to the end. In fact, the firm advertised that all its hulls were very flared at the bow for safer, dryer rides. The last Gar Wood photo I obtained was shot in February, 1941 and showed a 1941 22' three-cockpit runabout with folding convertible top in place at full speed near Marysville. The roof appears to attach above the "V" windshield allowing full movement of air through the

Posh 1937 26' custom Landau hardtop at Lake Tahoe, California

Aerial view of 1938 Gar Wood "V" drive runabout

A little "cheese cake" 1937 style at New York Boat Show—19' Gar Wood Custom Runabout

New 1938 22' Gar Wood Streamliner. Note unusual trim running down center of front deck.

Factory view of new 1939 Gar Wood 22' 3-cockpit "V" drive runabout

3 Gar Wood 24' Sedans owned by U.S. Corps of Engineers on Missouri River at Kansas City, Missouri

1940 All-varnished 24' Gar Wood sedan

1940 Gar Wood assembly line

1941 30' Gar Wood all-varnished overnighter cruiser with twin Gray 8-175 engines

1941 22' Gar Wood runabout with folding top in place

1940 view of Gar Wood plant at Marysville, Michigan

1941 24' Gar Wood cruiser

boat to cool passengers on board. I hope you enjoyed these views of other Gar Wood speedboats. I think they help to fill in some of the years not illustrated in *Volume I* as well as adding to material on some years that were covered. Gar Wood boats were truly the "Commodore's Fleet". I am very glad to see increasing numbers of both antique and classic Gar Woods showing up at major boat shows everywhere. We hope to have at least three or more at our Antique Boat Show here in Minnesota this year.

SUNFLOWER BOAT WORKS
Lake Tomahawk, Wisconsin

We now will cover a small regional builder, Sunflower Boat Works, which to many readers of *Volume I* was totally new. Mr. Ben B. Bryan, Jr. who owned the Gar Wood Limo. shown in the last section also owned the finest of all Sunflower craft, the 23' Helen Mary shown on page 56 of *Volume I*. Ben sent two excellent views of the Helen Mary—one tied to his dock, and another with him at the controls, out for a fast ride. Ben revealed the following information about his beloved Helen Mary.

Helen Mary—sleek Sunflower Craft runabout powered by eight-cylinder Gray Phantom engine

Close-up of Helen Mary tied to the dock

First of all, he said the engine was not a Packard as mentioned, but a Phantom Gray Marine. It was mounted further forward than required, thus slowing the boat down to speeds considered safe by Ben so his children could use the boat without fear of accidents. Fabian Woodzicka estimated the boat would travel over 50 m.p.h. with the engine mounted slightly further aft. As it worked out the boat still turned an honest 40 m.p.h. which was fast enough for the Ben Bryan, Jr. family. Again, thanks to Ben Bryan, Jr. who, though retired and living in a retirement home, is still sharp as a tack and enjoys talking about his speedboats that gave him and his family such pleasure years ago. Ben, in closing, told me he has tried to find his old Helen Mary, but with no luck. Most likely the boat has been destroyed or at least "retired" to some shed or old barn where it might be just waiting for a new and eager owner to get her restored and back into the water. I also must note at this time that Todd Warner of Lake Minnetonka Restoration Company looked at the "Torpedo-stern" Sunflower shown at the bottom of page 58 in *Volume I*. He said a tree had fallen on the boat and nearly every piece of hardware had been stripped from the boat so he decided it was too far gone to restore. Others have been looking for Sunflower craft runabouts but with no luck to date. I am sure there must be one or two still in use somewhere up in northern Wisconsin.

HAFER CRAFT BOAT COMPANY
Spirit Lake, Iowa

A friend of mine who has antique boats in California as well as Okoboji, Iowa decided he wanted to obtain a small Hafer runabout to add to his collection. Upon searching around town the fellow stumbled onto a nice little 16' split-cockpit model that had been in storage for some years but in mint condition. It even had its original storage cradle and he was able to buy it at a very reasonable price. In talking with his good friend Dick Clarke back out in Lake Tahoe about his little "gem", Dick decided he, too, wanted a Hafer for his collection. Upon investigating further, a boat was found for Clarke

6000 square feet of ground floor used in the building and care of Hafer Craft launches.

170

Work room of Hafer Craft, looking toward the lake

Some 24' family launches built in 1908 by Hafer Craft

Another view of the family launch by Hafer Craft

and late in the fall of 1977 both little boats were trucked west to California. Dick Clarke's boat now resides in the Sierra Boat Company's showroom. These two Hafer Crafts are probably the only Hafer Crafts west of Iowa. My friend from California obtained an old 1908 Hafer catalog and was able to make four photos showing the old building, boats under construction, and completed 1908 launches shown here. I really enjoyed the photo showing the completed launches lined up in the plant built in the winter of 1908. I also just recently received a photo of a 16' Hafer outboard built in 1938 which is still in excellent shape and is used every summer over at Okoboji. So, I guess the Hafer clan knew how to build boats that lasted and kept their value over the years. Last fall I visited Glen Hafer and he enjoyed seeing the book and the report on Hafer Boat Company which he operated with his father.

Now we will look at a few of the custom builders from *Volume I*, starting with Steblow Boat Company of Kenosha, Wisconsin.

STREBLOW BOAT COMPANY
Kenosha, Wisconsin

I have talked with Larry Streblow since *Volume I* came out and he and his son Randy are as busy as ever. Larry was supposed to send new 1978 photos of Streblow boats, but to date nothing has arrived. Larry chided me for not mentioning his son in *Volume I*. Young Randy started helping his dad when he was just 14 years old with various jobs around the shop. Today Randy is Larry's right hand man and the fellows tell me that this year they hope to build one boat each month, concentrating on a 23' utility as their main model. A dealer who sells Streblow boats who was left out of *Volume I* was Coleman Ford of Mississippi. I am sorry for that omission. Their complete address will be found in the rear portion of this book under restoration shops, etc. The only new Streblow photo I could find shows the auto influence in 1963 when the tail fin was in vogue. This was

1960's era 19' Streblow Rebel utility

a 19' Streblow utility type which looked much like the Streblows of today. On the color jacket of this book you will see a Streblow runabout, so the firm is not totally missing from this book. A new 1978 dealer is the Wawassee Boat Company of Syracuse, Indiana.

HUTCHINSON BOAT WORKS
Alexandria Bay, New York

No other single boat mentioned in *Volume I* caused a greater stir than the mighty Lockpat III, the massive 48'

Hutchinson shown on pages 76 and 77 in that book. First of all, I am very glad to say the boat is still very much "alive" and safely tucked in a boat house in Michigan. I only hope that some time in the future she will be brought out, dusted off and put back into use. Just after *Volume I* was published I was fortunate in obtaining more information concerning Lockpat III in her early

1948 48' Hutchinson speedboat, Lockpat III

days. It seems the boat was built for C. P. Lyon in 1948 by Hutchinson Boat Works, Inc., and was called The Pardon Me. Mr. Lyon maintained a summer home on the St. Lawrence River where the boat was kept but because of illness the boat was sold and moved to Detroit where its new owner Dick Locke took over. It was estimated the boat cost over $48,000 to build in 1948. The Lockpat III was run over the July 4th weekend, 1978 at Harsens Island, Michigan with great success! I understand her new owner plans to use her and have her refinished.

The next firm we shall revisit is among the speedboat builders of Canada—Greavette.

GREAVETTE BOATS, LIMITED
Gravenhurst, Ontario

A little more material has come in on Greavette Boats, Ltd., including several photos showing a 1952 23' Streamliner and a larger view of a beautiful 1953 26' three-seater runabout. One Canadian reader advised me that Greavette built its first "Disappearing Propeller Boat" in 1937 and the final ones were sold in 1958, not 1956 as was mentioned in *Volume I*. I stand corrected,

23' 1952 Greavette streamliner

even though all dates, etc., came from the Greavette Boat Company itself. Greavettes are still some of the most beautiful speedboats ever built. Their hull design was never copied and is just as unique now as it was 40 years ago. Greavette boats are still very much in use all over Canada, and a few are starting to show their "faces"

1953 26' Greavette runabout

south of the border, in this country. My same friend from Canada also corrected my error when I stated that Minett-Shields boats were built in Port Carling, Ontario. This was untrue as they were built at Bracebridge, Ontario. Earlier in Chapter IV of *Volume II* you read the review of Minett which I hope was accurate in such details.

DITCHBURN BOAT COMPANY
Gravenhurst, Ontario

I have fared better concerning Ditchburn and have gathered a whole "raft" of photos showing their fine looking launches and speedboats down through the years. My friend in Canada also advised me that Ditchburn started back in 1875 when the four Ditchburn brothers started building boats at Rosseau, Ontario. Perhaps it was 1907 when they later moved to Gravenhurst. Quite a rivalry arose between Greavette, Ditchburn and Minett-Shields as all were located close to each other in the Canadian province of Ontario. The Miss Vancouver, a 1928 34' Ditchburn thrilled the world by cruising halfway around the world from Vancouver over to the East Coast of the United States without major problems. Antique boat shows in Canada have always been popular and you will see a good selection of photos shot by

28' 1927 Ditchburn classic launch

1929 Ditchburn runabout

1928 Viking Ditchburn launch

Famous old Ditchburn racer, the Rainbow IV of Canada

Custom-built 34' runabout which traveled over half way around the world—1928 Ditchburn

173

Close-up of 31' classic Vernon, Ditchburn launch

CANADIAN BOATING magazine at the 1977 Gravenhurst Antique Boat Show. In 1978 a bigger show is planned with up to 150 boats being on display. I would love to be able to attend that show as Canada has loads of great, old mahogany speedboats in many locations. I also came across a photo of a 1931 24' Autocraft built by Peterborough Canoe Company of Canada, as well as a 1925 ad for Gidley launches built at Penetang, Ontario. Thus the Canadians have done (and are still doing) much to preserve wooden launches and speedboats up north. As I said, right now Canada is a real "hot bed" of activity in wooden boats.

Probably the ultimate brand of boat covered in *Volume I* would be Riva of Italy. Just a mention of that name conjures up ideas of luxury wooden speedboats streaking along the Riviera.

Antique Ditchburn launch

1930 40' Ditchburn hydroplane with two 150 h.p. Sterling Petrol engines.

Vernon, 31' Ditchburn launch

Brice, classic Ditchburn launch under power

1931 Commodore, 31' Ditchburn runabout

1937 20' Ditchburn runabout

Rare 1937 Ditchburn 225 class hydroplane

174

1931 24' Autocraft by Peterborough Canoe Company

MOTORBOATING...

the Summer Sport Supreme Offers Kingly Relaxation!

WHAT an unmatched thrill it is to skim through blue waters or leisurely cruise among green islands in a staunch, graceful craft of your own... what healthful recreation! *It is the ultimate in sophisticated pleasure.*

You really owe it to yourself and your family to enjoy this glorious sport *this summer*—with the motorboat which has won a priceless reputation for beauty, for dependability, for economy...

The GIDLEY

For the name Gidley for many years has been identified with superbly built watercraft—from the smallest runabout to the lordly lake cruiser. Such a long period of boat-building experience has created facilities and standardized methods which make a Gidley boat a long-time investment in economy.

Grace of design, beauty of equipment, attractiveness of build, dependability and power of motor—all inevitably point to the Gidley as the boat of your choice, whether you desire a custom or a standard model.

Write, wire or phone for complete illustrated literature.

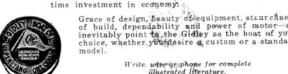

GIDLEY BOAT CO., LIMITED
PENETANG · ONTARIO

1925 Gidley, a Canadian launch

RIVA
Cantieri, Sarnico, Italy

I am very sorry to say that I have not gathered much new material on Riva except for a few more photos, starting about 1960. My own favorite view shows the Riva storage building at Monte Carlo. Wow! Not a plastic boat anywhere.... For those readers desiring to order an Aquarama Special shown on the jacket of *Volume I*, the selling price was $76,000 apiece in 1977 but production is already sold out through 1978. Better luck next time! Only 150 vessels are built each year by Riva—the bulk now of fiberglass—and as we have seen, the Riva

1960 20' Ariston runabout by Riva

Truly excellent storage building at Riva on the Riviera

population here in the states has crept up to about 150 boats at this time. It is very difficult to obtain lists of Riva clients but here are a few for starters: John Wayne, Evel Knievel, Shah of Iran, Sean Connery, Richard Burton, Rex Harrison, Bridgitte Bardot, Sophia Loren and Anita Ekberg. Riva announced it will publish a new magazine, *SYMBOL*, to be sent to all Riva boat owners and Rolls-Royce and Porche auto owners.

Thus we can see that Riva is not suffering these days as sales of the luxury craft go on and on. A new Midwest dealer for Riva has been appointed in Prairie View, Illinois. Their complete address is shown in the back part of this book. Though most of us will only dream of owning a Riva, their numbers increase steadily and before long I am sure they, too, will start to appear at antique boat shows all over this country.

Well, that covers all the firms that we reviewed in *Volume I*. I hope the material shown in this chapter will better illustrate those firms. Like any book, I have ended up with some good photos which fit into no real category which I still want to include, so I have decided to call this section "The United Nations of Real Runabouts". My purpose is to show you examples of speedboats built in other countries so that we can better appreciate the

175

1965 view of Riva Service Center at Monte Carlo

1965 Riva factory view showing boats being framed and planked

1960 26' Atlantico by Italcraft of Rome—twin 155 h.p. engines

1960 Italcraft's Bucaniere, a 20-footer that will do about 36 m.p.h.

1935 30' sedan runabout built in Germany.

Luxury 1950 Pedrazzini of Switzerland, 23' 6" runabout

176

1949 20' Argentine inboard runabout Nautical Baader of Tigre, Argentina—41 m.p.h. Scripps Zephyr engine.

Muller-Herzog of Switzerland 25' runabout—48.5 m.p.h.

Swiss Boesch Model 560 runabout 18½' long.

Cantieri-Taroni of Italy—18' single seat 1949 runabout

1960 19' Windermere English runabout

1931—The English-built Rytecraft runabout powered with an American 40 h.p. Lycoming engine.

popularity of the Real Runabout—not just here, but all over the globe. Some you may have seen or have been aware of, but I am sure many are new firms to you, just as they were to me.

The final photos shown here are of American boats which I felt too good not to use. Several—such as Stan-Craft, Chase-Emerson, and Aeolian—were new to me. The Fay-Bow 18' and 23' runabouts also were of great interest as most people only remember the older Fay-Bowen launches, etc. The last two photos show examples of other large speedboats. I think the 50' Vee-bottom hull would be the largest around. The Flying Pony used to be a Navy P.T. boat which was converted after World War II for pleasure boat rides.

1947 22' Stan-Craft Torpedo

1931 17' 6" Chase-Emerson runabout

1931 26' Aeolian runabout by Aeolian Company of New York City

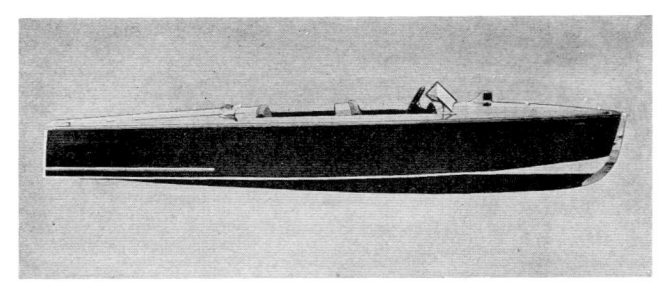

1931 18' Fay-Bow runabout with 40 h.p. Lycoming engine

1931 23' Fay Bow runabout

FOR SALE

Brand New—*Never Used*—50-Foot Vee-Bottom Runabout
One of the world's finest and most beautiful speed boats
Constructed of specially selected solid Honduras mahogany
Suitable for single, twin or triple screw power up to 5,000 H.P.
Perfect hull for sightseeing or thrill rides.

Could this be the largest speedboat ever built?

57-passenger runabout, Flying Pony, 45' long with 1400 h.p. Packard for power.

That pretty well wraps up Chapter V. I hope you enjoyed all photos and bits of news in this section, and we now shall move to the final portion of the book, Chapter VI, the Technical Section.

CHAPTER VI
TECHNICAL SECTION

This section of the book was not included in *Volume I*. In this chapter we shall cover a varied amount of material such as a complete breakdown of 1935 Chris-Craft engine facts. We list a Chris-Craft serial-number breakdown; also a complete chart of Chris-Craft prop and shaft sizes from 1927 through 1935. Much of this material has never been printed before and it should be of interest to many collectors. You will note a greatly expanded listing for old boat and engine parts as well as more than twice as many firms listed who sell boats, do refinishing and complete restorations, etc. This field is expanding greatly right now. I am sure you may know of firms who are not listed here that should be. If so, send me their names, addresses, phone numbers, and just what services they offer and it will appear in other upcoming volumes. Many readers of *Volume I* asked for more information on what I call "the modern-classic" speedboats like Century. Therefore, I have covered Century for every year, starting in 1954 up through 1968 when they built their last inboard from wood. Each year tells changes made, engine sizes, upholstery colors as well as a photo of each model for each year. Much time was spent compiling this section, but I hope you, the readers, as well as Century fans will enjoy it. Finally, a big thanks to Tony Brown, antique boat restoration expert, for writing a down-to-earth, easy-to-follow beginner's guide to refinishing an inboard. Many of the newer fans in our hobby have been requesting such a feature, so we included it in this book.

TECHNICAL DATA SECTION

PROPELLER WHEEL DATA

YEAR	ENGINE MAKE	ENGINE MODEL	H.P.	SHAFT SIZE & TAPER	WHEEL #	WHEEL SIZE
15.5 Runabout and Utility						
1931	Gray	4-43	43	1" standard	7507	11-1/2 x 13
1932-33	Chrysler	Four	55	1" standard	7509	12 x 13
1933	Gray	C-4, C-5	50-55	1" standard	7510	12 x 12
1934	C.C.	B	55	1" standard	7524	11 x 11-7/8
1934	Gray	Phantom-32	32	1" standard	7530	10 x 10 LH
16' Runabout and Utility						
1934-35	C.C.	B	55	1" standard	7524	11 x 11-7/8
1934-35	Chrysler	Ace-PC	70	1" standard	7526	12 x 14
1935	C.C.	C	45	1" standard	7535	11 x 10
17' Runabout						
1930	Gray	4-41	41	1" standard	7510	12 x 12
1931	Gray	4-43	43	1" standard	7510	12 x 12
18' Runabout and Utility						
1931	Gray	6-63	63	1" standard	7509	12 x 13
1932-33	Chrysler	Four	55	1" standard	7509	12 x 13
1931-32	Chrysler	Crown-CM	85	1" standard	7509	12 x 13
1933	Chrysler	Ace-PC	67	1" standard	7509	12 x 13
1934-35	Chrysler	Ace-PC	70	1" standard	7526	12 x 14
1933-34-35	Chrysler	Crown-CI, CA	85-92	1" standard	7526	12 x 14
1934-35	C.C.	B	55	1" standard	7524	11 x 11-7/8
19' Runabout						
1935	Chrysler	Ace-PC	70	1" standard	7526	12 x 14
1935	Chrysler	Crown-CA	92	1" standard	7526	12 x 14
20' Runabout						
1930-31	Chrysler	Crown-KM	75	1" standard	7510	12 x 12
1931	Chrysler	Crown-CM	85	1" standard	7509	12 x 13
21' Runabout and Utility						
1932	Chrysler	Crown-CM	85	1" standard	7509	12 x 13
1932-33-34	Chrysler	Imperial-LM	125	1" standard	7511	15 x 14
1933-34-35	Chrysler	Crown-CI, CA	85-92	1" standard	7526	12 x 14
1934-35	C.C.	B	55	1" standard	7524	11 x 11-7/8
1935	Chrysler	Ace-PC	70	1" standard	7526	12 x 14
22' Runabout						
1927	Scripps	F-6	110	1.25" standard	7534	15 x 20
1927	Kermath	70	70	1.25" standard	7533	15 x 18
1927	Chrysler*	Imperial-EM	100	1.25" standard	7514	15 x 14
1927	Chrysler**	Imperial-EM	100	1" standard	7511	15 x 14
1928-29	Chrysler	Royal-JM	82	1" standard	7532	14 x 13
1928-29-30-31	Chrysler	Imperial-LM	106-125	1" standard	7511	15 x 14
1930	Chrysler	Chrysler-KM	75	1" standard	7510	12 x 12
1931	Chrysler	Crown-CMM	85	1" standard	7509	12 x 13
1935	Chrysler	Crown-CA	92	1" standard	7526	12 x 14
1935	Chrysler	Imperial-LM	125	1.25" standard	7514	15 x 14
1935	Chrysler	Majestic-YM	150	1.25" standard	7508	14-1/2 x 16

*Before #1160.
**After #1160.

PROPELLER WHEEL DATA—CONTINUED

YEAR	ENGINE MAKE	ENGINE MODEL	H.P.	SHAFT SIZE & TAPER	WHEEL #	WHEEL SIZE
24' Runabout						
1928-29-30-31	Chrysler	Imperial-LM	106-125	1" standard	7511	15 x 14
1931	Chrysler	Majestic-YM	150	1.25" standard	7508	14-1/2 x 16
25' Runabout						
1932-33-34	Chrysler	Imperial-LM	125	1.25" standard	7514	15 x 14
1932-33-34-35	Chrysler	Majestic-YM	150	1.25" standard	7508	14-1/2 x 16
1932-33	Scripps	202	200	1.25" standard	7512	17-3/8 x 22
26' Runabout						
1927	Curtiss	OX-5	90	1.25" standard	7531	18 x 23 LH
1927 through 31	Kermath	150-200-225	150-225	1.25" standard	7518	17-1/2 x 24
1928-29	Chrysler	Imperial-LM	120-106	1" standard	7519	16 x 13
1930-31	Chrysler	Imperial-LM	125	1.25" standard	7520	16 x 13
1929-30-31	Scripps	202	200	1.25" standard	7512	17-3/8 x 22
1929-30-31	C.C.	A-70, A-120	250	1.25" standard	7513	18-1/2 x 24
1930-31	Chrysler	Majestic-YM	150	1.25" standard	7508	14-1/2 x 16
27' Runabout						
1932-33-34-35	C.C.	A-120	250	1.25" standard	7513	18-1/2 x 24
28' Runabout						
1929-30-31	Kermath	200-225	200-225	1.25" standard	7518	17-1/2 x 24
1929-30-31	Scripps	202	200	1.25" standard	7512	17-3/8 x 22
1929-30-31	C.C.	A-70, A-120	250	1.25" standard	7513	18-1/2 x 24
24' Cruiser and Utility Cruiser						
1934	C.C.	B	55	1" standard	7527	14 x 10
1934	Chrysler	Ace-PC	60	1" standard	7527	14 x 10
1934	Chrysler	Crown-CI	85	1" standard	7527	14 x 10
25' Cruiser and Utility Cruiser						
1935	C.C.	B	55	1" standard	7527	14 x 10
1935	Chrysler	Ace-PC	70	1" standard	7527	14 x 10
1935	Chrysler	Crown-CA	92	1" standard	7527	14 x 10

MODEL RECORD BY HULL NUMBER

HULL SIZE	STANDARD HULL NUMBER	GROUP NUMBER LIMIT
26' Runabout	#1	#999
22' Runabout	1000	1999
24' Runabout	2000	2999
28' Runabout	3000	3999
30' Runabout	4000	4999
38' Cruiser	5000	5999
48' Cruiser	6000	6999
20' Runabout	7000	7999
34' Cruiser	8000	8999
26' Runabout	9000	9999
26' Runabout	10000	10999
22' Runabout	11000	11999
36' Cruiser	12000	12999
31' Cruiser	13000	13999
17' Runabout	14000	14999

15.5' Runabout	15000	15999
16' Dual Runabout	16000	17999
18' Runabout	18000	18999
21' Standard Runabout	20000	20999
21' Runabout	21000	21999
22' Runabout (1935)	22000	22999
24' Cruiser	24000	24199
25' Cruiser	24200	24999
25' Runabout	25000	26999
27' Runabout	27000	28000
16' Runabout	30000	32999
18' Dual Runabout	33000	34999
21' Utility	35000	39999
15.5 Runabout	40000	40999
15.5 Utility	41000	41099
16' Utility	41100	44999
18' Utility	45000	46999
30' Cruiser	47000	47999
19' Dual Runabout	48000	48999

LIFTING RING DIMENSIONS

A - Overall Dimension
B - Stern to Aft Lifting Ring
C - Distance Between Lifting Rings
D - Forward Lifting Ring to Bow

Size Boat	A	B	C	D
16' Runabout	16'	2-1/2"	13' 8-1/2"	2' 1"
16' Utility	16'	2-1/2"	13' 8-1/2"	2' 1"
18' Runabout	18'	2-1/2"	15' 7-3/4"	2' 1-3/4"
18' Utility	18'	2-1/2"	15' 8-1/2"	2' 1"
19' Runabout	19'	2-1/2"	16' 11-1/2"	1' 10"
21' Utility	21'	2-1/2"	19' 1-1/2"	1' 8"
22' Runabout	22'	1' 6-1/2"	18' 7-1/2"	1' 9-7/8"
25' Runabout	25'	2'	17' 6"	5' 6"
25' Utility Cruiser	25'	5"	22' 4"	2' 3"
27' Runabout	27'	2' 8-3/4"	18' 6-1/4"	5' 9"

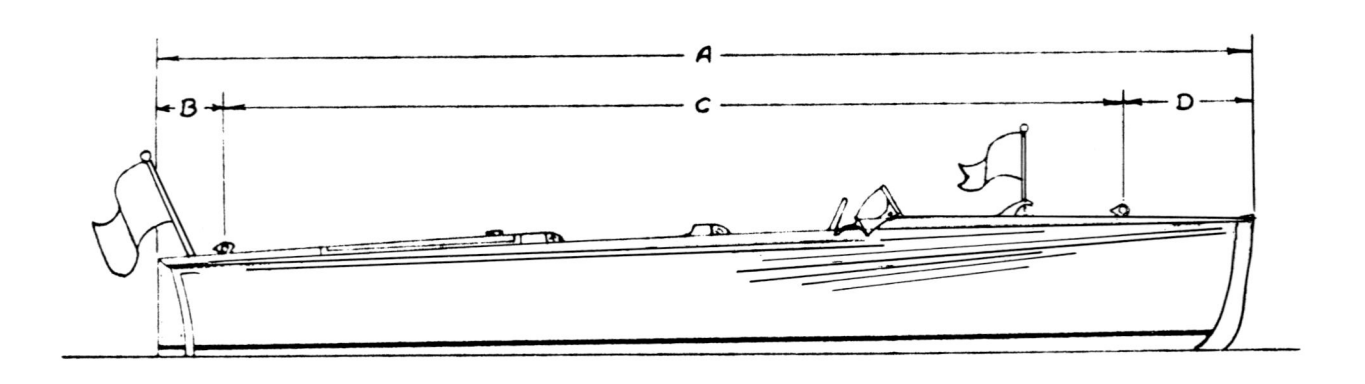

Chris-Craft with ***LEVEL RIDING***

Chrysler—Model Crown-KM

Superseded by Crown—CMM

MOTOR SPECIFICATIONS

Type—L-Head, Vertical, 4-cycle Bore—3 1/8"
Cylinders—6 Stroke—4 3/8"
Brake Horsepower—75
Minimum R. P. M. (Idling Speed)—400
Piston Displacement—195 cu. in.
Compression Ratio—6:1
Weight: Motor and Trans.—625 lbs.

ELECTRIC SYSTEM—6-VOLT

Generator—Delco-Remy, Model 947-C
Starter—Delco-Remy, Model 714-K (Bendix Engagement)
Distributor—Delco-Remy, Model 632-K
Coils—Delco-Remy, Model 2195
Remote Control Switch—Delco-Remy, Model 1336
Battery—Willard WS 1.13—86 A. H.
Generator Charging Rate—8-10 Amperes maximum
Generator Cuts in at—1000 R. P. M.

OIL SYSTEM—HIGH PRESSURE

20 Pounds (Minimum)—Idling Speed
40 to 60 Pounds—Maximum Speed

CARBURETOR

Holly Downdraft, Model D-3, 1 1/2"

WATER TEMPERATURE

Water Temperature—140°-160° Average

REVERSE GEAR

Make—Chrysler
Ahead Ratio—Direct Reverse Ratio—90%

CLEARANCE AT OPERATING TEMPERATURES

Intake Valve—.006 Exhaust Valve—.008
Piston Clearance: At Top—.022; At Skirt—.003
Ring Gap—.007 to .015 Ring Side Clearance—.0015
Crank Pin Bearing Clearance: End—.003
Rod to Shaft—.001 to .00275
Main Bearing Clearance: End—.004
Shaft to Bearing—.002 to .003

VALVE TIMING

Intake Valve opens—6° ATDC; closes—46° ABDC
Exhaust Valve opens—42° BBDC; closes—8° ATDC

Chris-Craft with ***LEVEL RIDING***

Chrysler—Model Crown-CMM

Supersedes Crown—KM

MOTOR SPECIFICATIONS

Type—L-Head, Vertical, 4-cycle Bore—3 1/4"
Cylinders—6 Stroke—4 3/8"
Brake Horsepower—85
Minimum R. P. M. (Idling Speed)—400
Piston Displacement—217.8
Compression Ratio—6:1
Weight: Motor and Trans.—625 lbs.

ELECTRIC SYSTEM—6-VOLT

Generator—Delco-Remy, Model 947-C
Starter—Delco-Remy, Model 714-K (Bendix Engagement)
Distributor—Delco-Remy, Model 632-K
Coils—Delco-Remy, Model 2195
Remote Control Switch—Delco-Remy, Model 1336
Battery—Willard SW. 1.13—86 A. H.
Generator Charging Rate—8-10 Amperes maximum
Generator Cuts in at—1000 R. P. M.

OIL SYSTEM—HIGH PRESSURE

20 Pounds (Minimum)—Idling Speed
40 to 60 Pounds—Maximum Speed

CARBURETOR

Holly Downdraft, Model D-3, 1 1/2"

WATER TEMPERATURE

Water Temperature—140°-160° Average

REVERSE GEAR

Make—Chrysler
Ahead Ratio—Direct Reverse Ratio—90%

CLEARANCE AT OPERATING TEMPERATURES

Intake Valve—.006 Exhaust Valve—.008
Piston Clearance: At Top—.022; At Skirt—.003
Ring Gap—.007 to .015 Ring Side Clearance—.0015
Crank Pin Bearing Clearance: End—.003
Rod to Shaft—.001 to .00275
Main Bearing Clearance: End—.004
Shaft to Bearing—.002 to .003

VALVE TIMING

Intake Valve opens—6° ATDC; closes—46° ABDC
Exhaust Valve opens—42° BBDC; closes—8° ATDC

Chris-Craft with ***LEVEL RIDING***

Chrysler—Model Crown-CA

Supersedes Crown—CI

MOTOR SPECIFICATIONS

Racing Class F

Type—L-Head, Vertical, 4-cycle Bore—3 3/8"
Cylinders—6 Stroke—4 1/2"
Brake Horsepower—92
Minimum R. P. M. (Idling Speed)—400
Piston Displacement—242
Compression Ratio—6:1
Weight: Motor and Trans.—625 lbs.

ELECTRIC SYSTEM—6-VOLT

Generator—Delco-Remy, Model 947-C
Starter—Delco-Remy, Model 714-K (Bendix Engagement)
Distributor—Delco-Remy, Model 632-K
Coils—Delco-Remy, Model 2195
Remote Control Switch—Delco-Remy, Model 1336
Battery—Willard SW. 1.13—86 A. H.
Generator Charging Rate—8-10 Amperes maximum
Generator Cuts in at—1000 R. P. M.

OIL SYSTEM—HIGH PRESSURE

20 Pounds (Minimum)—Idling Speed
40 to 60 Pounds—Maximum Speed

CARBURETOR

Zenith Updraft

WATER TEMPERATURE

Water Temperature—140°-160° Average

REVERSE GEAR

Make—Chrysler
Ahead Ratio—Direct Reverse Ratio—90%

CLEARANCE AT OPERATING TEMPERATURES

Intake Valve—.006 Exhaust Valve—.008
Piston Clearance: At Top—.022; At Skirt—.003
Ring Gap—.007 to .015 Ring Side Clearance—.0015
Crank Pin Bearing Clearance: End—.003
Rod to Shaft—.001 to .00275
Main Bearing Clearance: End—.004
Shaft to Bearing—.002 to .003

VALVE TIMING

Intake Valve opens—6° ATDC; closes—46° ABDC
Exhaust Valve opens—42° BBDC; closes—8° ATDC

Chris-Craft with ***LEVEL RIDING***

Chrysler—Model Imperial

MOTOR SPECIFICATIONS

Type—L-Head, Vertical, 4-cycle Bore—3 5/8"
Cylinders—6 Stroke—5"
Brake Horsepower—125
Minimum R. P. M. (Idling Speed)—500
Piston Displacement—309 cu. in.
Compression Ratio—5.4:1
Weight: Motor and Trans.—925 lbs.

ELECTRIC SYSTEM—6-VOLT

Generator—Delco-Remy, Model 947-C
Starter—Delco-Remy, Model 724-C (Bendix Engagement)
Distributor—Delco-Remy, Model 656-T
Coils—Delco-Remy, Model 2195
Remote Control Switch—Delco-Remy, Model 1336
Battery—Willard SJWR 6—147 A. H.
Generator Charging Rate—8-10 Amperes maximum
Generator Cuts in at—1000 R. P. M.

OIL SYSTEM—HIGH PRESSURE

20 Pounds (Minimum)—Idling Speed
60 to 75 Pounds—Maximum Speed

CARBURETOR

Holly Downdraft, Model DD-5, 2"

WATER TEMPERATURE

Water Temperature—140°-160° Average

REVERSE GEAR

Make—Chrysler
Ahead Ratio—Direct Reverse Ratio—90%

CLEARANCE AT OPERATING TEMPERATURES

Intake Valve—.008 Exhaust Valve—.010
Piston Clearance: At Top—.025; At Skirt—.004 to .005
Ring Gap—.005 to .010 Ring Side Clearance—.0015
Crank Pin Bearing Clearance: End—.003; Rod to Shaft—.002
Main Bearing Clearance: End—.004; Shaft to Bearing—.002

VALVE TIMING

Intake Valve opens—6° ATDC; closes—46° ABDC
Exhaust Valve opens—42° BBDC; closes—8° ATDC

Chris-Craft with ***LEVEL RIDING***

Chrysler—Model Majestic

MOTOR SPECIFICATIONS

Type—L-Head, Vertical, 4-cycle Bore—3 1/2"
Cylinders—8 Stroke—5"
Brake Horsepower—150
Minimum R. P. M. (Idling Speed)—500
Piston Displacement—384 cu. in.
Compression Ratio—5.5:1
Weight: Motor and Trans.—1125 lbs.

ELECTRIC SYSTEM—6-VOLTS

Generator—Delco-Remy, Model 947-C
Starter—Delco-Remy, Model 924-C (Bendix Engagement)
Distributor—Delco-Remy 660-F
Coils—North East 21670
Remote Control Switch—Delco-Remy, Model 1336
Battery—Willard SJWR6—147 A. H.
Generator Cuts in at—1000 R. P. M.
Generator Charging Rate—8-10 Amperes maximum

OIL SYSTEM—HIGH PRESSURE

15 Pounds (Minimum)—Idling Speed
60 to 75 Pounds—Maximum Speed

CARBURETOR

Holly Downdraft, Model DD-5, 2"

WATER TEMPERATURE

Water Temperature—140°-160° Average

REVERSE GEAR

Make—Chrysler
Ahead Ratio—Direct Reverse Ratio—90%

CLEARANCE AT OPERATING TEMPERATURES

Intake Valve—.008 Exhaust Valve—.010
Piston Clearance: At Top—.020; At Skirt—.004 to .005
Ring Gap—.005 to .010 Ring Side Clearance—.0015
Crank Pin Bearing Clearance: End—.003; Rod to Shaft—.002
Main Bearing Clearance: End—.004; Shaft to Bearing—.002

VALVE TIMING

Intake Valve opens—6° ATDC; closes—46° ABDC
Exhaust Valve opens—42° BBDC; closes—8° ATDC

Chris-Craft with ***LEVEL RIDING***

Chris-Craft Marine—Model A-70

Superseded by Model A-120

MOTOR SPECIFICATIONS

Type—V-90° Bore—5"
Cylinders—8 Stroke—5 1/4"
Brake Horsepower, Updraft Carburetor—225; Downdraft—250
Minimum R. P. M. (Idling Speed)—500
Piston Displacement—824.67 cu. in.
Compression Ratio—5.6:1
Weight: Motor and Trans.—1625 lbs.

ELECTRIC SYSTEM—12-VOLT

Generator—Delco-Remy, Model 955-W
Starter—Delco-Remy, Model 347 (Bendix Engagement)
Distributor—Delco-Remy, Model 4040
Coils—Delco-Remy, Model 178-E
Remote Control Switch—Delco-Remy, Model 1335
Battery—National 12-Volt—120 Ampere Hours (2 6-volt used)
Generator Charging Rate—8 to 10 Amperes maximum
Generator Cuts in at—800 to 1200 R. P. M.

OIL SYSTEM—HIGH PRESSURE

20 Pounds (Minimum)—Idling Speed
40 to 60 Pounds—Maximum Speed

CARBURETOR

Updraft Model—Schebler S 2 1/4"
Downdraft Model—Holly DD-5 2 1/4"

WATER TEMPERATURE

Water Temperature—135°-150° Average

REVERSE GEAR

Make—Christ-Craft
Ahead Ratio—Direct Reverse Ratio—80%

CLEARANCES AT 60° FAHRENHEIT

Intake Valve—.015 Exhaust Valve—.020
Piston Clearance: At Top—.032 to .035; At Skirt—.012 to .015
Ring Gap—.018 Ring Side Clearance—.0015
Crank Pin Bearing Clearance: End—.008; Rod to Shaft—.002
Main Bearing Clearance: End—.008; Shaft to Bearing—.005
Piston Pin Clearance
Light sliding fit through connecting rod bushing. Without oil.
Light press fit through piston. At room temp. 70°F. Without oil

VALVE TIMING

Intake Valve opens—.15° ATDC; closes—57° ABDC
Exhaust Valve opens—39° BBDC; closes—10° ATDC

While it is not absolutely necessary, we highly recommend the use of Ethyl gasoline.

Chris-Craft with **LEVEL RIDING**

Chris-Craft Marine—Model A-120
Supersedes Model A-70
MOTOR SPECIFICATIONS

Type—V-90° Bore—5"
Cylinders—8 Stroke—5¼"
Brake Horsepower—250
Minimum R. P. M. (Idling Speed)—500
Piston Displacement—824.67 cu. in.
Compression Ratio—5.6:1
Weight: Motor and Trans.—1750 lbs.

ELECTRIC SYSTEM—12-VOLT
Generator—Delco-Remy, Model 955-W
Starter—Delco-Remy, Model 458 (Bendix Engagement)
Distributor—Delco-Remy, Model 4064
Coils—Delco-Remy, Model 178-E
Remote Control Switch—Delco-Remy, Model 1335
Battery—National 12-Volt, 120-Ampere Hours (2 6-volt used)
Generator Charging Rate—8 to 10 Amperes maximum
Generator Cuts in at—800 to 1200 R. P. M.

OIL SYSTEM—HIGH PRESSURE
20 Pounds (Minimum)—Idling Speed
40 to 60 Pounds—Maximum Speed

CARBURETOR WATER TEMPERATURE
Downdraft Model Water Temperature—
Holly DD-5—Size 2¼" 135°-150° Average

REVERSE GEAR
Make—Chris-Craft
Ahead Ratio—Direct Reverse Ratio—80%

CLEARANCE AT 60° FAHRENHEIT
Intake Valve—.015 Exhaust Valve—.020
Piston Clearance: At Top—.032 to .035; At Skirt—.012 to .015
Ring Gap—.018 Ring Side Clearance—.0015
Crank Pin Bearing Clearance: End—.008; Rod to Shaft—.002
Main Bearing Clearance: End—.010; Shaft to Bearing—.003
Piston Pin Clearance
  Light sliding fit through connecting rod bushing. Without oil.
  Light press fit through piston. At room temp. 70°F. Without oil.

VALVE TIMING
Intake Valve opens—15° ATDC; closes—57° ABDC
Exhaust Valve opens—39° BBDC; closes—10° ATDC
  While it is not absolutely necessary, we highly recommend the use of Ethyl gasoline.

Chris-Craft with **LEVEL RIDING**

Gray—Model 4-43
MOTOR SPECIFICATIONS

Type—L-Head, Vertical, 4-cycle Bore—3⅝"
Cylinders—4 Stroke—4¼"
Brake Horsepower—45
Minimum R. P. M. (Idling Speed)—500
Piston Displacement—152.08 cu. in.
Compression Ratio—4.2:1
Weight: Motor and Trans.—455 lbs.

ELECTRIC SYSTEM—6-VOLT
Generator—Auto-Lite, Model GAL-4305
Starter—Auto-Lite, Model MAJ-4013 (Bendix Engagement)
Distributor—Auto-Lite, Model IGC-4047B
Coils—Auto-Lite, Model IG-4066
Battery—National,
Generator Charging Rate—12 Amperes maximum
Generator Cuts in at—800 R. P. M.

OIL SYSTEM—HIGH PRESSURE
5 Pounds (Minimum)—Idling Speed
20 to 30 Pounds—Maximum Speed

CARBURETOR WATER TEMPERATURE
Tillotson, S-18-B 1" Water Temperature—
  140°-160° Average

REVERSE GEAR
Make—Paragon
Ahead Ratio—Direct Reverse Ratio—88%

CLEARANCE AT 60° FAHRENHEIT
Intake Valve—.010 to .012 Exhaust Valve—.010 to .012

VALVE TIMING
Intake Valve opens—10° BTDC; closes 50° ABDC
Exhaust Valve opens—50° BBDC; closes—10° ATDC

NOTE—For bearing clearances, write direct to Gray Marine Motor Co., Detroit, Michigan. Be sure to give model and serial number of engine.

Chris-Craft with **LEVEL RIDING**

Gray—Model 6-63
MOTOR SPECIFICATIONS

Type—L-Head, Vertical, 4-cycle Bore—3 1/16"
Cylinders—6 Stroke—3⅞"
Brake Horsepower—65
Minimum R. P. M. (Idling Speed)—500
Piston Displacement—200.6 cu. in.
Compression Ratio—5:1
Weight: Motor and Trans.—658 lbs.

ELECTRIC SYSTEM—6-VOLT
Generator—Auto-Lite, Model GAL-4320
Starter—Auto-Lite, Model MAS-4014 (Bendix Engagement)
Distributor—Delco-Remy, Model 639-U
Coils—Auto-Lite, Model IG-4065
Remote Control Switch—None
Battery—National
Generator Charging Rate—12 Amperes maximum
Generator Cuts in at—800 R. P. M.

OIL SYSTEM—HIGH PRESSURE
5 Pounds (Minimum)—Idling Speed
20 to 30 Pounds—Maximum Speed

CARBURETOR WATER TEMPERATURE
Tillotson Up-draft, Water Temperature—
  Model J5-AX, Size 1½" 140°-160° Average

REVERSE GEAR
Make—Paragon
Ahead Ratio—Direct Reverse Ratio—88%

VALVE CLEARANCE AT OPERATING TEMPERATURES
Intake Valve—.007 to .009 Exhaust Valve—.007 to .009

VALVE TIMING
Intake Valve opens—7° ATDC; closes—45° ABDC
Exhaust Valve opens—42° BBDC; closes—TDC

NOTE—For bearing clearances, write direct to Gray Marine Motor Co., Detroit, Michigan. Be sure to give model and serial number of engine.

Chris-Craft with **LEVEL RIDING**

Scripps—Model 202
MOTOR SPECIFICATIONS

Type—L-Head, Vertical, 4-cycle Bore—5"
Cylinders—6 Stroke—5¾"
Brake Horsepower—200
Minimum R. P. M. (Idling Speed)—500
Piston Displacement—678 cu. in.
Compression Ratio—6:1
Weight: Motor and Trans.—1175 lbs.

ELECTRIC SYSTEM—12-VOLT
Generator—Delco-Remy, Model 955-W
Starter—Delco-Remy, Model 347 (Bendix Engagement)
Distributor—Delco-Remy, Model 5298
Coils—Delco-Remy, Model 529-C
Remote Control Switch—Delco-Remy, Model 1335
Battery—National, Model H3-21-M (2 6-volt used)
Generator Charging Rate—8 Amperes maximum
Generator Cuts in at—800 R. P. M.

OIL SYSTEM—HIGH PRESSURE
15 Pounds (Minimum)—Idling Speed
60 to 80 Pounds—Maximum Speed

CARBURETOR WATER TEMPERATURE
Holly Downdraft, Water Temperature—
  Model DD-5, 2" 90°-140° Average

REVERSE GEAR
Make—"Joes" Self-Centering Duplex Clutch
Ahead Ratio—Direct Reverse Ratio—88%

CLEARANCE AT 60° FAHRENHEIT
Intake Valve—.010 Exhaust Valve—.018
Piston Clearance: At Top—.030 to .035; At Skirt—.008 to .009
Ring Gap—.015 to .018 Ring Side Clearance—.0015
Crank Pin Bearing Clearance: End—.0045 to .010
  Rod to Shaft—.0015 to .0033
Main Bearing Clearance: End—.004 to .008
  Shaft to Bearing—.0015 to .0035

VALVE TIMING
Intake Valve opens—7° ATDC; closes—52° ABDC
Exhaust Valve opens—45° BBDC; closes—6° ATDC

Chris-Craft with **LEVEL RIDING**

Kermath Model—150
MOTOR SPECIFICATIONS

Type—Valve in head Bore—5"
Cylinders—6 Stroke—5½"
Brake Horsepower—150
Minimum R. P. M. (Idling Speed)—300
Piston Displacement—648 cu. in.
Compression Ratio—5.3:1
Weight, Motor and Trans.—1350 lbs.

ELECTRIC SYSTEM—12 VOLTS
Generator—Delco-Remy, Model 945-R
Starter—Delco-Remy, Model 347 (Bendix Engagement)
Distributor—Delco-Remy, Model 4012
Coils—Delco-Remy, Model 2185
Remote Control Switch—Delco-Remy, Model 1335
Battery—Exide, 12-Volt
Generator Charging Rate—10 Amperes maximum
Generator Cuts in at—600 R. P. M.

OIL SYSTEM—HIGH PRESSURE
10 Pounds (Minimum)—Idling Speed
40 Pounds—Maximum Speed

CARBURETOR WATER TEMPERATURE
Schebler, Type SX-382, Water Temperature—
  Size 1½" 120° Average

REVERSE GEAR
Make—Joes
Ahead Ratio—Direct Reverse Ratio—85%

CLEARANCE AT 60° FAHRENHEIT
Intake Valve—.015 Exhaust Valve—.020
Piston Clearance: At Top—.018; At Skirt—.007 to .009
Ring Gap—.014 to .016 Ring Side Clearance—.0015
Crank Pin Bearing Clearance: End—.006; Rod to Shaft—.002
Main Bearing Clearance: Front—.041; Intermediate—.010; Shaft to bearing—.002

VALVE TIMING
Intake Valve opens—10° ATDC; closes—45° ABDC
Exhaust Valve opens—45° BBDC; closes—8° ATDC

Chris-Craft with **LEVEL RIDING**

Make—Kermath
Model—200-1929; 225-1930
MOTOR SPECIFICATIONS

Type—Valve in head Bore—5"
Cylinders—6 Stroke—5¾"
Brake Horsepower—200-1929; 225-1930
Minimum R. P. M. (Idling Speed)—300
Piston Displacement—672 cu. in.
Compression Ratio—5.3:1
Weight of Motor and Trans.—1350 lbs.

ELECTRIC SYSTEM—12 VOLTS
Generator—Delco-Remy, Model 945-R
Starter—Delco-Remy, Model 458 (Bendix Engagement)
Distributor—Delco-Remy, Model 4012-1929; No. 4059-1930
Coils—Delco-Remy, Model 178-E
Remote Control Switch—Delco-Remy, Model 1335
Battery—Exide, 12 Volts
Generator Charging Rate—10 Amperes Maximum
Generator Cuts in at—600 R. P. M.

OIL SYSTEM—HIGH PRESSURE
10 Pounds (Minimum)—Idling Speed
30 to 40 Pounds—Maximum Speed

CARBURETOR
1929—1½" Schebler 1930—Holley Downdraft Duplex
  Type SX-382 Type DD-5—2"

WATER TEMPERATURE
Water Temperature—120° Average

REVERSE GEAR
Make—Joes
Ahead Ratio—Direct Reverse Ratio—85%

CLEARANCE AT 60° FAHRENHEIT
Intake Valve—.015 Exhaust Valve—.020
Piston Clearance: At Top—.018; At Skirt—.007 to .009
Ring Gap—.014 to .016 Ring Side Clearance—.0015
Crank Pin Clearance: End—.006; Rod to Shaft—.002
Main Bearing Clearance: Front—.041; Intermediate—.010; Shaft to Bearing—.002

VALVE TIMING
Intake Valve opens—TDC; closes—55° ABDC
Exhaust Valve opens—48° BBDC; closes—5° ATDC

See the nearest Chris-Craft Dealer — Buy Now!

HARRIS & GILCHRIST
Birmingham, Ala.
ROBERTSON'S AUTO REPAIR
Dothan, Ala.
BRYAN MOTORS SALES & SERVICE
Florence, Ala.
QUIGLEY MOTORS
Mobile, Ala.
J. B. CARL
Tuscaloosa, Ala.
MILAM & HASTINGS MARINE SERVICE
Hot Springs, Ark.
JOHN G. RAPP CO.
San Francisco, Cal.
H. G. McKINNEY & CO., Inc.
Wilmington, Cal.
MARTIE RUTTNER
Denver, Colo.
GRAND LAKE BOAT SERVICE
Pueblo, Colo.
ALFRED H. HIGSON
Danbury, Conn.
G. W. VOORHEES
Devon, Conn.
WESTON M. JENKS
East Hartford, Conn.
ESSEX MARINE RAILWAY
Essex, Conn.
FRANKLIN G. POST & SON, Inc.
Mystic, Conn.
MACKENZIE MACHINE & MARINE WORKS
New Haven, Conn.
LOUIS J. GARDELLA
Norwalk, Conn.
MUZZIO BROS. YACHT YARD
Stamford, Conn.
WM. E. WALSH
Lewes, Del.
MARINE CONSTRUCTION CO.
Wilmington, Del.
FLOOD GATE SALES AGENCY, INC.
Washington, D. C.
PAUL N. BEALL
Bradenton, Fla.
GINGRAS BOAT WORKS, Inc.
Cocoa, Fla.
HOWARD BOAT WORKS, Inc.
Daytona Beach, Fla.
BASSETT BOAT WORKS
Eustis, Fla.
KNIGHT BOATS & MOTORS, Inc.
Jacksonville, Fla.
MIAMI CHRIS-CRAFT CO., Inc.
Miami Beach, Fla.
JACK SIMMONS
Tallahassee, Fla.
ATLANTA OUTBOARD MARINE
Atlanta, Ga.
HIGHTOWER STORE
Damascus, Ga.
HALL'S BOAT HOUSE
Lakemont, Ga.
SEA ISLAND YACHT YARDS
St. Simons Island, Ga.
PERRY'S MARINE SERVICE
Thunderbolt, Ga.
JOHNSTON'S SPORT SHOP
Champaign, Ill.
CHRIS-CRAFT BOAT SALES, Inc.
Chicago, Ill.
SHAFFER BOAT CO.
Decatur, Ill.
HEWES BOAT CO., Inc.
Fox Lake, Ill.
GREAT LAKES COMPANY
Macomb, Ill.
GEO. W. BRICKNER, Jr.
Peoria, Ill.
MARINE SERVICE CO.
Springfield, Ill.
MEYER BOAT LIVERY
Angola, Ind.
E. C. MERTENS BOAT AGENCY
Evansville, Ind.
MACY'S WAWASEE SLIP
Syracuse, Ind.
PRIMM CHRIS-CRAFT SALES
Davenport, Iowa
IOWA BOAT CO.
Des Moines, Iowa
WILSON BOAT WORKS
Okoboji, Iowa
T. W. MAXWELL
Shenandoah, Iowa
BLACK MOTOR CO.
Corbin, Ky.
BLACK MOTOR CO.
Cumberland, Ky.
BLACK MOTOR CO.
Harlan, Ky.
L. R. PINKSTON
Lexington, Ky.
FALLS CITY BOAT WORKS
Louisville, Ky.
BLACK MOTOR CO.
Middlesboro, Ky.
COLLET BROS.
Owensboro, Ky.
ASHCRAFT-BABB CAR CO.
Paducah, Ky.
ELMER & HARRY SHUTTS
Lake Charles, La.
HOWARD GRIFFIN
Monroe, La.

HIGGINS INDUSTRIES, Inc.
New Orleans, La.
S. & L. SERVICE & STORAGE CO.
Shreveport, La.
ALBERT G. FROST
Portland, Maine
JOHN W. BRAMBLE
Baltimore, Md.
MURPHY'S GARAGE
Berlin, Md.
J. W. HALLOWELL & SONS
Federalsburg, Md.
HUBERT M. BOWMAN
McHenry, Md.
BAY BOAT WORKS
North East, Md.
STEARNS MARINE CO.
Boston, Mass.
AURA STEWART
Algonac, Mich.
NATE'S MOTORBOAT SERVICE
Ann Arbor, Mich.
MILLER BOAT CO.
Charlevoix, Mich.
MAJESTIC MARINE SALES & SERVICE
Cheboygan, Mich.
CLYDE BOAT WORKS
Detroit, Mich.
FISHER BOAT WORKS, Inc.
Detroit, Mich.
GREGORY BOAT CO.
Detroit, Mich.
HANSEN BOAT LIVERY
Detroit, Mich.
J. L. HUDSON CO
Detroit, Mich.
MOTOR BOAT SALES & SERVICE
Detroit, Mich.
ZUP'S BOAT LIVERY
Elk Rapids, Mich.
COTTER'S BOAT HOUSE
Essexville, Mich.
EVINRUDE-ELTO FLINT SALES
Flint, Mich.
SMITH'S SUPER-SERVICE STATION
Hancock, Mich.
MELCHING BOAT WORKS
Harbor Springs, Mich.
E. J. MERTAUGH BOAT WORKS
Hessel, Mich.
JUSTIN P. FLEMING
Jackson, Mich.
P. O. SEXTON
Lansing, Mich.
SCHWARZ MOTORS SALES
Leland, Mich.
HAROLD ROLSTON
Maple City, Mich.
HOWARD V. GROESBECK
Mt. Clemens, Mich.
RALPH ENGLE
Oden, Mich.
L. M. PETERS
Pontiac, Mich.
SEELEY E. MOSHER
Port Huron, Mich.
GLENN M. TODD
Richland, Mich.
JAMES A. STACKHOUSE
Rochester, Mich.
WARD J. BLUNT
Saginaw, Mich.
SOO CHRIS-CRAFT SALES
Sault Ste. Marie, Mich.
E. J. BAUMAN MARINE CO.
Spring Lake, Mich.
HARMON DUDD
Three Rivers, Mich.
MURRAY BOAT CO.
Traverse City, Mich.
W. J. MASTERS
Walloon Lake, Mich.
WYANDOTTE BOAT BASIN, Inc.
Wyandotte, Mich.
MINNETONKA BOAT WORKS,
Wayzata, Minn.
A. L. GROTHER MOTOR CO.
Higginsville, Mo.
STAR BOAT & MOTOR CO.
Kansas City, Mo.
SCHNEIDER SALES & SERVICE
St. Louis, Mo.
HERRICK MOTOR CO.
Springfield, Mo.
BOULDER CITY BUILDERS SUPPLY CO.
Boulder City, Nev.
BROWN MOTORS, Inc.
Reno, Nev.
CHARLES W. ROWELL
Sunapee, N. H.
IRWIN CORP.
The Weirs, N. H.
DALE YACHT BASIN
Bayhead, N. J.
FEUERBACH & HANSEN
Brielle, N. J.
THROPP BOAT WORKS
Forked River, N. J.
C. C. GALBRAITH & SON, Inc.
Keyport, N. J.
HOCKENJOS BOAT CO.
Lake Hopatcong, N. J.

LONGPORT MARINE CO.
Longport, N. J.
STICKLE BROS., Inc.
Newton, N. J.
ZOBEL'S SEA SKIFF & YACHT WORKS
Sea Bright, N. J.
J. SALVESEN & SON
Stone Harbor, N. J.
HENRY WURFEL, JR.
Trenton, N. J.
GREER LOAN CO.
Santa Fe, N. Mexico
HOMAN BOATS, Inc.
Amityville, L. I., N. Y.
C. M. WEEKS CO., Inc.
Babylon, L. I., N. Y.
ROY M. BREWSTER
Bay Shore, L. I., N. Y.
RICHARD COLLINS
Blue Mountain Lake, N. Y.
LAMB BROS.
Bolton Landing, N. Y.
BUFFALO MARINE MART
Buffalo, N. Y.
RICH MARINE SALES
Buffalo, N. Y.
E. T. WALDORF
Canandaigua, N. Y.
DAN GETTINGS
Carthage, N. Y.
W. I. VAN DUSEN
Catskill, N. Y.
DUNHAM SALES CO., Inc
City Island, N. Y.
GEO. W. MERCIER
Clayton, N. Y.
HENDERSON BOAT CO.
Cleverdale-on-Lake George, N.Y.
QUEENS MARINE SALES & SERVICE
College Pt., L. I., N. Y.
H. J. McDONALD, Inc.
East Rockaway, L. I., N. Y.
LYON BROS.
E. Setauket, L. I., N. Y.
HADCOCK BROS.
Fair Haven, N. Y.
CHATFIELD'S MARINE SALES
Freeport, N. Y.
COL. S. TOOEY
Geneseo, N. Y.
BOURNE BOAT & STORAGE YARD
Geneva, N. Y.
BAIR & EDGERTON BOAT WORKS
Glen Cove, L. I., N. Y.
L. C. BOLLER
Gowanda, N. Y.
HOCKENJOS BOAT CO.
Greenwood Lake, N. Y.
E. JOHNSON BOAT YARDS
Ithaca, N. Y.
L. S. AERO MARINE, Inc.
Jamestown, N. Y.
GEORGE & BLISS, Inc.
Lake Placid, N. Y.
C. G. YAGER
Liberty, N. Y.
ORIENTA BOAT YARDS
Mamaroneck, N. Y.
BENNETT BOAT CO.
Mayfield, N. Y.
CHARLES W. BLIVEN & CO.
New Rochelle, N. Y.
CHRIS-CRAFT CORP.
New York, N. Y.
HARRY R. STOKES, Inc.
New York, N. Y.
SUTTER BROS.
New York, N. Y.
E. H. TUCKER
New York, N. Y.
WEXLER & SPORTY, Inc.
New York, N. Y.
WARDS SPTG. GOODS STORE
Ogdensburg, N. Y.
PATCHOGUE YACHT BASIN
Patchogue, L. I., N. Y.
J. S. BANKER
Plattsburg, N. Y.
HERMAN CLEMONS
Pulaski, N. Y.
ROCHESTER MARINE CO.
Rochester, N. Y.
WM. EDGAR JOHN & ASSOCIATES, Inc.
Rye, N. Y.
FRANK M. BAKER
Saranac Lake, N. Y.
HARRY E. DUSO
Saranac Lake, N. Y.
GEORGE HELFER
Sodus Point, N. Y.
THE BOAT SHOP
Southold, L. I., N. Y.
SYRACUSE MOTOR MARINE CORP.
Syracuse, N. Y.
EASTERN BOAT WORKS
Ticonderoga, N. Y.
UTICA AUTO-ELECTRIC SERVICE
Utica, N. Y.
HARRY H. HENRY
Watervliet, N. Y.
L. I. BOAT & MOTOR SALES
W. Sayville, L. I., N. Y.

LUDLOW MARINE BASIN
Yonkers, N. Y.
PIERCE MARINE CORP.
Youngstown, N. Y.
CONTRACTORS SERVICE, Inc.
Charlotte, N. C.
KINSTON ELECTRIC CO.
Kinston, N. C.
C. C. MOTOR CO.
Raleigh, N. C.
WILMINGTON IRON WORKS
Wilmington, N. C.
SAYRE BROS.
Buckeye Lake, Ohio
MARINE SALES & SERVICE, Inc.
Cincinnati, Ohio
CLEVELAND YACHT & SUPPLY CO.
Cleveland, Ohio
OUTDOORS
Columbus, Ohio
GALLIPOLIS DEPT. STORE
Gallipolis, Ohio
WM. R. BROWN
Lakeside, Ohio
SCHULER MARINE SALES
Russells Point, Ohio
WORTHY R. BROWN & SON
Sandusky, Ohio
BODETTE MARINE SUPPLY CO.
Toledo, Ohio
HERMAN MARINE SERVICE
Toledo, Ohio
GEORGE'S CABINET & BOAT SHOP
Ardmore, Okla.
SPAVINAW SPORT SHOP
Spavinaw, Okla.
TULSA MARINE SUPPLY CO.
Tulsa, Okla.
NORTHWEST TRUCKSTELL SALES
Portland, Oregon
STAFFORD H. JENNINGS
Portland, Oregon
ERIE-CHRIS-CRAFT SALES CO.
Erie, Pa.
ESSINGTON YACHT YARD
Essington, Pa.
JOHN D. GROVE SONS
Huntingdon, Pa.
WARREN HENWOOD, Inc.
Lancaster, Pa.
BAEHR BROS.
McKeesport, Pa.
E. J. WINKELEMAN
Oakmont, Pa.
GEORGE O. RAGNER
Pittsburgh, Pa.
DOUDS-GEORGE, Inc.
Rochester, Pa.
PACKARD LACKAWANNA AUTOMOBILE CO.
Scranton, Pa.
ZOPF'S GARAGE
Wilkes-Barre, Pa.
THE ANCHORAGE, Inc.
Providence, R. I.
DOUGLAS H. PATON & CO., Inc.
Providence, R. I.
PAUL MOTOR CO., Inc.
Charleston, S. C.
OLIVER MOTOR CO.
Columbia, S. C.
THE BROAD STREET GARAGE
Chattanooga, Tenn.
KAYLOR RADIO & BOAT CO.
Knoxville, Tenn.
GRAHAM BOAT CO.
Memphis, Tenn.
ROY NOWLIN BOAT & CYCLE CO.
Nashville, Tenn.
BOATS & MOTORS, Inc.
Austin, Texas
DAVIDSON MOTOR CO.
Breckenridge, Texas
SAN ANTONIO MACHINE & SUPPLY CO.
Corpus Christi, Texas
CRADDOCK MOTOR CO.
Crockett, Texas
SLATER BOAT CO.
Dallas, Texas
STEAKLEY CHEVROLET CO.
Denison, Texas
DON THOMPSON, Inc.
El Paso, Texas
MARION HERRING BOAT WKS.
Fort Worth, Texas
LECHENGER MARINE STORE
Houston, Texas
HUNDLEY BOAT CO.
Lake Dallas, Texas
O. H. SHELTON GARAGE
Longview, Texas
D. M. PICTON & CO., Inc.
Port Arthur, Texas
SAN ANTONIO MACHINE & SUPPLY CO
San Antonio, Texas
SAN ANTONIO MACHINE & SUPPLY CO.
Waco, Texas
THE ROCKY MOUNTAIN MOTOR BOAT CO.
Logan, Utah
CHAMPLAIN MARINE CO., Inc.
Burlington, Vt.
CHAMPLAIN MOTORS, Inc.
St. Albans, Vt.

JETT & CO., Inc.
Norfolk, Va.
MOTOR BOAT SALES AGENCY
Richmond, Va.
MOTOR BOAT MARINA, Inc.
Seattle, Wash.
E. H. GEIL CHRIS-CRAFT SALES & SERVICE CO.
Spokane, Wash.
KANAWHA FLYING SCHOOL
Charleston, W. Va.
THE SPORT MART
Charleston, W. Va.
EARLE ROGERS CO.
Wheeling, W. Va.
DELAVAN LAKE BOAT CO.
Delavan, Wis.
HARVEY J. LHOST
Green Bay, Wis.
BROOKS GARAGE & BOAT CO.
Green Lake, Wis.
BERG'S, Inc.
Madison, Wis.
RUGGLES MARINE MART
Milwaukee, Wis.
THOMPSON'S BOAT MART
Minocqua, Wis.
CLARK & LUND BOAT CO.
Oshkosh, Wis.
CHAINEY & CHAINEY
Spread Eagle, Wis.
TWO RIVERS AUTO SERVICE CO.
Two Rivers, Wis.
WAUSAU BOAT CO.
Wausau, Wis.
L. B. CLARKSON
Sydney, N. S. W., Australia
MASTERS HDWE. CO.
Hamilton, Bermuda
EDWARDO FERNANDES & CIA
Bahia, Brazil
J. A. BARROS
Rio de Janeiro, Brazil
MESBLA S/A
Rio de Janeiro, Brazil
VERDIER & CIA, Ltda.
Sao Paulo, Brazil
M. M. ALEXANDER, Ltd.
Kingston, Jamaica, B. W. I.
G. H. PAGE
Winnipeg, Man., Canada
LLOYD'S TOURIST EMPORIUM
Fort Frances, Ont., Canada
LEO J. GALLAGHER
Kingston, Ont., Canada
MINAKI BOAT HOUSE
Minaki, Ont., Canada
E. R. FRALING
Minett, Ont., Canada
H. R. ARCHER MOTOR SALES
Port Perry, Ont., Canada
RIVERSIDE BOAT AGENCY
Riverside, Ont., Canada
OGILVIE & LE PAN
Toronto, Ont., Canada
STEWART C. KNOX
Montreal, Que., Canada
BESA & COMPANY, Ltd.
Santiago, Chile
THE KOWLOON MOTOR BUS CO., Ltd.
Hong Kong, China
ERNESTO V. DUPERLY & CO.
Bogota, Colombia
CUBAN DIESEL ELECTRIC CO.
Havana, Cuba
ARTHUR BRAY
London, England
P. & E. MEYER & CO
Fort de France, Martinique, F. W. I.
COURCOUMELIS, PHOCAS & CO.
Athens, Greece
M. MESSINESI
Athens, Greece
R. A. NICOL
Guatemala City, Guatemala
HAWAIIAN TUNA PACKERS, Ltd.
Honolulu, Hawaii
ANDRE J. H. CEURVORST
Amsterdam, Holland
HILLS BROTHERS EASTERN CO., Inc.
Basrah, Iraq
K. YAMAMOTO
Tokyo, Japan
CASA MOLINA FONT
Merida, Yucatan, Mexico
MEXICAN MACHINERY CO.
Tampico, Mexico
AUTO HALL
Casablanca, Morocco
VICTOR MENOZZI
Lima, Peru
LUNETA MOTOR CO.
Manila, P. I.
SOBRINO DE IZQUIERDO, Inc.
San Juan, Porto Rico
WILLIAMS, HUNT & CO., Ltd.
Johannesburg, South Africa
GARAGE KASINOPLATZ
Berne, Switzerland
SLAZENGERS, Ltd.
Istanbul, Turkey
J. RAMIREZ MAC GREGOR
Maracaibo, Venezuela
CASANOVA & CIA
Maracay, Venezuela

★ ★ **CHRIS-CRAFT** ★ ★

Complete list of Chris-Craft Dealers in 1940

185

EXPANDED LISTINGS OF RESTORATION SHOPS, DEALERS AND OLD PARTS SOURCES

A LIST OF FIRMS SPECIALIZING IN ANTIQUE AND CLASSIC BOATS

Following is a listing of some companies who restore and service various kinds of boats. Since I have not had dealings with most of these firms, I cannot guarantee their work. If interested, you will have to check them out for yourself.

MIDWESTERN STATES

ANTIQUE AUTO & BOAT
RESTORATION SHOP
c/o Art Iles
1816 East 91st Street
Indianapolis, IN 46240
(317) 846-1624

(Offers restorations and repairs, also sells some old hardware)

CHAMBERLIN RESTORATION CO.
115 Olive Street
Cartersville, IL 62918
(618) 985-6119

(Complete boat restorations, sales and repairs—Chris-Craft exclusively)

CUTHBERTSON BOAT YARD
6231 Duke Road
Pearl Beach, MI 48052
(313) 794-4552

(Expert restoration and wood work)

E. J. MERTAUGH BOAT WORKS
c/o Jim Mertaugh
Hessel, MI 49745
(906) 484-2434

(First franchised Chris-Craft dealer in U.S., 1925. Offer complete restoration shop, sales, repairs and storage of antique and classic boats. Has good supply of parts for Chris-Craft A-120 and A-70 engines)

FONTANA MARINE SERVICE
c/o James A. Humphrey
Fontana, WI 53125
(414) 275-5708

(Sales, service and restoration work on wooden boats. Also a dealer for Streblow inboards)

GAGE MARINE
c/o Bill Gage
Williams Bay, WI 53191
(414) 245-5501

(Former custom builder, now restores and maintains classic and antique sales and dockage)

GREGORY'S
9666 E. Jefferson
Detroit, MI 48233
(313) 823-1900

(Established in 1912—sell Chris-Craft and offer all sorts of parts, sales, supplies, service, refinishing, storage and dockage. They are a Chris-Craft parts depot)

HUGO'S BOAT WORKS
Onamia, MN 56359

(Builds cedar-strip fishing boats, runabouts and also repairs and refinishes wooden boats)

ISLAND MARINA
Dave Lorimer
15806 Rt. #84 North, Box 297-A
East Moline, IL 61244
 (309) 755-0492

(Does restoration work on Chris-Craft runabouts and cruisers. Also storage, dockage and marine lift)

KEN'S MARINE SERVICE
165 Woodpecker Ridge Road
Tonka Bay, MN 55331

(Offer complete refinishing, restorations, engine repairs, etc.)

KRAMER BOAT COMPANY, INC.
c/o Vernon Kramer
82 N. Route #12
Fox Lake, IL 60020
 (312) JU7-2623

(Oldest Century dealer in U.S. Has sold Century ever since 1927. Also sold Gar Wood in the past. Offer sales, storage and refinishing of wooden speedboats. Also possible source for old boat and/or engine parts)

LUND BOAT WORKS, INC.
East Public Dock
Erie, PA 16507
 (814) 455-1782

(Rebuild, renovate or redesign classic wooden boats—mostly cruisers)

MACY'S WAWASEE SLIPS
R.R. #4
Syracuse, IN 46567

(Long-time Chris-Craft dealer—offer sales, service, storage, dockage and care of antique and classic boats. Do refinishing also)

MARTIN'S SPORT AFLOAT
c/o Ted Dallum
Lakefront Store
Nisswa, MN 56468
 (218) 963-2292

(Offers complete refinishing, repairs, engine work, storage and sales. Former Century and Chris-Craft dealers)

MINEOLA MARINE, INC.
c/o Pete Jakftas
117 Cora Avenue
Fox Lake, IL 60020
 (312) 587-2777

(Offer complete restorations, repairs, refinishing, dockage, winter storage plus the sale of lots of old engines, engine parts and hardware—mainly Chris-Craft. Total business geared towards restorations with no boat sales but limited brokerage. Offer towing and salvage services)

MINNETONKA BOAT WORKS, INC.
Wayzata, MN 55391
 (612) 473-7305

(Rebuild, refinish wooden boats. Also an excellent engine and boat parts department)

MINNETONKA RESTORATION CO.
c/o F. Todd Warner
6033 Cherrywood Road
Mound, MN 55364
  (612) 472-4187

(We buy, sell, and brokerage antique and classic runabouts. Also have some old parts.)

NAGAWICKA MARINA
1764 Milwaukee Street
Delafield, WI 53018

(Does wood boat refinishing, etc.)

OKOBOJI BOATS, INC.
c/o Bob Schneider
Box 414
Okoboji, IA 51355
  (712) 332-2144

(Century dealer since early 1930's. Maintain, store and dock wooden boats. Also offer good selection of old boat hardware)

RUSSELL MARINA, INC.
5442 County Highway N.
Madison, WI 53718
  (608) 249-7633

(Offer complete refinishing of wooden boats as well as dockage, storage and sales of some wooden boats, engines and parts, etc.)

ST. CLAIR FLATS MARINA
c/o Pete Henkle
7650 S. Channel Drive
Harsens Island, MI 48028
  (313) 748-3600

(Sales, restoration and storage of wooden boats. Nation's largest selection of genuine Scripps new and used engine parts. Also some old boat hardware)

SAYRE BROTHERS MARINE
c/o Bud Sayre
212 North Bank
Buckeye Lake, OH 43008
  (614) 928-3691

(Franchised Chris-Craft dealer since 1926. Began operations in 1904. Offer complete restorations, some old parts and very extensive selection of wood speedboats for sale year around)

ARNOLD E. SODERLAND
3200 Snelling Avenue
Minneapolis, MN 55401
  (612) 721-1356

(Offers complete wood boat restorations)

STREBLOW BOATS, INC.
2317 Springbrook Road
Kenosha, WI 53140
  (414) 694-3222

(Probably one of only a handful of firms still turning out fine mahogany speedboats. Several sizes offered plus refinishing and repairs to all types of wooden power boats)

LEO M. TASSIER BOAT SHOP
Cedarville, MI 49719
  (906) 484-2573

(This firm restores and maintains inboard runabouts. Offer storage, engine and hull restorations, upholstery, etc. Open year around)

THE BOAT SHOP
522 Baker Street
Lake Geneva, WI 53147
  (414) 248-3590

(Storage, repairs and sales of wooden boats. 100% restoration. Large supply of old boat hardware, etc.)

TOM'S MARINE HARDWARE
c/0 Tom Flood
30060 S. River Road
Mt. Clemens, MI 48045
(313) 468-6769

(Tom's dad worked for Hacker Boat Company for 35 years. Tom is a possible source for some old Hacker parts or for help concerning restoration of old Hacker Craft boats)

WAWASEE BOAT COMPANY, INC.
Route #1, Box 92
Syracuse, IN 46567
(219) 457-4404

(Former Gar Wood dealer, now sell, service, dock and store wood and fiberglass boats. Do offer excellent refinishing and restoration work. Check concerning possible old boat or engine parts. Now dealers for Streblow Boats of Wisconsin)

WILSON BOAT WORKS
Arnolds Park, IA 51331
(712) 332-5626

(Complete restorations, repairs, sales and storage of wooden boats. Chris-Craft dealer since 1932)

WEST COAST STATES

ASPEN ANTIQUE BOAT WORKS
1730 Pomona Street #12
Costa Mesa, CA 92661

(Specializes in mahogany inboard speedboat restorations)

EDGEWATER YACHT SALES, INC.
c/o Ken Underwood
Box 943
Bridgeway at Turney
Sausalito, CA 94965
(415) 332-2822

(Specializes in restoring inboard speedboats, mainly Chris-Craft)

GRAND LAKE MARINA
Grand Lake, CO 80447
(303) 627-3401

(Offer complete boat restorations, repairs as well as restores Chris-Craft engines. Oldest exclusive Chris-Craft dealer in U.S. since 1934. Also offers storage)

NORTH SHORE BOAT LANDING
Lake Arrowhead, CA 92352

(Refinish wooden boats; also have some old boats for sale)

PHILBRICK BOAT WORKS
603 Embarcadero
Oakland, CA 94606
(415) 893-9443

(Build beautiful all-mahogany 20½' inboard runabouts with 250 h.p. Chrysler engines. Boats are sold factory-direct; the firm has been building boats since 1934)

SIERRA BOAT COMPANY
c/o Dick Clarke
Box 69
Carnelian Bay, CA 95711
(916) 546-2552

(Largest complete restoration, dealership operation in the U.S. Also sell, store and maintain wooden boats. Sell new Century boats; Riva service center; Philbrick runabout dealer)

THE BOAT HOUSE
8188 Belvedere
Unit-D
Sacramento, CA 95826
(916) 455-BOAT

(Restore wooden runabouts, cruisers, etc. Also sell old parts, some engines, supplies and advise do-it-yourself restoration people. Have just added windshield brackets and other hardware made to the firms' own specifications)

EASTERN STATES

BACK BAY BOATS
c/o George Johnson
Bay Street Box 792
Wolfeborrow, NH 03894
(603) 569-4095

(Sells, buys classic and antique Chris-Craft runabouts; also has large stock of old boat hardware, engine parts, etc. for sale. Now making one type of pre-war Chris-Craft windshield brackets and two post-war types; also wood Chris-Craft flag staffs, bow and stern, plus other hardware—contact George for details)

BAKER BOAT WORKS
Westport, MA 02790
(617) 636-3272

(Build wooden skiffs, canoes, etc. Also restore antique and classic sail boats, etc.)

JAY BROWN
Box 979
Bangor, ME 04401
(207) 942-4209

(Sells antique mahogany runabouts; also sells supplies, parts, etc. Sells duplicate black-ribbed flooring for speedboats; buys boats. Located 10 minutes from Bangor International Airport and two miles off Interstate 95)

H. CHALK & SONS, INC.
c/o Duane J. Chalk
Fishers Landing, NY 13641
(315) 686-5622

(Specializes in restoration of Fitzgerald and Lee boats, plus sells boat and engine parts and old outboard motor parts. Many old Chris-Craft engine parts)

CHANNEL MARINE CORPORATION
Channel Lane
Weirs Beach, NH 03426
(603) 366-5541

(Century dealer offers sales, service and refinishing for wooden boats; also some old parts, etc.)

DUNHAM'S BAY BOAT COMPANY
Road #1, Route #9 L
Lake George, NY 12845
(518) 656-9244

(Former Century dealer—now offers restoration and refinishing work on wooden boats as well as dockage and storage)

FISHERS MARINA, INC.
East side of Lake George
Star Route Pilot Knob Road
Glen Falls, NY 12801
(518) 656-9981

(Does refinishing and repairs on wooden boats)

GOODHUE & HAWKINS
Seewall Road
Wolfeboro, NH 03894
(603) 569-2371

(Former builder of "Laker" boats. Now offer sales, storage and repair of antique and classic boats)

HALL'S BOAT CORPORATION
Drawer 321
Lake George, NY 12845
(518) 668-5437

(Established in 1908; offers storage, service and restoration work)

HARVARD FORDMAN
87 Gold Street
Lakeport, NH 03426
(603) 524-7189

(Antique boats bought, sold and restored)

HUTCHINSON BOAT WORKS
Crossmon and Bethune Street
Alexandria Bay, NY 13607
(315) 482-9931

(Former custom speedboat builder, built Lockpat III; now offer sales, storage and service)

IRWIN MARINE, INC.
c/o Jim Irwin
Lakeport, NH 03426
(603) 524-6661

(Founded in 1921, Chris-Craft dealer from the early days. Offer complete sales, service and refinishing of wooden boats. Also provide storage and sell parts)

LAKE KEUKA MACHINE WORKS
799 E. Lake Street
Penn Yan, NY 14527
(315) 536-2620

(Complete restorations, custom overhauls, parts, assemblies, antique engines)

LAKEWOOD SALES, INC.
Holiday Harbor
Celoron, NY 14720
(716) 484-7175

(Chris-Craft dealers; also offer parts, sales and service plus refinishing)

LAMB BROTHERS INC.
Main Street
Bolton Landing, NY 12814
(518) 644-5411

(Former Chris-Craft dealer; still sell some antique boats and offer service too)

H. B. MARCH
Box 641
Newport, VT 05855

(Old-time Chris-Craft dealer; sell some boats and parts; do restoration and refinishing work)

MARINE CUSTOMIZING
Box 199
Cleverdale, NY 12820
(518) 656-9657

(Specializes in sales of antique and classic power and sail craft)

MARINE RESTORATIONS, INC.
c/o Earl Lewis
Box 228
Jamesburg, NJ 08831
(201) 521-1128

(Complete restorations, refinishing, upholstery, engines rebuilt—plus boat sales)

MOORING POST MARINA, INC.
Cleverdale on Lake George
New York 12820
(518) 656-9206

(Chris-Craft dealer—offers sales, service, dockage and refinishing)

MORGAN MARINE BASE
c/o Bill Morgan
Silver Bay, NY 12874
(518) 543-6666

(Boat carpentry, refinishing, machine work, upholstery and chroming service. Specialize in Hacker Craft restorations. Also offer excellent reproduction Hacker Craft step pads, vents, etc.)

OSBORNE'S GARAGE & MARINE, INC.
Sunapee Harbor
Sunapee, NH 03782
(603) 763-2611

(Restores all types of antique and classic boats. Also sell old boat and engine parts)

PILOT KNOB BOAT COMPANY
c/o Phil Austin
On Lake George
Pilot Knob, NY 12844
(518) 656-9211

(Offer sales, service and restoration work. Also currently sell Century boats and provide storage)

ST. LAWRENCE RESTORATION CO.
411 Franklin Street, Box 310
Clayton, NY 13624
  (315) 686-5950

(Complete carpentry, refinishing, upholstery and chroming services. Also complete restoration of antique boats plus sell both restored and unrestored boats. Large selection of old engines, boat parts—plus boat magazines; specialize in Gar Wood restorations)

VELEZ MARINE BASE
c/o Luey Velez
Port Henry, NY 12974
  (518) 546-7588

(Located on Lake Champlain; sell, store, repair and refinish wooden boats and sell some old parts for engines, boats, etc.)

WAYNE'S MARINE, INC.
c/o Wayne Mocksfield
Henderson Cove
Lake Hopatcong, NJ 00849
  (201) 663-3214

(Specialize in restoring Chris-Craft, Dodge, Fay-Bowen boats; also store boats and sell some old parts)

SOUTHERN STATES

ALRED MARINA
Route 6
Guntersville, AL 35976
  (205) 582-4400

(Offer complete restorations, repairs, refinishing. Chrysler engine repairs, old parts for boats, etc. Dockage and storage)

AQUARIUS YACHT SALES, INC.
Suite F-3105, U.S. 19 South
New Port Richey, FL 33552
  (813) 848-1065

(Firm selling all types and sizes of classic, modern, etc. power boats)

VINTAGE BOAT WORKS
Box 90412
Nashville, TN 37209
  (615) 352-8290

(Complete restorations, rebuilding service and sales)

CANADIAN LOCATIONS

DUKE MARINE SERVICES
c/o Ed Skinner
Box 148
Port Carling, Ontario POB IJO
(705) 765-3141

(Former location of Duke Boats. Now exclusively into storage, repairs and restorations of antique and classic motor boats)

OGILIVE BLOSS LTD., YACHT BROKERS
1 Port Street East
Port Credit, Ontario L5G 4NI
(416) 278-2333

(Specialize in the sale of antique and classic power and sail craft of all sizes. Good selection of the more rare Canadian speedboats at most times)

ANTIQUE AND OLD INBOARD PARTS[1]

Crown Engine & Parts, Inc.
1802 River Road
Fawn Lake, NJ 17410

Frank's Marine Service #2
Route #7
Rutherford, NJ 07000

Marine Parts
Box 540
Warsaw, IN 46580

Marine Sales & Repair Company
30040 S. River Road
Mt. Clemens, MI 48043

Rogers Marina
Alexandria Bay, NY 13607

Wilmington Marine Supply
2423 E. Anaheim Boulevard
Wilmington, CA 90744

MANUFACTURERS AND PARTS SUPPLIERS[2]

Bolts, Bronze

Parker Merrick Company
245 S.W. 32nd Street
Ft. Lauderdale, FL 33335

Wilcox-Crittenden Company
Box 111
Middletown, CT 06457

Bolts, fastners

Linger Fastner Company
5657 Thunder Hill Road
Columbia, MD 21045
  (Screws, nuts, bolts)

Marine Screw-Bolt
Box 421
Valley Stream, NY 11580

Ships Tender
344 City Island Avenue
City Island, NY 10464

Bolts, stainless steel

Allmetal Screw Products Company, Inc.
821 Stewart Avenue
Garden City, NY 11530

Nautical Development Company, Inc.
405 Main Street
Port Washington, NY 11050

Southern Screw Division
Box 1460
Statesville, NC 28677

---

[1] "Boat Keeping", *MOTOR BOATING AND YACHTING*, (Oct. '74), 40.
[2] "Advertisement", *ANTIQUE BOATING*, I, (April '74), 2.

CASTINGS AND PATTERNS[3]

Hinckley Foundry & Marine
13 Water Street
New Market, NH 03857
(All types of bronze, brass, aluminum patterns and castings)

CHROMING AND ELECTROPLATING

G. & H. Metal Finishers, Inc.
282 Dakota Street
Peterson, NJ 07503

Cycle Chrome
2430 Washington Street
Syracuse, NY 13206

CONVERTIBLE TOPS & CANVAS WORK AND UPHOLSTERY

Cardinal Canvas Company
1301 James Avenue
Albert Lea, MN 56007
(507) 373-2158
(Custom fitted and built mooring and storage covers, convertable tops, side curtains.)

Coe Restoration Services
"The Leather Man"
Steve L. Coe
2117 Iuga Avenue
Columbus, Ohio 43216
(614) 268-9665
(Offers expert marine upholstering—leather, a specialty)

Geordie Magee
Brewerton, NY 13029
(315) 686-7679
(Offers custom canvas, upholstery work for power & sail craft—serve north and central New York with four mobile units)

Lakeside Upholstery
Norowal Marina
Bolton Landing, NY 12814
(518) 644-9438
(Custom boat interiors, tops and all types of mooring covers)

Mance Marine Basin, Inc.
End of Anthony Street
Alexandria Bay, NY 13607
(Custom tops, boat cushions, etc.)

Smith Accessories
Hauge on Lake George
Lake George, NY 12814
(518) 543-6446
(Custom convertible tops, wicker chairs, instruments restored, castings made.)

William C. Smith
15 Normandy Parkway
Morristown, NY 13664
(201) 267-7499
(Makes and sells reproduction custom roadster tops for Chris-Craft, Gar Wood and Hackers)

The Upholstery Shop
6535 Redman Lane
Excelsior, MN 55331
(612) 474-1850
(Does all types of marine upholstery)

DECALS AND NAME PLATES

Jay Fisher
Acken Drive 4-B
Clark, NJ 07066
(201) 388-6442
(Offers nameplates for Chris-Craft and Fay-Bowen boats. Send stamped, self-addressed envelope for more information, prices, etc.)

Dave L. Nelson
306 W. Washington
Appleton, WI 54911
(1930's era Chris-Craft decals)

William C. Smith
15 Normandy Parkway
Morristown, NJ 07690
(Reproduction Fay-Bowen nameplates)

ENGINE AND ENGINE PARTS

Automotive Division Bikes, Inc.
7011 S. Stoney Island
Chicago, IL 60607
(312) DO 3-8005
(Authorized sales, service and parts depot for Interceptor, Universal, Gray Marine, Crusader, Flagship, Palmer)

Barr Marine Products Company
Cornwells Heights, PA 19020

---

[3] "Advertisement", *ANTIQUE BOATING, IV,* (Summer '76), 33.

(Manufacturer's direct replacement water-cooled manifolds, for Chrysler 283, 400, 413, 426 and 440 c.i. engines. This unit will replace early and late style Chrysler manifolds)

Chrysler Marine Engines
Marysville Marine Distributors
Box 126
Marysville, MI 48040
(313) 364-7653
(Sell gasoline engines from 130 to 375 h.p. Also Chrysler engine parts and replacement gears and outdrives)

Crusader Engines
Thermo Electron Corporation
15 Mile Road
Sterling Heights, MI 48077
(313) 264-1200
(Manufacturer and dealer of Crusader engines; parts through dealers)

Gray Marine Company
339 W. 20th Avenue
Oskosh, WI 54901
(414) 231-4560
(Since 1906 offered all types and sizes of heavy duty inboard engines. Offer parts, service through authorized dealers)

Lawton Marine Sales & Service
Box 569, 489 S. Clay Street
Coldwater, MI 49306
(517) 279-9736
(New, used and rebuilt engines, instruments for Chris-Craft, Gray, Chrysler and Interceptor)

Mohawk Marine Engine Company
18-02 River Road
Fairlawn, NJ 07410
(201) 796-1630
(Complete selection of gas and diesel engines for repowering, etc.)

Osco Motors Corporation
Souderton, PA 18964
(Offer engines, manifolds, and much more)

Stokes Marine Supply
740 W. York Avenue
Pawtucket, RI 02861
(401) 725-5790
(New and rebuilt engines, leading brands, expert service, large inventory of obsolete and hard to find engine parts. Big catalog, $1.00)

Travelers Marine Engine Company
215 Hudson Avenue
Freeport, NY 11520

(516) 868-1193
(Distributors for Palmer, Crusader engines, parts, service transmission parts for Paragon, Borg-Warner)

Universal Motors
1552 Harrison Street
Oshkosh, WI 54901

ENGINE MANUFACTURER PARTS AND SUPPLIERS

Barr Marine Products Company
Box 408
Cornwells, PA 19020
(See other listing for firm)

Chris-Craft
Box 860
Pompano Beach, FL 33061

Chris-Craft Sales Center
Algonac, MI 48001
(313) 794-4944
(Sell all types of Chris-Craft engine parts, refinishing supplies, hardware, decals and much, much more)

Hercules
Hercules Motor Company
White Motor Company
5826 W. Ogden
Chicago, IL 60600
   Or 101-11th Street, S.E.
   Canton, OH 44702

Interceptor
10400 W. North Avenue
Melrose Park, IL 60160

Kermath
Granite Star Machine Company, Inc.
124 Joliet Street
Box 779
Manchester, NH 03105

Lehman Manufacturing Company
800 E. Elizabeth Avenue
Linden, NJ 07036
(See dealer listing elsewhere)

Palmer Engine
New England Marine Engine & Supply Company
River Road
Cos Cob, CT 06807

Red Wing Engines
Red Wing Engine Parts
211 Main Street
Red Wing, MN 55066

Scripps Engine Parts
Scripps Marine Engine Company
7650 S. Channel Drive

Harsens Island, MI 48028
(313) 748-3600

ENGINE PARTS

Atlantic Engine Sales Company
741 S. Ocean Avenue
Freeport, NY 11520
(Over 2,000 engines for use and parts)

B. & B. Marine
125 S. 16th Street
Lindenhurst, NY 11757
(516) 226-6042
(Carry parts for Chrysler—Ace, Crown, Royal straight 8 engines)

Bayview Marine
781 Oakland Beach Avenue
Warwick, RI 02886
(401) 737-2522
(Complete prop, shaft and coupling repairs; sell Columbian props)

Bob's Marine Service
3030 W. Commodore Way
Seattle, WA 98101
(Sell Chris-Craft, Chrysler and Crusader engine parts)

Cleveland Yacht Supply
3027 Detroit Avenue
Cleveland, OH 44101
(Old line Chris-Craft dealer; also sell Chris-Craft and Gray engine parts)

Clinton Reef Marine Sales
Lakeshore Drive West
Port Clinton, OH 43452
(419) 734-3107
(Carry parts for Chris-Craft, Gray Flagship, Chrysler, Interceptor, Crusader; also manifolds, alternators and starters)

DiPietro-Kay Corporation
914 Cromwell Avenue
Rocky Hill, CT 06067
(203) 563-2167
(Largest stock in New England for Chrysler engines. Also props, hydraulic gears, etc.)

G. A. Plumb, Inc.
Foot of Sunrise Avenue
Old Saybrook, CT 06475
(Sell new, used inboard engines)

H. & H. Prop Shop, Inc.
1 Essex Street Extension
Salem, MA 01970
(617) 744-3806
(Prop sales, repairs, shafts, couplings, stuffing boxes, rudders, struts. All types bronze bolts, lags, fasteners)

J. D. Brown & Associates
Box 979
Bangor, ME 04401
(Service for selling boats, parts; write for list)

Jefferson Beach Marine Store
2400 Jefferson Avenue
St. Clair Shores, MI 48080
(Chris-Craft and Chrysler parts)

Jerry's Marine Service
100 S.W. 16th Street
Ft. Lauderdale, FL 33315
(Complete stock of parts, manuals for Interceptor)

Ted Larter
Main Street
Dunstable, MA 01827
(Kermath engines bought, sold, rebuilt)

Lehman Marine Engine Center
800 E. Elizabeth Avenue
Linden, NJ 07026
(201) 486-5758
(Offer Chris-Craft, Econ-o-Power conversion engines, hardware, instruments, controls, exhaust and fuel systems)

Marine Associates
R.R. #1
Hudson, WI 54016
(715) 386-5144
(Dealers only—props, rudders and shafts, sold, repaired, etc.)

Marine Division
Transmission Clinic
2706 Portage
Kalamazoo, MI 49001
(616) 345-0629
(Repair and sales of marine transmission parts, etc. new and rebuilt; exchange units on hand also rebuilt)

Marine Engine Sales & Service, Inc.
300 State Street
Annapolis, MD 21403
(301) 268-3072
(Dealers for Chrysler, Crusader, Volvo, Palmer-Warner gears, etc.)

Marine & Industrial Engines, Inc.
170 Granite Avenue
Dorchester, MA 02124
(617) 436-8300
(Distributor for Chrysler engines; Paragon & Warner transmissions; Stewart-Warner gauges, manifolds, pumps, parts)

Marine Manifold Corporation
134 Verdi Street

E. Farmingdale, NY 11735
(515) 694-0714
(Exhaust manifolds, elbows, piping, headers for most V-8 engines)

Marine Parts N.W., Inc.
817 Republican Street
Seattle, WA 98109
(206) 624-6431
(Dealers only—Chris-Craft and Owens engine parts, Osco replacement manifolds and Atomic 4 engines and parts)

Marine Sales & Repairs
Mt. Clemens, MI 48043
(Old, rare engine and boat parts)

Marine Transmission Service
801 Penn Avenue
Linden, NJ 07036
(201) 486-5705
(Complete marine transmission service, sales, parts, repairs, exchanges, rebuilding, adaptions)

Midwest Marine Supply
St. Clair Shores, MI 48080

Rex Marine Center
144 Water Street
Norwalk, CT 06854
(212) MO 5-6055
(Sell Chrysler, Crusader, OMC engines. Also sell Chris-Craft, Chrysler parts—check with them for more information)

Rodi Boat Company
2550 S. Ashland Avenue
Chicago, IL 60608
(312) 666-6670
(Large Chris-Craft dealer since 1930's. Good source for "hard-to-find" Chris-Craft engine and Paragon gear parts)

Sante Marine Prop, Inc.
13368 Madison Avenue
Cleveland, OH 44107
(216) 226-4444
(Oldest prop repair firm for pleasure boats in Ohio; also sell new props)

Strater Auto & Marine
15020 Woodworth
Cleveland, OH 44110
(216) 249-9952
(Interceptor engine parts)

Travelers Marine Engine Company
355 Atlantic Avenue
Freeport, NY 11520
(516) 868-1139
(Carry genuine, original parts for Palmer, Interceptor engines. Also sell, service the same brands)

Vanek's Engine Specialists
2038 5th South Lake
Lake Tahoe, CA 95730
(Inboard engines a specialty; some parts)

LUMBER

General Woodcraft
100 Blinman Street
New London, CT 06326
(203) 442-5301

Georgia-Pacific Corporation
900 S.W. 5th Avenue
Portland, OR 97204

Maurice L. Condon, Inc.
260 Ferris Avenue
White Plains, NY 10603

J. G. Peterson
2247 S. Michigan Avenue
Chicago, IL 60616
(312) 842-2700

West Coast Forest Industries
10550 S.W. Allen Boulevard
Beaverton, OR 97005

STEP PADS

C. J. Gothardt
49 Carey Road
Needham, MA 02194
(1920's and 1930's era Chris-Craft reproduced step pads)

Richard Hopgood
200 Governors Drive A-32
Winthrop, MD 02152
(Gar Wood, Baby Gar and Chris-Craft reproduced step pads)

Morgan Marine Base
Silver Bay, NY 12874
(Hacker reproduced step pads and other parts)

TRUCK MOVEMENT OF BOATS

Boat Haulers, Inc.
23829 Little Mack Avenue
St. Clair Shores, MI 48080
(313) 776-6263
(Offer complete boat moving services from canoes to yachts. Agent K.A.T.)

Custom Boat Hauling
J. A. Vorhees Company
13972 Peninsula Drive
Traverse City, MI 49684
(616) 223-4370
(Custom boat hauling to 8' beam, customer supply trailer or cradle; call concerning rates)

Morrison Truck Service
Box 252
Mound, MN 55364
(612) 471-9770
(Moving large and small boats their specialty)

Nap & Paul's Marine Transportation
385 Main Street
E. Hartford, CT 06108
(203) 568-9320
(Offer moving services for your boat)

MISCELLANEOUS SERVICE AND EQUIPMENT LISTING

Century Boat Company

Conrad Adamski
Customer Service
Box 190
Manistee, MI 49660
(616) 723-9975
(Contact concerning material on Century boats; also possible lead on older Century boat and engine parts)

Antique Boating "T" Shirts

Z. M. Klos
100 Prospect Street
Glastonbury, CT 06033
(Colorful blue, brown and white "T" shirts to let everyone know you are an antique boater. Order by size, $5.95 plus 55¢ postage)

T-Shirts and Caps

Wooden Boat Magazine
Box 78
Brooklin, ME 04616
(Nice painter's cap with "Wooden Boat" logo—$1.00 each, minimum order $5.00)
"T" shirts for wooden boat fans. Cool cotton, silk screened with "Wooden Boat" logo. Black or white—$5.50 each, post paid. Order by size; allow 5 weeks for delivery)

Lap Robes

LeBaron Bonney
14 Washington Street
Amesbury, MA 01913
(Offer 4 distinct plaid color combination lap robes. Large size 60" by 60"—write for information)

LATE ARRIVALS

Kits Marine Ltd.
1502 W. 2nd Avenue
Vancouver, B.C. V6J 1h2
(604) 736-0166
(Complete marine hardware store. Also sell all types of marine lumber, etc.)

The Wooden Boat Shop
c/o Land Washburn
1007 Northeast Boat Street
Seattle, WA 98105
(206) 634-3600
(Offer wooden boats for sale. Oar, paddle and sail varieties; also woodworking tools, good boat hardware and reference books)

WOOD BOATS—Ship Carpenters
114 Water Street
Norwalk, CT 06854
(203) 866-5285

Ray W. Vandermeer
3305 South "G" Street
Oxnard, CA 93030
(Offer hand woven manila boat fenders in sizes from 3" x 10" through 8" x 24". Write directly for prices and details)

Bay Harbor Marina
Wilder Road at Saginaw River
Bay City, MI 48707
(517) 684-5022
(Offer good boat repair and restoration)

Suburban Boats
5060 Delhi Pike
Cincinnati, OH 45238
(513) 451-5060
(Offer excellent refinishing; also brokerage of wooden boats and repair of Chris-Craft engines)

Boat Catalogs Unlimited
Bob Speltz
505 Albert Lea Street
Albert Lea, MN 56007
(507) 373-2145
(I will swap excellent Xerox copies of catalogs with you. Also I will buy, sell or trade extra catalogs. I have over 100 that can be copied. Let me hear what you have to trade and what you want)

Svobodas' Watergate Marina
2500 Mississippi River Boulevard
St. Paul, MN 55116
(612) 698-0738
(Full service marina offering complete repair and refinishing of wood, steel and "glass" boats. Dockage, storage, engine repairs, etc.)

Minnetonka Top and Interiors
Joe Sanko
4750 Kildare Road
Mound, MN 55364
(612) 472-1282
(Specializes in upholstery of antique boats)

Greenwood Marina
c/o Jim Bean
21945 Minnetonka Boulevard
Excelsior, MN 55331
(Offers complete covered dockage, storage, gas, repairs, refinishing, etc. Caters to wooden boat owners)
(612) 474-9963

Pal Remanufactured Engines
129 Front Street South
Orillia, Ontario, Canada L3V 6J8
(705) 226-7376
(Engine repair; large supply of old engines—gas and diesel; also parts, etc. for sale. Call for more information)

Joe Morrison
Chris-Craft Sales Center
Algonac, MI 48001
(Helpful with Chris-Craft parts orders, engine manuals, etc.)

Afton Chris-Craft
Box 67
Afton, MN 55001
(612) 436-8827
(Large Chris-Craft dealer; offers dockage, storage, repairs, engine work, refinishing)

Race IV Ltd.
Rt. #1, Box 105
Prairie View, IL 60069
(312) 634-0814
(Midwest dealer for Riva yachts. Sell and service Riva boats only)

Bonnie Castle Yacht Basin
Alexandria Bay, NY 13607
(315) 482-2526
(Chris-Craft master dealer—offer dockage, repairs, storage, refinishing, etc.

Wilmington Marine Supply
2423 East Anaheim
Wilmington, CA 90744
(213) 435-9149
(Used marine gas engine parts for most makes)

Bristol Services
Costa Mesa, CA 92626
(714) 892-8541
(Sell Gray Marine engines up to 350 h.p.; also genuine new parts distributor)

Gasket King
18 Hastings Avenue
Toronto, Ontario, Canada M4L 2L2
(416) 466-6775
(Sell all types of engine gaskets for marine engines from 1904 through 1940)

Russ Young
109 S. 9th Street
Clear Lake, IA 50428
(515) 357-2597
(Does refinishing at his home. Has done this work for years)

Gray Marine Engine Manuals
Bob G. Falcone
2711 James Street
Syracuse, NY 13206
(1939-1958 all models, complete Xerox copy of original 78-page manual and trouble-shooting guide. Send $18.00 with name and address)

Delavan Lake Boat Company
c/o Bob Welch
Rt. #5, Box 179
Delavan Lake, WI 53115
(414) 728-5885
(Former old Chris-Craft dealer, still refinish, store and sell wooden power boats. Some old engine and boat hardware too)

Pierce Marine Corporation
555 Water Street
Youngstown, NY 14174
(716) 745-7000
(Chris-Craft dealer. Carry parts, offer service, storage, etc.)

Riverview Yacht Basin
18 Petten Street Extension
Rochester, NY 14612
(716) 663-0088
(Chris-Craft dealer. Offer storage, dockage, engine parts, used wood boats, etc.)

Gunderland Marine Supply Company
Box 9758, Cantwell Lane
Corpus Christi, TX 78408
(512) 882-4231
(Possible good source for old Chris-Craft engine parts)

Marine Manifold Corporation
134 Verdi Street
East Farmingdale, NY 11735
(516) 694-0714
(Will manufacture manifolds to replace those which are worn out or no longer available from the builder)

Geneva Lake Boat Company
523 South Shore Drive
Fontana, WI 53125
(Former Lyman, Century and Shepherd dealer. Still store, repair, dock and refinish wooden-power and sail boats)

Morris Boat Works
c/o Ray McLarney
Penatang, Ontario, Canada
(519) 549-2509
(Restore wooden cruisers and runabouts, does repair and refinishing also)

Thompson's Boat House
Owner, Tom E. Kuyper
406 - 9th St. N.E.
Waseca, MN 56093
(507) 835-2419
(Longest continuous operating wooden boat rental in Minnesota. Open year around. Sells wooden fishing boats on occasion)

Gerage Canvas & Boat Reupholstering
c/o Leonard Gerage
Rt. #5, Box 232
Antioch, IL 60002
(Specializes in Chris-Craft interiors)

Barbary Coast Yacht & Ship Brokers
c/o Barry Maynard, President
25 Third Street
San Rafael, CA 94901
(415) 457-9772
(Main distributor for the new Philbrick runabouts. Contact directly for name of nearest dealer. A new 27' three-cockpit runabout to be offered in the very near future.)

1959 CENTURY DEALER LIST

ALABAMA

Buck's Service—Alexandria City
Point Clear Boat Works—Battles Wharf
Inland Marine—Birmingham
Buck's Boats—Gadsden
Dixie Marine, Inc.—Montgomery
Crow Supply—Troy

ARIZONA

The Boat House—Phoenix

ARKANSAS

Holiday Beach, Inc.—Hot Springs
McGille & Prickett—Pine Bluff

CALIFORNIA

Otto Galey—Bakersfield
Balboa Boat Sales—Balboa Island
Bert's Hobbies & Sporting Goods—Berkeley
Jules Resort—Clear Lake
Humbolt Marine Supply—Eureka
Winther Brothers, Inc.—Fresno
Sierra Boat Company—Lake Tahoe
Bahia Marine—Long Beach
Louis Thomas Marine Center—Los Angeles
Peninsula Boat Sales—Monterey
Yates & Cochrane—Napa
B. & W. Sportsman—Paso Robles
Bridge Bay Boats—Redding
Norby's Marine—Roseville
Sun Harbor Marine, Inc.—San Diego
Bay City Marine, Inc.—San Francisco
North Marina Boat—Santa Monica
Stephens Marine Supply—Stockton

COLORADO

McCune Outboard Marine—Denver
Frank Ulrich Boat Company—Ft. Collins

CONNECTICUT

The Lake Marine Base, Inc.—Danbury
A. T. Howe Boat Company—East Hartford
Essex Boat Works—Essex
Thurston Outboard Marine—Niantic
Norwalk Boat Works—South Norwalk
Westbrook Boat & Engine—Westbrook
Adams & Podloff—West Haven
F. C. Bachman Boat Company—Wolcott

DISTRICT OF COLUMBIA

Katemac Marine, Inc.—Washington

FLORIDA

Gulls' Bay Marine—Clearwater
Sea Horse Marina—Daytona Beach
Daniels Brothers—Ft. Meyers
Gator Marine—Gainsville
Norton Marine Supply—Jacksonville
Charles L. Cooper—Lakeland
Boat Sales & Supply—Lantana
Santana Marine Service—Miami
Enterprise Marine Service—North Miami
Bob Weins' Marine Service—Ocala
Olcott Boat & Motor Sales—Orlando
Gulf Marina, Inc.—Panama City
J. C. Dixion Marine—Perry
Dunham Marina—Pompano Beach
Johnstone Maximo Boat Basin—St. Petersburg
Flagg Marine Company—Sarasota
Williams Brothers Marine—Tampa
100 Lakes Marine Sales & Service—Winter Haven

GEORGIA

Albany Outboard Marine—Albany
Russell-Daniel, Inc.—Athens
Cutter's, Inc.—Atlanta
C. K. Fields Marine Service, Inc.—Augusta
Tri-State Marine, Inc.—Bainbridge
Marine-Craft—Columbus
Deluxe Tire & Appliance—Toccoa

IDAHO

Buell J. Clement—Caldwell
Tobler's Boat Docks—Hayden Lake
Andy's Dock—McCall

ILLINOIS

Hansen Marine Service—Cary
Baily & Himes, Inc.—Champaign
Art Johnson—Chicago
Russ Leonard Boats & Motors—Chicago
Masters Marine—Chicago
Kramer Boat Company—Fox Lake
Century Boat Sales—Havana
Rowlett Motor Sales—Kewanee
Bruce Marine Service—McHenry
Wegstein Boats & Motors—Peoria
Quality School Supply—Pleasant Hill
J. Kenneth Johnson—Pontiac
Thompson Marine Sales—Rock Falls
Active Marine—Rockford
Earl C. Ritchie—Savanna
Donaldson's—Springfield

INDIANA

Fix Motor Sales—Attica
Owens Marine & Sporting Goods—Bedford
Wally's Boating Agency—Evansville
Harrington Boat Company—Fremont
Indianapolis Boat Company—Indianapolis
Fishburn's Marine—Knox
Burnham Marine Supply—Lafayette
Williams Boat Mart—La Porte
Tippecanoe Boat Company—Leesburg
Lowell T.V.—Lowell
McVicker's Sporting Goods—Marion
Williams Boat Mart—Michigan City
Tall Timbers Marine Supply—Monticello
New Albany Motor Company—New Albany
Wayne Marine Sales—Richmond
Rochester Flying Service—Rochester
Bullock's Marine Service—South Bend
Wawasee Boat Company—Syracuse
Paitson Brothers Hardware Co., Inc.—Terre Haute
Knob Hill Marina—Unionville

IOWA

Dehner Seed & Supply Company—Burlington
Brad's Marine Service—Cedar Rapids
Touristville Boat Company—Clear Lake
Lorenz & Jones—Des Moines
Ed's Boat Line—Guttenberg
Coyner's Marina—Burlington
Okoboji Boat Works—Okoboji
Lakeside Boat & Bathing Company—Storm Lake
Waterloo Boat & Motor Company—Waterloo

KANSAS

Automotive Parts Company, Inc.—Great Bend
United Marine Company, Inc.—Kansas City
B. & G. Sporting Goods—Topeka
Sports Craft Supply—Wichita

KENTUCKY

Taylor Marine—Beaver Dam
Henderson Boat Club—Henderson
Herrington Woods Marina—Lexington
Marine Sales & Service, Inc.—Louisville
Brandon Brothers Distributing Company—Murray

LOUISIANA

Anchor Marine, Inc.—Baton Rouge
Harris Marine Sales, Inc.—Baton Rouge
Howard Griffin—Monroe
Donovan Boat Supplies—New Orleans
S. & L. Marine Company, Inc.—Shreveport

MAINE

Johnson Marine Service—Belgrade Lakes
Cobb Buick—Caribou
Wassokeag Boat Sales—Manset
Hartley's Marina, Inc.—Raymond

MARYLAND

Morton & Loose Company—Baltimore
Delphey's Sports Store—Frederick
Georgetown Yacht Basin—Georgetown
Delphey's—Hagerstown
Sweene's Boat & Motor Service—McHenry
McDaniel Yacht Basin—North East

MASSACHUSETTS

Corsil's Marine Service—Arlington
Beverly Marine Basin, Inc.—Beverly
Ryder's Cove Yard—Chatham Port
Boston Boat Sales—Dorchester
Armand M. Rousel—Dracut
Dennis Marine—East Dennis
Capt. Joseph J. O'Connell—Fall River
Mercury Marine Sales—Hadley
Jesse White—Mendon
Fernold's Marine—Newbury
The Mariner—Plymouth
Glenny's Marine, Inc.—Shirley
Wareham Marine & Supply Company—Wareham
White's Marine—Webster
Dann Dee Marine, Inc.—Wellesley

MICHIGAN

Locke's Marina—Alanson
Lacrosse Boat Works—Alpena
Claey's Marine—Anchorville
Plowdrey's Marine Service—Bay City
Redfern Marine Inc.—Bellaire
Bob Hayward Marine, Belleville
Beulah Boat Shop—Beulah
Williams Sport Shop—Cadillac
Purdy Marine Sales & Service—Cassopolis
Texaco Marine Service—Cedarville
Clare Sportsman Shop—Clare
Skipper Peterson Boat Sales—Detroit
Emerald City Boat Harbor—Detroit
Lake Fenton Boat Sales—Fenton
Jim Robbins Company—Ferndale
Glen Craft Marine Shop—Glen Arbor
North Shore Marina—Grand Haven
Beyer's Marina—Grand Haven
Irish Boat Shop—Harbor Springs
Seeley Marine—Hillsdale
Easter Marine Sales—Holland
Johnson's—Ironwood

Gus Blacksmith's—Ithica
Van Camp Boat Company—Jackson
S. J. Wilkinson—Kalamazoo
Albert Marine Sales—Lansing
Stander Motor Sales—Leland
Cartier's Marina—Ludington
Friedrich's Sporting Goods—Manistee
Fred Minster Boat Sales—Manitou Beach
Midway Marine Sales—Mt. Clemens
Hobart's Marine Sales & Service—Mullett Lake
Roberts Boat Livery—Onekama
Inland Lakes Sales—Pontiac
Dock's Sporting Goods—Port Huron
S. J. Wilkinson—Richland
Rockford Boat Sales—Rockford
Higgins Lake Boat Yard—Roscommon
Robinson Sales—Saginaw
Gun Lake Marine Supply—Shelbyville
Parker Marine Sales & Service—Stuart
Tawas Boat & Marine Supplies—Tawas City
Sattler's Marina—Traverse City
O. C. Howey—Trenton
Si's Marine Service—Walloon Lake
Chalmer Bait & Tackle—White Lake
Jim's Outboard Service—Wyandotte

MINNESOTA

Tonka Bay Boat Works, Inc.—Excelsior
Falls Marine—International Falls
Inland Marine Corporation—Minneapolis
Nisswa Marine, Inc.—Nisswa
Wilson Boat Works—Rochester
Sunnyside Marine—Stillwater
Virginia Boat Company—Virginia
Central Motor Company—Winona

MISSISSIPPI

Gimma Marine—Biloxi
McClure Motors—Corinth
Hammett Supply Company—Natchez
Anderson's Sporting Goods—Yazoo City

MISSOURI

Cape Boating Company—Cape Girardeau
United Marine Supply—Kansas City
Malibu Beach Boat Sales & Service—Osage Beach
Boathouse—St. Charles
Missouri Boat & Motors—St. Louis
Fallin Motor Mart, Inc.—Springfield

MONTANA

Jim Rothrock's Montana Marina—Billings
Triangle Hardware—Chester
Jerry's Boat & Motor Service—Helena
Service Boat Company—Lakeside

NEBRASKA

Kimball Auto Service—North Platte
Omaha Century Boat Sales—Omaha
Alexander Pontiac—Superior

NEVADA

Lake Mead Marina—Boulder City

NEW HAMPSHIRE

Eldridge Marine—Dover
Cole's Marine—Sunapee
Channel Marine Corporation—The Weirs

NEW JERSEY

Brown's Boat Yard—Brant Beach
Lyndhurst Marine—Lyndhurst
Barres Brothers—Mt. Arlington
N. J. Yacht Sales Corporation—Point Pleasant Beach
Harbor Marine, Inc.—Somers Point
Zeller Cruiser Sales Company, Inc.—Toms River

NEW YORK

Dutchess Marine Company—Beacon
L. Potter Inc.—Bethpage, L.I.
Jewell's Sport Shop—Binghamton
Georgia's Marine Service—Branchport
Brobeil Marine Service—Buffalo
Rake's Marina—Canandaigua
1,000 Islands Marina—Clayton
Cooperstown Marina—Cooperstown
Davis Boat & Motor Company—Cuba
William E. Peters—Elmira
Hadcock Brothers—Fair Haven
Boat Sales & Transport Company—Freeport, L.I.
West Shore Marine—Greenwood Lake
Hummel's Marine Supply Company—Howard Beach
Augie's Boat Shop—Huntington, L.I.
Freeman's Motor Marine—Ithica
Almgren's Marine, Inc.—Jamestown
Dunham's Bay Boat Company, Inc.—Lake George
Orienta Marine Sales, Inc.—Mamaroneck
Dashner & Bubel Marine—Oswego
Gerry Finke's Marine—Ravena
Harrison Marine Service—Rochester
Morgan Marine—Lake George
Keough Marine Sales Company—Saranac Lake
Traswell Marine—Skaneateles
Utica Electric & Boat Sales—Utica
Ulrich & Lieblin—Southland, L.I.
Inland Marine Harbor—Waterloo
Grabau Boat Company—Youngstown

NORTH CAROLINA

Hiller-Taylor Company—Durham
Sparky's Harley-Davidson Sales—Greensboro
Tar Heel Boating, Inc.—Henderson
Hill's, Inc.—Raleigh
Bills Marine—Rockingham
Short's Boat & Motor Service—Shelby
Park Boat Company—Washington

NORTH DAKOTA

Overold Motors, Inc.—Fargo
Frasaker Motor Company—Minot

OHIO

Outboard Sales & Service—Akron
Archbold Sales & Service—Archbold
Bray's Marine Service—Cincinnati
Maplewood Marine Sales—Chesapeake
W. C. Kennedy & Son Company—Columbus
Gibson Brothers—Dover
Ribar Brothers—Hamilton
Huron Marine Park—Huron
Lancaster Marine Sales—Lancaster
Lake Erie Marine Corporation—Perrysburg
Major Marine Sales—Russell's Point
Brenner Marine, Inc.—Toledo
Netzlev Boat & Motor Sales—Troy
E. G. Smith & Son—West Carrollton
Youngstown Boat Supply Company—Youngstown

OKLAHOMA

Century Boats of Oklahoma—Tulsa

OREGON

The Sportsman—Florence
Don J. Diver Marine Supply—Klamath Falls
Oregon City Marine Mart—Oregon City
D.D.F. Company—Umatilla

PENNSYLVANIA

Skyline Motors—Beaver Falls
Reinmanns Marine Service—Conneaut Lake
Great Lakes Marine—Erie
Lake Harbor Boat Service—Greentown
Woolbert's—Kingstown
Gordon Boat Company—Philadelphia
Motor Boat Sales—Pittsburgh
Scott Motor Boat Sales—Point Marion
Reading Boat Works—Reading
Paragon Marine & Supply Company—Scranton
Engle Marine Sales—Washington
Byron Resh Boats—Wrightsville

RHODE ISLAND

Dawson Motors, Inc.—Warwick

SOUTH CAROLINA

Rankin's Boats & Motors, Inc.—Anderson
Roddey Motor Company—Columbia

SOUTH DAKOTA

Swenson Boat Sales—Watertown

TENNESSEE

Chicamuga Boat Docks—East Chattanooga
Wilson Outdoor Equipment—Jackson
Bayless Motor & Marine Service—Knoxville
Russell Hardwick Boats & Motors—Memphis
Bob's Sporting Goods—Nashville
Perryville Boat Docks—Perryville

TEXAS

Lake Phanton Fishing Village—Abilene
Bennett Boat Docks—Austin
Reynolds Brothers—Corpus Christi
Keeland-Overstreet Hardware Company—Crockett
Emerson Marine Sales—Dallas
Dusek & Miller—Denison
Harmar Boats, Inc.—Ft. Worth
C. B. Delhomme, Inc.—Houston
Cliff's Marine & Supply—Jacksonville
Godwin-Paxton Boat Company—Lubbock
Don Maxwell Company—Odessa
Strand's Speedboat Service—Orange
Bunyard Electric Company—San Angelo
Ray Russell—San Antonio
Denison Service Station—Snyder
G.F.C. Marine Sales—Texarkana
Alexander Boat Works—Tow
Auto Electric Service Company—Wichita Falls

UTAH

Howard Construction—Murray
P.W. Jack Preece—Murray
Wilson Transport Supply—Salt Lake City

VERMONT

Thayer Marine Company—Burlington
Wilson's Sporting Equipment—Rutland
Simpson Motors, Inc.—St. Albans
C. H. Danna, Jr.—St. Johnsbury

VIRGINIA

Colonial Yacht Club & Marina—Colonial Beach
Hampton Roads Marina—Hampton
Frantz Supply Company—Salem
Fletcher Equipment Company—Suffolk

WASHINGTON

Velrob Manufacturing Company—Everett
Metz Marina, Inc.—Kennewick
Lake Washington Yacht Basin, Inc.—Seattle
Earl's Marina—Spokane
Trudeaus Outboard Service—Spokane
Musty's Marina—Wenatchee

WEST VIRGINIA

Lucenti Motor & Marine Sales—Charleston
Wood's Boat House—Fairmont

WISCONSIN

Koch Stroker Marine Service, Inc.—Appleton
Eisle Marine Sales—Appleton
Safford's Sport Sales & Service—Beloit
Reed's Marine Sales—Delavan Lake
Joe's Marine Service—Eagle River
Lane-O-Lakes Motor Company—Land-O-Lakes
Valley Marine Mart—Menasha
Mail's Marine Mart, Inc.—Minocqua
Murphy & Son Marine Company—Neenah
Kinn Motors—Oconomowoc

Oshkosh Marine Mart—Oshkosh
Jim Rohan & Company—Racine
Kunz Marine Service—Sarona
Matt's Marine Service—Sheboygan
Reny's Gitchie Gumee—Sturgeon Bay
Al's Boat Shop—Twin Lakes
Russell Marina—Madison
Lakewood Sporting Goods, Inc.—Wausau
Gage Marine Corporation—Williams Bay

SOME FOREIGN CENTURY DEALERS

Andre Coutau Ing. S.I.A.—Geneva, Switzerland
Establishments G. De Beve—Costermansville, Belgian Congo, Africa
Morad Bin Yousuf Behbenani—Kuwait, Arabia
Cliftciler Ticaret, T.A.S.—Istanbul, Turkey
H. E. Heacock—Manila, Philippines
Transport & Engineering—Cairo, Egypt
Yacht Haven—Nassau, Bahamas
L. C. De Calirmont—Havana, Cuba
Fisher Faeh, Y. Cla, S.C.—Guatemala, C.A.
B.A.M.R. Pty. Ltd.—Cape Town, Belgian Congo, Africa

1954 marked the end of an era with Century. Following that year, a number of new models were to appear and some would see their last appearance in 1954. Let's review below the complete Century 1954 fleet of speedboats.

MODEL		LENGTH	ENGINE OPTIONS AND H.P.	COLOR COMBINATION	COLOR UPHOLSTERY
Resorter	Utility	16'	25 Gray through 112 h.p. Gray	Varnished hull, two-toned decks	Pastel shades
Resorter	Utility	18'	27 Gray through 140 h.p. Gray	Varnished hull, two-toned decks	Pastel shades
Resorter	Utility	20'	100 Gray through 145 h.p. Norberg	Varnished hull, two-toned decks	Pastel shades
Sea Maid	Runabout	18'	60 Gray through 160 h.p. Gray	Varnished hull, two-toned decks	Pastel shades
Sea Maid	Runabout	20'	100 Gray through 160 h.p. Gray	Varnished hull, two-toned decks	Pastel shades
Viking	Utility	19'	25 Gray through 60 h.p. Gray	White hull, varnished decks	Red or green

1954 16' Century resorter

1954 20' Century resorter with sun top

1954 20' Century Sea Maid runabout

1954 19' Century Viking

The newest Century in 1954 was the 19' Viking Sea Skiff, a boat for family fun and cruising, fishing, etc. The Sea Maid 18' and 20' would not remain in the Century line for 1955. No longer would they be the "queens" of the Century fleet. All 1954 Centuries were built of mahogany and all were varnished except for the lapstrake Viking. Century collectors today find especially the Sea Maids from 1954 to be very popular collectors' pieces.

Now let's move on to 1955 and see what the changes were going to be.

COLLECTORS' GUIDE TO MODERN CENTURY INBOARDS

It seems that since *Volume I* was published, a great deal of interest has surfaced in Century mahogany speedboats. For that very reason I am going to include at this point a year-by-year review of Centuries from 1955 through 1968, when the last wooden Centuries were built. A special "thank you" here to Jon and Tim Paske, both real Century buffs who are proud owners of a beautiful Resorter and a Sea Maid. These two men have helped in much of the gathering of background material for this section as well as giving me encouragement to do this section.

1955 was a milestone in the existence of the Century Boat Company. In that year a complete new line of super luxury speedboats was offered. I shall list below all the 1955 models along with color combinations, engine sizes, etc., plus small photos of each boat. I hope you enjoy this idea.

MODEL	LENGTH	ENGINE OPTIONS AND H.P.	COLOR COMBINATION	UPHOLSTERY COLORS
Resorter	16'	Gray 75, 100, 112, 135. Chrysler 100	Varnished hull, two-toned decks	Dark red with white trim
Resorter	18'	Gray 100, 110, 112, 135, 140 Chrysler 110, 125	Varnished hull, two-toned decks	White with green and other pastel shades
Arabian	18'	Gray 112, 135, 140, 160 Chrysler 125	Blue with gray stain	Dark blue with white
Coronado	20'	Gray 135, 175 Chrysler V-8 200 Cadillac V-8 230 Nordberg 155	Varnished hull and decks, white trim	Dark green with white
Viking	19'	Gray 45, 60, 75	White painted hull, varnished decks	Dark red

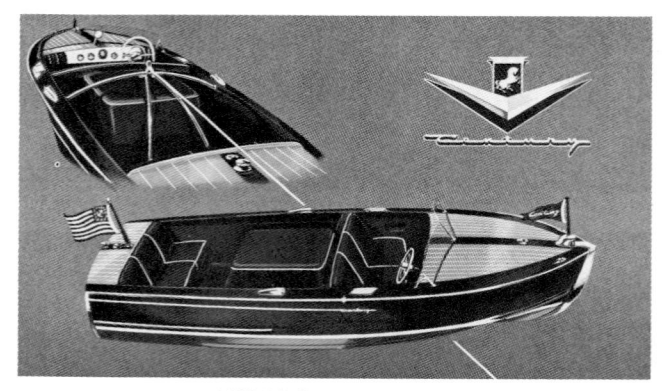

1955 16' Century Resorter

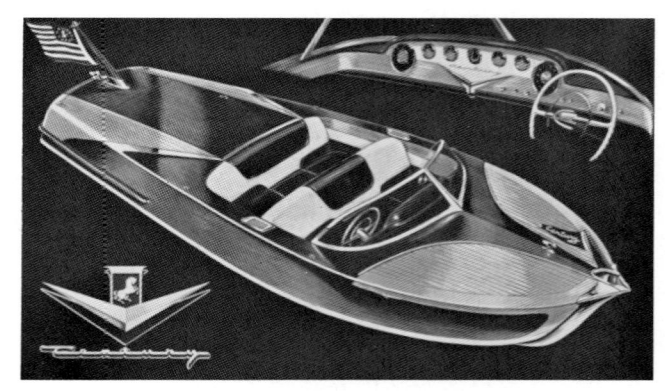

1955 18' Century Arabian runabout

1955 18' Century Resorter

1955 20' Coronado speedboat

206

1955 Century Viking 19' utility

Some changes in 1955 included the use of a new ski tow bar on the Resorter 16'. That year also saw the use of new pennant poles, steering wheels, and hardware designs. Arabian replaced the former Sea Maid while the all-new luxury 21' Coronado made its debut. A deluxe padded hardtop roof for the Coronado was also available. The Coronado would remain in the Century line in one design or another through the early 1970's. Century offered a very deluxe watercolor portfolio for 1955 showing all the new 1955 models. This material has become of great interest to literature collectors.

1956 also saw some changes in the Century inboards. Below is a listing of all the models.

MODEL	LENGTH	ENGINE OPTIONS AND H.P.	COLOR COMBINATION	UPHOLSTERY COLORS
Resorter	16'	Gray 110, 112, 135 Chrysler 110	Varnished hull, two-toned decks	Red with white piping
Resorter	18'	Gray 135, 140, 175 Chrysler 135, V-8 200 Cadillac V-8 250 Nordberg 155	Varnished hull, deck and transom	Red with white
Arabian	18'	Gray 135, 140 Nordberg 155 Chrysler 135, V-8 250 Cadillac V-8 250	Blue with gray stain	Blue with white
Coronado	21'	Gray 135, 175 Nordberg 155 Chrysler 135, V-8 200 Cadillac V-8 250 and 285	Varnished hull and decks, with white trim and hardtop	Green with white
Viking	19'	Gray 60, 75	White painted hull, varnished decks	Red
Vagabond	18'	Gray 60, 75	White painted hull, varnished cabin top and decks	Red

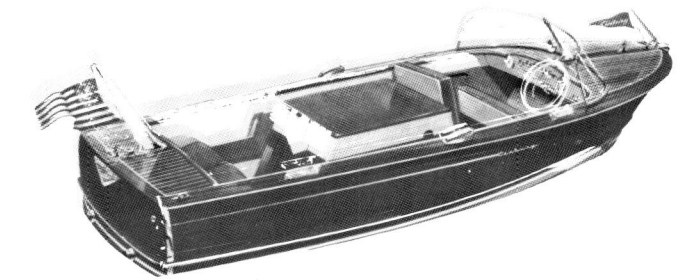

1956 16' Century Resorter

1956 18' Century Resorter

To begin with, the old 16' Resorter for 1956 received its first wraparound windshield along with a more streamlined chrome cutwater. The 18' Resorter was also restyled with a wraparound windshield, new bow and stern light poles, and new deck hardware. Front decks were more flared and streamlined. The biggest change in the sleek Arabian 18' was that you could now order it with the big Cadillac 250 h.p. V-8 in 1956. Everything else on the Arabian, including its

1956 18' Century Arabian

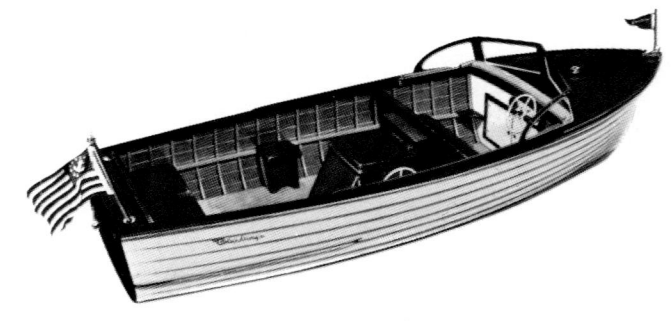

1956 19' Century Viking

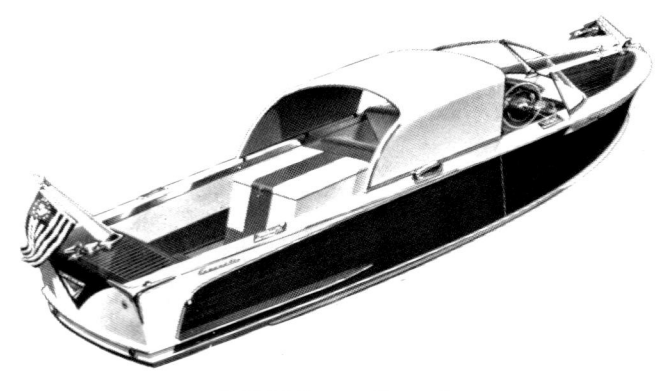

1956 21' Century Coronado

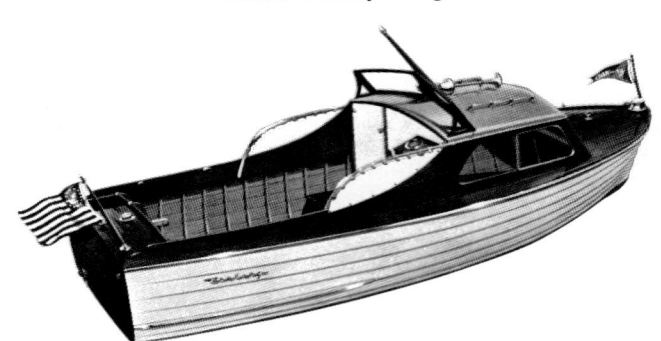

1956 18' Century Vagabond cruiser

color, was the same as in 1956. The big Coronado 21' also was pretty much as it was in 1955. Its hardtop roof was redesigned and you could get a 285 h.p. Cadillac in it too. The Viking 19' utility remained unchanged from 1955 except for a larger optional Gray 75 h.p. The other new model for 1956 was the 18' Vagabond, Century's first small cabin cruiser. This boat was stylish but remained in the line only in 1956.

1957 would see larger lapstrake cuddy cabins introduced to replace the small Vagabond. In 1957 Century also showed a rather revised line of runabouts and utilities. The photos in this section will show you just what changes did occur. The complete Century listing for 1957 follows.

MODEL	LENGTH	ENGINE OPTIONS AND H.P.	COLOR COMBINATION	UPHOLSTERY COLORS
Resorter	16'	Gray 110, 112, 135 Chrysler 110, 135 Interceptor V-8 185	Varnished hull, two-toned decks	Red with white, green with white, yellow with green
Resorter	18'	Gray 135, 175 Chrysler 135, V-8 200 Cadillac V-8 265 Nordberg 155 Interceptor V-8 215	Varnished hull, two-toned decks	Red with white, green with white, yellow with brown
Arabian	18'	Gray 135 Chrysler 135, V-8 200 Cadillac V-8 265, 300 Nordberg 155 Interceptor V-8 215	Varnished hull, two-toned decks	Yellow with brown
Coronado	21'	Gray 135, 175 Chrysler 135, V-8 200 Cadillac V-8 265 and 300 Nordberg 155 Interceptor V-8 215	Varnished and white sides, vinyl front deck, varnished rear	Red with white

1957 16' Century Resorter

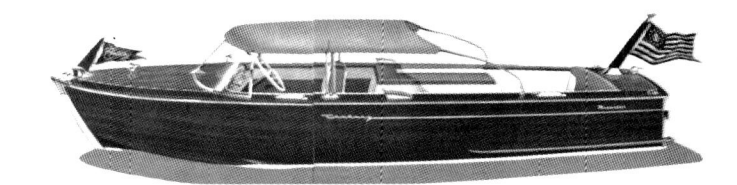

1957 18' Century Resorter

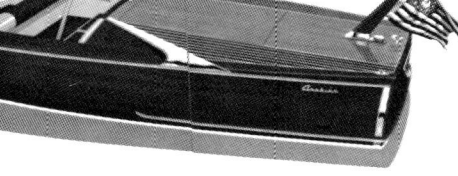

1957 18' Century Arabian

1957 21' Century Coronado

The 1957 16' Resorter received considerable design changes. It was given a more modern, streamlined cutwater and more raked wraparound windshield than in 1956. New deck hardware, running lights, and bow flag poles were also used; no more king plank in two-tone shades on the Resorter 16'. More upholstery options were also added. The biggest changes in the Resorter 18' were upholstery colors and a new V-8 engine. The Arabian 18' was the same as 1956 except it was now varnished for the first time. A somewhat larger 215 h.p. V-8 could also be ordered in the Arabian for 1957. The Coronado 21' was completely restyled in shades of brown, gold and white. The hardtop roof was designed with glass side windows and a sliding plexiglass section overhead. The front deck was covered with white vinyl and the rear deck was still varnished. All in all, 1957 proved to be a year of change with Century; customers appeared to like what they saw as sales were at a record high.

Several other last minute changes for 1957 included an all-new metal-framed windshield on the 19' Viking; optional ski bars were available for the Resorter 16' and Arabian 18' runabout.

For 1958 Century offered some new faces in its lineup. Several models would prove to be popular and are now real collectors' pieces. Let's see what 1958 had to offer.

MODEL	LENGTH	ENGINE OPTIONS AND H.P.	COLOR COMBINATION	UPHOLSTERY COLOR
Resorter	16'	Gray 116, 118, 136 Chrysler 110, 135 Interceptor V-8 150, 185	Varnished hull and decks	Red with white, green with white, brown with white
Resorter	19'	Gray 136, V-8 225 Chrysler 135, V-8 225 Cadillac V-8 275 Interceptor V-8 215	Varnished hull and decks, white trim	Copper, metallic red with white, green with white
Arabian	18'	Gray 136, V-8 225 Chrysler 135, V-8 225, 275 Cadillac V-8 275 Interceptor V-8 215	Varnished hull and decks	Yellow with brown
Coronado	21'	Gray 136, V-8 225 Chrysler 135, V-8 225, 275 Cadillac V-8 275, 300 Interceptor V-8 215	Varnished hull, white vinyl decks and trim	Red with white
Viking	19'	Gray 60, 75	White painted hull, varnished decks	All red

1958 16' Century Resorter

1958 18' Arabian by Century

All-new 1958 19' Century Resorter

1958 21' Coronado by Century

1958 19' Viking by Century

1958 also found three lapstrake utilities in the Century lineup. They were the Nordic 19', Viking 19', and Raven 22'. The Coronado 21' remained much like the 1957 version. However, a brand new Resorter 19' was added, replacing the familiar old Resorter 18'. The new boat had an "aircraft carrier" type front deck plus an all-new sliding roof for easier entry and exit from the craft. Only minor changes appeared elsewhere in the 1958 line. In fact, 1958 was the year Century probably did the smallest amount of changing in its boats for almost any year we shall review. As we mentioned before, Century sales in the late 1950's were going "great guns" and the management team felt no urge to "rock the boat" in 1958 and lose a good thing.

1959 again saw changes in the Century speedboat lineup. The lapstrake selection was expanded while runabouts and utility models remained about the same.

MODEL	LENGTH	ENGINE OPTIONS AND H.P.	COLOR COMBINATION	UPHOLSTERY COLORS
Resorter	16'	Gray 116, V-8 225 Chrysler 135 Interceptor V-8 125, 165	Varnished decks and hull	Bright green with white
Resorter	19'	Gray 136, V-8 225 Chrysler 135, V-8 225 Interceptor V-8 215	Varnished decks and hull, white trim	White with red
Arabian	19'	Gray 136, V-8 225 Chrysler 135, V-8 225 Interceptor V-8 215	Varnished decks and hull, white trim	Bright red with white
Coronado	21'	Gray 136, V-8 225 Chrysler 135, V-8 225, 275 Interceptor V-8 215	Varnished hull with white trim, vinyl white decks and tops	White with red
Nordic	19'	Gray 109	White hull, varnished decks	All red

1959 16' Resorter by Century

1959 19' Arabian by Century

1959 19' Resorter by Century

1959 19' Nordic by Century

1959 21' Coronado by Century

The 1959 Resorter 16' was almost an exact copy of the 1958 model. This was also true for the 19' Resorter which mainly had new upholstery colors. The Arabian was a foot longer in 1959, lengthened to 19'; its decks were now vinyl down the center and varnished elsewhere. Everything else was about the same. The luxury Coronado received a complete new hull in 1959. The chrome cutwater on the bow extended out about 16" ahead of the nose and the all-new hardtop roof slid on its own track. The 1959 Coronado has been called one of the most stylish ever built by Century. In conclusion, the old Viking lapstrake boat was replaced by a new model called the Nordic 19'. A black hulled lapstrake 22' cuddy cabin cruiser called the Raven was offered for 1959 in two models.

Century, down through the years, normally changed only one or two models each year, not the whole fleet. In 1960, that practice was still in effect with the Arabian 19' getting a facelift.

MODEL	LENGTH	ENGINE OPTIONS AND H.P.	COLOR COMBINATION	UPHOLSTERY COLORS
Resorter	16'	110 h.p. through 170	Varnished hull, white vinyl deck	White with red
Resorter	19'	170 h.p. through 240	Varnished hull, white vinyl deck	White with orange
Arabian	19'	170 h.p. through 240	White hull, turquoise decks and trim	Turquoise with white
Coronado	21'	170 h.p. through 325	White hull, varnished trim, white vinyl decks, roof	White with red
Nordic	19'	100 h.p. through 135	White hull, varnished decks	All red

1960 16' Resorter by Century

1960 19' Resorter by Century

211

1960 19' Arabian by Century

1960 21' Coronado by Century

1960 19' Nordic by Century

A very rakish chrome cutwater and the front deck covered totally with white vinyl were the major changes in the 1960 Resorter 16'. The 19' Resorter also had new all-white vinyl front decks as well as a new built-on rear boarding ladder. A nice feature for sun bathers, etc., was a sun lounge deck that ran aft from the engine box to the edge of the rear deck. The Arabian 19' went back to a painted finish in turquoise and white instead of the old natural finish. Bow and stern poles were painted white; a new feature was the built-in boarding ladder. The interior seating, instead of the old twin-cockpit-forward style, was a new arrangement having twin bucket seats up front with small side seats on both sides aft and a folding activity table in between. The only real change in the Coronado 21' was a gold-painted stripe around the border on each side between the varnish and white trim. All other things remained the same as in 1959. Finally, the Nordic 19', new in 1959, received an all-new metal-framed wraparound skiff-type windshield as well as a new clipper-bow and deeper "V" hull rather than its old round one. Those were the big changes in 1960 at Century.

1961 was a year of new models for Century. No less than four brand new designs were brought out. Let's look at these exciting new boats at this time.

MODEL	LENGTH	ENGINE OPTIONS	COLOR COMBINATION	UPHOLSTERY COLORS
Corsair	16'	Gray, Interceptor engines	Varnished hull with white vinyl front deck, varnished aft deck	Dark red with white
Resorter	17'	Gray, Interceptor engines	Two-tone varnished hull, white vinyl decks	Dark red with white
Resorter	19'	Gray, Interceptor, Crusader engines	Varnished hull with white trim, white vinyl decks	White with orange
Sabre	18'	Gray, Interceptor, Crusader engines	Varnished hull with white trim, varnished decks, vinyl king plank	White with orange
Arabian	19'	Gray, Interceptor, Crusader engines	White hull, turquoise decks and trim	Turquoise with white
Coronado	21'	Gray, Interceptor, Crusader engines	Varnished hull with white trim, all vinyl deck and top with gull wings for entry-exit	Bright red with white
Nordic	19'	Gray engines	White painted hull, varnished decks	Bright red

1961 16' Corsair by Century

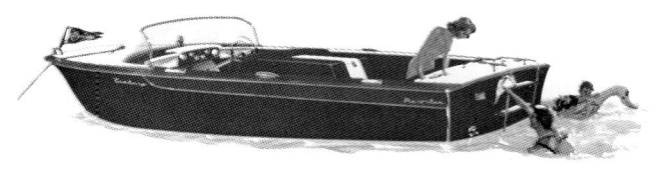

1961 17' Resorter by Century

212

1961 19' Resorter by Century

1961 19' Arabian by Century

1961 18' Sabre by Century

1961 21' Coronado by Century

1961 19' Nordic by Century

The Corsair 16' replaced the old Resorter 16' and was a very stylish utility. A sliding hardtop was also available for the boat. The Resorter 17' was also new and had a two-tone hull with wraparound windshield, vinyl deck and built-in boarding ladder. The only change in the Resorter 19' was a new, rakish windshield; all else remained the same. Another all-new model for 1961 was the sporty Sabre, The Sabre would eventually have a wood hull and fiberglass deck and top. This boat "broke the ice" for Century's use of fiberglass in their boats. A sleek gull-wing top was also offered. Sabres would appear in the line for some years to come. The Arabian was the same as in 1961 except it now had four bucket seats as opposed to the seats used in 1960. The big Coronado 21' was also restyled with less use of chrome trim, more varnish on the hull and not as much white paint; it had an all-new gull-wing type roof. The 1961 Coronado was less gaudy than before.

The Nordic 19' was given white vinyl decks in 1961 as well as another new windshield, a wooden-framed model. The other new speedboat for 1961 was the 16' 8" Ski Dart, a less expensive plywood constructed utility designed for water skiers. The boat came painted yellow and black with white upholstery. Well, that's about it for 1961—quite a few new "faces" that year.

1962 found a little change in the Century fleet. A new sled-type inboard-outboard utility was added called the Sun Sled. Other boats had slight modifications. Below is the complete 1962 Century runabout and utility list.

MODEL	LENGTH	ENGINE OPTIONS AND H.P.	COLOR COMBINATION	UPHOLSTERY COLOR
Resorter	16'	Engines up to 180 h.p.	Varnished hull, white vinyl decks	Red with white, green with white
Resorter	17'	Engines up to 240 h.p.	Varnished hull, white vinyl decks	Red with white
Resorter	19'	Gray and Chrysler from 225 h.p. to 260 h.p.	Varnished hull with white trim, white vinyl decks	Red, white and gray
Sun Sled	17'	Inboard-outboard power	Varnished hull and decks, green fiberglass bow	Turquoise and white
Sabre	18'	Engines from 190 h.p. to 240	Varnished hull, white fiberglass decks and roof	Brown, beige and bamboo
Coronado	21'	Engines up to 300 h.p.	Varnished hull, white trim and vinyl front deck	White with red

1962 16' Resorter by Century

1962 17' Resorter by Century

1962 19' Resorter by Century

1962 17' Sun Sled by Century

1962 18' Sabre by Century

1962 21' Coronado by Century

The old traditional 16' Resorter was back in the line for 1962. The Corsair 16' was dropped but would reappear later. The Resorter 17' did not have the same two-tone varnished upper hull sides it had in 1961 but all else remained the same. A brand-new unusual boat for 1962 was the Sea Sled, a kind of "far out" early tri-hull type inboard-outboard. The boat ran in the line for several years but was never very successful. The sleek 19' Resorter had a new paint job—less paint and more varnish on its hull sides with different upholstery colors too. The popular 18' Sabre, first introduced in 1961, was the same except for the upholstery color, etc. The old 19' Arabian runabout was dropped in 1962, leaving Century without a true runabout in its line. The Coronado 21' was exactly the same as 1961, as the boat had been completely restyled in that year. The plywood Ski Dart was dropped for 1962, but the lapstrake utility cruisers (including the Raven 19') replaced the old Nordic 19'. Century announced in 1962 that Cruise-Along cruisers were now sister ships of Century; 1963 would see these boats included in the Century catalog for the very first time.

1963 brought a few more changes. The Century cabin cruisers appeared in the new catalog and ranged in sizes from 26' through a 45' yacht. The color catalog for 1963 had a color cover resembling mahogany and was very nicely done. Below is the Century fleet for 1963.

MODEL	LENGTH	ENGINE OPTIONS AND H.P.	COLOR COMBINATION	UPHOLSTERY COLORS
Resorter	16'	Engines up to 180 h.p.	Varnished hull, white vinyl decks	White, orange and black White, green and black
Resorter	17'	Gray 215 V-8 Buehler Jet; also engines up to 240 h.p.	Varnished hull, white vinyl decks	Red with white
Resorter	19'	Gray and Chrysler engines to 280 h.p. V-8	Varnished hull, white trim and vinyl or varnished decks	Sky blue and white
Sun Sled	17'	Inboard-outboard power	Varnished hull and aft deck, green fiberglass front deck	White with red
Sabre	18'	Gray, Chrysler and Interceptor engines from V-8 190 to 210 h.p. V-8	Varnished hull, white fiberglass decks and roof	White with orange
Coronado	21'	Gray, Chrysler and Interceptor engines up to V-8 300 h.p.	Varnished hull, black trim, white vinyl decks	Pale yellow

16' Resorter in 1963 by Century

1963 Century 17' Resorter "Jet"

Queen of 1963 fleet—Century's 21' Coronado

Nicely designed 1963 19' Century Resorter

Unique 1963 17' Sun Sled inboard-outboard

1963 18' Sabre by Century

The 1963 16' Resorter was a carbon copy of the 1962 model. The biggest change in the 17' Resorter was that in 1963 it could be ordered with an all-new Buehler turbopower marine jet. Otherwise, the boat was about the same as in 1962. The only changes in the 19' Resorter were a new windshield and new upholstery colors. The Sun Sled was identical in 1963 also, even down to the use of the same colored photo in the catalog. The 1963 18' Sabre had a slight change in the design of its fiberglass decks as well as a brighter color combination. Showing the biggest change in 1963 was the 21' Coronado. The hull was completely restyled and it sported a massive fiberglass hardtop with windows as well as gull-wing exits. Black trim was used above the varnished hull sides with all-white vinyl decks. Three black Raven lapstrake inboards were also available for 1963, including a 26' with flying bridge controls.

1964 marked the beginning of the Resorter era. For the next several years, Century would be offering four or more models in the popular Resorter style. Other models were either added or dropped as in the past. Let's look to see just what was available.

MODEL	LENGTH	ENGINE OPTIONS AND H.P.	COLOR COMBINATION	UPHOLSTERY COLORS
Resorter	15'	Gray 80 h.p. Interceptor 160 h.p. V-8	Varnished hull, gray vinyl decks	Red with white
Resorter	16'	Gray V-8 178 h.p. Interceptor 170 h.p. V-8	Varnished hull and decks	White with red trim
Resorter	17'	Gray V-8 225, 238, 215 with jet, 220. Chrysler V-8 210. Interceptor V-8 240 h.p.	Varnished hull, dark blue vinyl decks	Turquoise, white and green
Resorter	19'	Gray V-8 220, 238, 280 Chrysler V-8 280 Interceptor V-8 240, 280	Varnished hull, blue fiberglass decks	Blue with white

Resorter	21'	Gray V-8 215, 225, 238, 280 Chrysler V-8 210, 280 Interceptor V-8 215, 240	Varnished hull, white vinyl decks	Red with white
Sabre	18'	Gray V-8 220, 225, 238 Interceptor V-8 240 h.p.	Varnished hull sides, white fiberglass decks and hardtop	Red with white
Ski Dart	17'	Gray V-8 175 Interceptor V-8 180	Lime with white painted hull and decks	Green and white
Coronado	21'	Gray V-8 238, 280, 310 Chrysler V-8 280, 325 Interceptor V-8 240, 280, 300, 310	Varnished hull, black upper trim, light gray vinyl decks, gold and gray padded hardtop	Gold, white and brown

1964 15' Century Resorter

1964 21' Century Resorter

1964 16' Century Resorter

1964 18' Sabre by Century

1964 17' Century Resorter

1964 17' Century Ski Dart

1964 19' Century Resorter

1964 21' Century Coronado

As you can see above, Century really expanded its line for 1964. To begin with, the 1964 Resorter 16' had all-varnished (rather than vinyl) decks once again. The 15' Resorter was a less deluxe boat and new in the lineup. It was to compete with large outboards and inboard-outboards of that era. The 17' Resorter also was about the same except for upholstery, engine options, etc. The 19' Resorter no longer had its aircraft-carrier-type, squared-off front deck but had a one-piece deck of blue fiberglass. An all-new 21' open Resorter was also added in 1964. This boat was aimed at the owner who wanted a boat the size of the Coronado, but not quite so fancy or high in price. The 18' Sabre was almost identical for 1964 except its hardtop was now all-white fiberglass rather than two-tone as in the past.

The plywood Ski Dart appeared in the line in 1964. This plywood model was designed to appeal especially to water skiers. Power options ran up to the 180 h.p. V-8 Interceptor. The only change in the 21' Resorter was its new gold and white hardtop and interior upholstery colors. The hull finish and design were the same as in 1963.

Century cruisers were still big business in 1964. A nice selection of color photos was shown in the catalog. Several small Raven-type lapstrakes remained in the Century runabout fleet while the other cruisers were being made out in Maryland under the cruiser division.

1965 showed a rather large fleet offered by Century. Below is a breakdown of models.

MODEL	LENGTH	ENGINE OPTIONS AND H.P.	COLOR COMBINATION	UPHOLSTERY COLORS
Resorter	15'	Gray 80 h.p. Interceptor V-8 165	White decks, varnished hull	White with red
Resorter	16'	Gray V-8 175 Interceptor V-8 170	Varnished decks and hulls	Various colors
Resorter	17'	Gray V-8 220, 238 Chrysler V-8 210 Interceptor V-8 240	White decks, varnished hull	Various colors
Resorter	19'	Gray V-8 220, 238, 280 Chrysler V-8 280 Interceptor V-8 240, 280	Vinyl decks, varnished hull	Various colors
Resorter	21'	Gray V-8 220, 238, 280 Chrysler V-8 280 Interceptor V-8 240, 280	Vinyl decks, varnished hull	Winter green and silver
Sabre	18'	Gray V-8 220, 238 Chrysler V-8 210 Interceptor V-8 240	Vinyl covered decks, varnished hull	Spark red, platinum deck and roof
Ski Dart	17'	Gray V-8 175 Interceptor V-8 190	Blue with white enamel hull and decks	White with blue
Bronco	17'	Interceptor V-8 165 with Eaton I.O. V-8	Metalic red hull and decks	Black
Coronado	21'	Gray 238, 280, 310 Chrysler V-8 280, 325 Interceptor V-8 240, 280, 330	Platinum decks, black top, varnished hull	Spark red

1965 15' Century Resorter

1965 16' Century Resorter

1965 Century 17' Resorter

1965 17' Century Ski Dart

1965 19' Century Resorter

1965 17' Century Bronco

1965 21' Century Resorter

1965 18' Century Sabre

1965 21' Century Coronado

Nine speedboats were offered by Century in 1965. All four Resorters from 15' through 19' were unchanged in design; the 21' Resorter was the same except for upholstery color and power options; the Sabre 19' remained virtually unchanged; the 17' Ski Dart was the same except for a new paint job. A rather unique new boat for 1965 was the 17' Bronco two-seat inboard-outboard runabout. The large Coronado 21' was restyled to be somewhat similar to the hull of some years before. The hull was now varnished, with gold upper planking, black vinyl top and bright red upholstery.

1966 found Century introducing its very first all-fiberglass inboard utility, the Fibersport 17'. From that year on, more and more fiberglass models would be added to the line until not a wood speedboat remained by 1969.

MODEL	LENGTH	ENGINE OPTIONS AND H.P.	COLOR COMBINATION	UPHOLSTERY COLORS
Resorter	15'	Interceptor V-8 165	Varnished hull, platinum deck, black trim	Sky blue
Resorter	16'	Interceptor V-8 190 Gray V-8 185	Varnished hull, platinum deck, black trim	Bright red
Resorter	17'	Interceptor V-8 210, 250 Gray V-8 220, 238 Chrysler V-8 210, 235	Varnished hull, platinum deck, black trim	Russet

218

Resorter	19'	Interceptor V-8 250, 285 Gray V-8 238, 280 Chrysler V-8 290	Varnished hull, platinum deck, black trim	Wintergreen
Resorter	21'	Interceptor V-8 250, 285 Gray V-8 238, 280 Chrysler V-8 290	Varnished hull, platinum deck, black trim	Wintergreen
Sabre	18'	Interceptor V-8 210, 250 Gray V-8 220, 238 Chrysler V-8 235	Varnished lower hull, platinum decks and fiberglass decks	Spark red
Ski Dart	17'	Interceptor V-8 190 Gray V-8 185	White hull and blue decks	White with blue
Bronco	17'	Interceptor I.O. 165 V-8 240 with "V" drive	White hull and red decks	Metallic red
Coronado	21'	Interceptor V-8 250, 285, 300, 330. Gray V-8 238, 280 Chrysler V-8 290, 300, 325	Varnished lower hull, platinum upper hull sides and decks, black top	Spark red

1966 15' Century Resorter

1966 16' Century Resorter

1966 17' Century Resorter

1966 Century 21' Resorter

1966 19' Century Resorter

1966 18' Sabre speedboat by Century

17' Century Bronco

219

1966 17' Century Ski Dart

1966 21' Century Coronado

The 1966 and 1965 were virtually alike except for modern squared-off type front deck and side air vents. The new fiberglass Fibersport 17' was identical to the wooden 17' Resorter. Century cruisers ranged in size from 27' to 33' in length. The Raven lapstrake hulls still were offered in 19', 22' and 27' lengths. All in all, 1966 was virtually unchanged from the year before.

1967 found quite a few new fiberglass Centuries being offered as well as the reappearance of the 19' Arabian in either wood or fiberglass. Other new models also appeared.

MODEL	LENGTH	ENGINE OPTIONS AND H.P.	COLOR COMBINATION	UPHOLSTERY COLORS
Resorter	15'	Engines up to 210 V-8	Varnished hull, platinum decks	Dark blue
Resorter	16'	Engines up to 210 V-8	Varnished hull, platinum decks	Dark blue
Resorter	17'	Engines up to 300 V-8	Varnished hull, platinum decks, black top	Spark red
Resorter	19'	Engines up to 300 V-8	Varnished hull, blue vinyl decks	Wintergreen
Sabre	18'	Engines up to 300 V-8	Varnished lower hull, platinum vinyl deck and platinum fiberglass upper hull and roof	Spark red
Arabian	19'	Engines up to 300 V-8	Varnished hull, blue vinyl decks, black convertible top	Dark blue
Coronado	21'	Engines up to 335 V-8	Varnished hull, white waterline platinum decks, black hardtop roof	Wine color

1967 15' Resorter by Century

1967 17' Century Resorter

1967 16' Century Resorter

1967 19' Resorter by Century

1967 18' Sabre by Century

1967 19' Arabian by Century

1967 21' Coronado by Century

Most of the 1967 Centuries were little changed over 1966. The sleek Arabian 19' had been restyled with a nice aft sunbathing pad, wood boarding platform and rear deck rails. The other wood Resorters had minor changes in deck hardware and windshield design. The Resorter fiberglass 17' was unchanged while new to the line was an unusual 20' Trident tri-hull with lowering forward ramp. A 19' Arabian in fiberglass also was added along with a 19' fiberglass Resorter. The large Century wooden cruisers were dropped from the line and the Venture 27', an open type day cruiser, was the biggest cabin cruiser still offered. 1968 would mark the last year Century would ever offer wooden inboards and with that an era in fine wood boat building came to an end. . . . Let's move on and view that final year.

Century Boat Company offered its last wooden inboards in the season of 1968. After that time no others would be built. By 1968 the fiberglass versions were beginning to appear in both the Arabian and Resorter Series. Below is a rundown of what was offered.

MODEL	LENGTH	ENGINE OPTIONS AND H.P.	COLOR COMBINATION	UPHOLSTERY COLORS
Resorter	15'	Engines to 210	Varnished hull, blue vinyl decks	Dark blue vinyl
Cheetah*	16'	Engines to 210	Green fiberglass hull and decks	Green with white vinyl
Resorter	17'	Engines to 300	Varnished hull, white vinyl decks	Dark red vinyl
Resorter	19'	Engines to 300	Varnished hull, white vinyl decks	Dark green and white vinyl
Arabian	19'	Engines to 300	Varnished hull, blue vinyl decks	Dark blue and black vinyl
Coronado	21'	Engines to 335	Varnished hull, white vinyl decks, white vinyl roof	Wine and white vinyl

*Replaced the former 16' Resorter.

1968 15' Century Resorter

1968 17' Century Resorter

221

1968 19' Century Resorter

1968 19' Arabian by Century

1968 21' Coronado by Century

The Coronado 21' now was equipped with a white vinyl top rather than black and white interior upholstery. The Resorter 16' was dropped and replaced by the new 16' all-glass Cheetah. We can see that starting back in 1954, Century expanded their offerings each season even with the rapid growth to fiberglass boats through the mid-1960's. Century was one of the last of the major firms to give up on wooden inboards, but starting in 1969 all their boats were fiberglass. Some of the old models remained in the line, others were dropped and new ones added. This report should be of value to Century owners, dealers and fans nationwide.

A WOODEN BOAT REFINISHING GUIDE

In this guide, the refinisher will assume the boat to be worked on needs a complete exterior refinish and is to be varnished.

Remove the hardware, label it and store it out of the way. Using a marine chemical stripper, remove the old finish. Three or more applications will be necessary. Apply the stripper thick and with a brush. Let it sit, but before the stripper dries scrape off the old finish with a flexible blade putty knife. Let the stripper do the hard work—excess scraping can splinter or chip the craft. When the boat appears clean, brush on stripper and scrub with bronze wool or burlap to clean out the grain. Scrape again. If you leave out this step the wood will have excess stain and be hard to sand. Wash the boat with water and a scrub brush. Let the wood dry.

If the deck is to be striped, clean out the seams with a file tang bent at a 90-degree angle and ground to the proper width. Clean well, and sand the edges of the seams smooth.

Depending on the condition of the wood, sand with production 80 paper and a good vibrating sander (*with the grain*) as much as possible. Sand with 100 production the same way. You want the surface uniform in color and smoothness. Any loose plugs must be removed, screws drilled deeper and replugged. Fill all dents and chips with a marine grade mender of the same color you intend your finished boat to be. Hand sand (*with the grain*), using 100 production paper. Take your time and be sure to remove all the electric sander marks. Wiping the wood with turpentine will enable the refinisher to see sanding marks. Clean with a vacuum the wood to be refinished.

If you want to lighten or even the color of the boat, bleach it. Use a two-part commercial bleach. Apply by brush, being careful not to let the bleach run—two to three coats are not that uncommon. Lightly hand sand the dried bleach residue off. Vacuum the wood to be stained.

After obtaining a marine stain, mix well or a leopard spotting effect may occur. Apply stain by brush. The stain has two jobs: (1) coloring the boat; and (2) filling in the grain. Push the stain into the grain by brushing with—and then against—the grain. Stir stain every other brush-full. Work an area until the first part you stained starts to get flat spots. Wipe excess stain off with burlap *across the grain.* Continue brushing stain, letting it dry and then wiping it off. After this horribly messy job is over, buff the stain with a terry cloth towel. Sight down the work under strong lighting to check flat spots. Rest for 24 hours.

Seal the surface with a marine clear sealer to insure adhesion of varnish coats. When sealer dries sand lightly with 220 paper *with the grain*, being careful not to scratch into your stain. Wipe with turpentine and then tack. Apply a 50% varnish-50% turpentine first coat. Let this sit a day. Sand lightly with 220, clean wood with turpentine and tack rag. Varnish with 25% turpentine mixture. Sand this 25% with 220 but sand harder to even the surface. Clean again. Fill the deck grooves with a seaming compound. Work this across the seam with a putty knife. Smooth out the seam with your finger, taking care to inlay the compound as deep as the seam is wide, on the dead seams, and deeper on the live ones. It will be easier to stripe if the seams are deep. Clean up with turpentine. Apply a 10% cut varnish coat and sand with 400 wet paper carefully. 400 wet cuts faster than 220 dry. Wipe as you go with a small squeegee. Clean wood with turpentine, then a tack rag. Next, varnish full strength. Let this sit at least two days. Sand again with 400 wet paper, dry surface as you go. Clean with turpentine and then tack rag. Take extra time to clean screw holes, vents, cracks and any place where dust hides. A stiff old toothbrush will be helpful with this. Wait for a very calm day and varnish once again. If you are happy with the finish, fine. If not, proceed as follows: Sand with 600 wet until not a shiny spot is to be found, but don't burn through. Then dry to check your work. Wash the boat with a soft scrub brush and hot water, clean everything and hose off. Squeegee the work dry.

Blow seams out with air. Clean work with turpentine and then take all the time in the world and tack the boat down. Make sure the refinisher and his clothes are spotless. Open a new can of varnish, strain and apply with a clean brush on a calm morning. Go away for a day.

Scrape, sand and caulk bottom. Wipe off with turpentine, and then paint. Be careful when sanding and painting. Most of the paint is made to kill bugs and plant life. I use a respirator, goggles and a large fan blowing under the boat. Stir the paint well, and stir as you use it.

If scribe marks for the waterline are intact, follow them. If not, follow the old line as best you can. Secure the tape below or above the waterline and walk it 8 or 10 feet out. Then stretch and put tape on the marks. Don't do this an inch at a time or your line will be jagged. Finish taping and press the tape on. Paint your line, and remove tape at right angles as soon as the paint is tacky.

Stripe the deck with a wheel or pinstripe brush. I like the brush, with full strength gloss paint and a jar of thinner to work with. The paint should just barely drip off the brush. Dip brush in paint, then rub it on a pallet. Dip brush in thinner and mix on the pallet until the brush is full. Clean up with a dry rag as you go.

Clean all hardware and replace. Be sure to bed all pieces that are on seams: the rub rails, the windshield and transom chrome. Use your discretion. Repack stuffing boxes, clean your boat up, and it's off to the water.

This is a short, basic guide article but I do hope it will be helpful to you in some way.

My thanks to you, Robert, you old "woodnut" you. A few closing suggestions:

1. Use the best materials and brushes.
2. Use original manufacturers colors.
3. Remove the engine and paint the bilge.
4. Rewire.
5. Re-upholster if needed.
6. New chrome as needed.
7. New screws throughout.
8. More varnish—we use eight coats on top of sealer.
9. Don't hurry.
10. Know what you are going to do before you do it.

—By Anthony W. Brown[*]
Brown Boats
6/78

[*]Anthony W. Brown, one of the head refinishers at Sierra Boat Co., Lake Tahoe, California—a true "craftsman" in every sense of the word!

CLUBS, MAGAZINE ARTICLES AND BOOKS OF INTEREST

APPENDIX

Listed below is an expanded selection of clubs to join as well as books you, the reader, might wish to add to your libraries along with a new group of interesting magazine articles covering antique boats in various forms. New clubs are springing up all over this country and elsewhere, and I feel nearly every former major speedboat builder will soon have a "fan club" of its very own.

ANTIQUE & CLASSIC BOAT SOCIETY
Box 831
Lake George, NY 12845

(Club formed in 1975 now boasts nearly 600 members with seven national chapters formed to date. The club publishes an excellent quarterly newsletter and an annual membership directory.)

ANTIQUE BOAT CLUB
P.O. Box 1386
Tallahassee, FL 32302

CLASSIC YACHT ASSOCIATION
Roy Newton
13967 Marquesas Way
Marina Del Ray, CA 90291

CLASSIC YACHT CLUB OF AMERICA
c/o Al Kmiec, Commodore
1433 Walker Avenue
Baltimore, MD 21239

CLAYTON ANTIQUE BOAT AUXILIARY
Clayton Shipyard Museum
Clayton, NY 13624

(Club operates exceptional boat museum and publishes good quarterly newsletter. This group staged the very first Antique & Classic Boat Show in 1961.)

THE ANTIQUE OUTBOARD MOTOR CLUB, INC.
c/o Allen Lebaugh
1009 7th Avenue
Council Bluffs, IA 51501

(A club of 1,000 members interested in the repair, restoration, collection and study of antique and classic outboard engines. Send s.s.a.e. for information. Publish quarterly magazine and newsletter 6 times a year.)

MATTHEWS BOATOWNERS ASSOCIATION
Box 254
Higganum, CT 06441

(New club formed in 1978 for Matthews owners and fans. Write directly for details.)

RICHARDSON BOAT OWNERS ASSOCIATION
John Dubickas
275 S. Meadow Drive
North Tonawanda, NY 14120

THE ELCO CLUB
Richard Cook, Commodore
12 W. Main Street
Mystic, CT 06355

CENTURY BOAT CLUB
c/o Bob Speltz — Membership Chairman
505 Albert Lea Street
Albert Lea, MN 56007
   (507) 373-2145

(A club that is made up of Century boat owners and buffs numbering over 1,100 members. Send s.s.a.e. for application and sample newsletter.)

MAGAZINE ARTICLES OF INTEREST

Shield, Harold D. "Antique Boat Show", *CANADIAN BOATING*, (September, 1977), 2-4.
O'Donovan, Bonnie. "Classics", *MOTOR BOATING & SAILING*, (July, 1977), 70-73.
"Growing Old Gracefully", *CANADIAN YACHTING*, (Fall, 1977), 39-41.
"The Antique Boat Movement", *MOTORBOAT*, (August, 1977), 36-40.
"The Perfect Yacht", *INLAND SEA*, (March, 1978), 33-35.
Barmonde, Peter. "Because They're the Best!", *WOODEN BOAT*, (August, 1978), 148-149.

BOATING MAGAZINES OF INTEREST TO WOODEN BOAT ENTHUSIASTS

SMALL BOAT JOURNAL Box 400 Benington, VT 05201	(A fine magazine aimed at the reader-owner of small pleasure crafts. Contact for current subscription fees etc.)
WOODEN BOAT Box 78 Brooklin, ME 04616	(Excellent slick paper quarterly with color covers and all types of reports on sailing, building and maintaining all varieties of wooden work and pleasure craft; also, reports on tools, methods of repair, etc. A must for wooden boat owners, builders and designers.) Write for subscription price.
NAUTICAL QUARTERLY 141 Lexington Avenue New York, NY 10016 (212) 689-8232	(A very outstanding all-new quarterly full of color photos; hard covers. It comes in its own protective hard box. No advertising in any issue. Plan to cover both power as well as sail. This is probably the finest, as well as most expensive boating publication on the market today.) Write directly for prices, etc.

BOATING BOOKS OF INTEREST TO WOODEN BOAT ENTHUSIASTS

Birt, Phillips D. *FAMOUS SPEEDBOATS OF THE WORLD*	(Book written in 1950's in England and traces the history of the major inboard racing boats like the Miss Americas, Miss Englands, Blue Bird, etc.)
Enlow, David & Dorothy. *SAVED FROM BANKRUPTCY*.	(Very interesting book—covers the life and times of the Correct Craft Boat Company and its founding family, the Meloons.) Order from— **CORRECT CRAFT BOAT COMPANY** Pinecastle, FL 32809 $3.95 each
Leather, John. *CLINKER BOAT BUILDING*	(Book covers all aspects of lapstrake construction.) Order from— **WOODENBOAT BOOKS** Box 268, Brooksville, ME 04617
Lewis, John. *RESTORING VINTAGE BOATS*	(Deals with classic restoration, both power and sail.) Order from— **WOODENBOAT BOOKS** Box 268, Brooksville, ME 04617 $20.00 each
Nations, David & Kevin Desmond. *THE GUINESS GUIDE TO WATERSKIING*	(New book tracing the history of water skiing from the 16th Century, and reveals the role of inboard runabouts in skiing.) Order from— **GUINESS SUPERLATIVES LTD.** London Road, Enfield, Middlesex, England EN2 6DJ

Desmond, Kevin. *THE WORLD WATER SPEED RECORD.*

(Traces history of speedboat racing from early 1900's up through the Blue Bird, etc. of the 1950's.)

Speltz, Robert. *THE REAL RUNABOUTS, Vol. I*

(Volume I is devoted entirely to the inboard speedboat. 310 photos, historical reports on various firms, parts and restoration shop listings, etc.)

Order from—
THE REAL RUNABOUTS, Vol. I
505 Albert Lea Street, Albert Lea, MN 56007
$17.95 post paid

(Also available at over 100 boat shops, bookstores and marinas nationwide.)

ALBUM OF ANTIQUE CHRIS-CRAFTS.

(Excellent soft cover photo album covering Chris-Craft fleet from the start up to 1958 or so. Of much interest to Chris-Craft fans.)

Order from—
C.C. ANTIQUE BOAT CLUB
Box 10245, Bradenton, FL 33507
$10.00 each

CHRIS-CRAFT OWNERS MANUALS—1929 & 1935

(Excellent 50- and 38-page manuals covering all aspects of "care and feeding" of your vintage Chris-Craft.)

Order from—
CHRIS-CRAFT ANTIQUE BOAT CLUB
c/o Howard Hallas, Secretary
Box 10245, Bradenton, FL 33507
$2.50 & $5.00 each

GOLD CUP REGATTA ANTIQUE SOUVENIR PROGRAM

(A most excellent fully illustrated 46-page book crammed with photos, historical material on the "Gold Cuppers". One book all fans should have. It reviews 1977 Gold Cup races on Lake George, New York.)

Order From—
ANTIQUE BOATING MAGAZINE
Box 199
Cleverdale, NY 12820
$1.50 each

HACKER CRAFT REPRODUCTION CATALOGS
1929, 1930, and 1931 issues

(Excellent reprinting, not Xerox copies of these valuable old catalogs. In black & white.)

Order from—
WILLIAM P. WILLIG
502 State Street, Schenectady, NY 12305
$7.50 each

THE CLASSIC BOAT

(A most excellent hard cover book, many color photos covering power as well as sail craft. A must for any serious collector.)

Order from—
TIME-LIFE BOOKS
Alexandria, VA 22313

BIBLIOGRAPHY

BOOK

Speltz, Robert. *THE REAL RUNABOUTS, Volume I.* Lake Mills, Iowa: Graphic Publishing Company. 1977.

MAGAZINE ARTICLES

ANCARROW

"Ancarrow Builds for Speed", *YACHTING*, (June '58), 91-93.
"Aquilifer", *MOTOR BOATING*, (August '57), 32-34.
"The Ancarrow Aquilifer", *YACHTING*, (February '58), 55.

BOESCH BOATS OF SWITZERLAND

"Boesch Customer Listing", (1970), 1-4.
"Boesch Historical Booklet", (1972), 1-10.
"Boesch Technical Facts Book", (1971), 1-4.

BROOKE BOATS OF ENGLAND

"A High-Speed Brooke Runabout", *THE MOTOR BOAT*, (June 22, 1928), 518-519.
"A 19-Foot Standardized Runabout", *THE MOTOR BOAT*, (June 6, 1930), 528-529.
"An 18-Foot Standardized Runabout", *THE MOTOR BOAT*, (August '27), 168-169.
"The Mermaids", catalog, 1933 issue.

CORRECT CRAFT BOATS

"Correct Craft for 1952", *MOTOR BOAT*, (March '52), 76.
"Correct Craft for 1954", *BOATS*, (October '54), 43.
"Correct Craft for 1956", *BOATING INDUSTRY*, (March '56), 175.

DART BOATS

"Dart Announces New Speed Tender", *POWER BOATING*, (May '30), 37.
"Dart Produces New Runabout", *POWER BOATING*, (September '29), 50.
"Dart Runabouts Changes Hands", *POWER BOATING*, (September '28), 34.
"New Indian Boat Company Owner", *MOTOR BOAT*, (November '47), 63.

DODGE BOAT COMPANY

"Death Last Headline on Horace Dodge", *THE DETROIT NEWS*, (December 22, '63), 2.
"Dodge Figureheads Set Fashion", *POWER BOATING*, (January '30), 34.
"Horace E. Dodge Announces Two New Watercars", *MOTOR BOATING*, (November '25), 98.
"The World's Largest Boat Plant", *MOTOR BOATING*, (January '31), 110-113.
"Water Cars Improved", *MOTOR BOATING*, (November '25), 140.
"Dodge Boats for 1930", catalog, 1930 issue.
"Dodge Boats for 1931", catalog, 1931 issue.
"Dodge Boats for 1932", catalog, 1932 issue.
"Dodge Boats for 1933", catalog, 1933 issue.
"Dodge Boats for 1934", catalog, 1934 issue.
"Dodge Boats for 1935", catalog, 1935 issue.

DUKE BOATS OF CANADA

"Duke Boats", *THE HERALD EXAMINER*, (November 2, '72), 1-2.
"Legacy of Boat-Building Experience", *THE MUSKOKA SUN*, (September 2, '76), 17-18.
"Tradition Ends—Duke Boats Sold. . . .", *PORT CARLING NEWS*, (April 28, '77), 25.

ENSIGN BOATS OF MICHIGAN

"16' Utility Inboard Added to '47 Ensign Line", *BOATING INDUSTRY*, (December '46), 45.

FAIRLINER BOATS

"Fire at Fairliner Boat Company", *MOTOR BOAT*, (November '50), 52-53.
"Letter", from Gean H. Arenz, (June 18, '77).
"Falls Flyer" by Larson Boat Company.
"Letter", from Glen Kraywinkle, (December '77).

GAGE-HACKER INBOARDS

"Gage Marine Corporation", *ANTIQUE BOATING*, (Spring '76), 13-15.
"Letter", from Bill Gage, (June 19, '78).

HIGGINS RUNABOUTS

"Andrew J. Higgins", *MOTOR BOAT*, (September '52), 38.

"Higgins for 1949", *MOTOR BOATING*, (January '49), 164.
"Higgins for 1950", *MOTOR BOATING*, (January '50), 119.
"Higgins for 1958", *BOATS*, (January '58), 78-79.
"Higgins Adds New Models", *MOTOR BOAT*, (January '49), 89.
"Higgins Eurekas", *MOTOR BOAT*, (January '41), 112.
"Higgins Launches", *MOTOR BOAT*, (June '53), 76.
"The Big Grandstand Builder", *MOTOR BOATING*, (June '38), 32-35, 108.

LEATHER RUNABOUTS OF ENGLAND

"Letter", from Mr. Leather, (Winter, '78).

LYMAN RUNABOUTS

"Lyman Boats", *MOTOR BOAT*, (January '51), 37-38.
"Lyman—Clinker Built Boats", *POWER BOATING*, (February '37), 64.
"Lyman—Clinker Built Craft", *POWER BOATING*, (January '38), 33.
"Lyman—Clinker Built Craft", *MOTOR BOAT*, (January '49), 121.
"Lyman Lapstrake" *MOTORBOAT*, (January '41), 14.
"Lyman for 1949", *MOTOR BOATING*, (January '49), 120.
"Lyman for 1950", *MOTOR BOATING*, (January '50), 94-96.
"Lyman for 1957", *BOATS*, (January '57), 201.
"The Lyman Story", *MOTOR BOAT*, (May '51), 24-25.
"The Wm. E. Lyman Story", *MOTOR BOAT*, (August '52), 56-58.

MARINER BOAT COMPANY OF MICHIGAN

"1956, 1957 Catalogs".

MERCURY BOATS OF CALIFORNIA

"Mercury, California Builder of Speed Boats", *MOTOR BOAT*, (January '52), 65.
"Mercury Runabouts", *BOATS*, (January '54), 100.
"Mercury Specifications", *MOTORBOAT*, (January '51), 102.
"Modern Runabouts", *MOTOR BOAT*, (February '49), 22.
"Mercury 1949", *MOTOR BOATING*, (January '49), 192.
"Mercury 1951", *MOTOR BOAT*, (January '51), 102.

MINETT-SHIELDS OF CANADA

"Letter", from Less Tennant, (April 21, '78).

PHILBRICK BOAT COMPANY

"Letter", from Don Philbrick, (December '77).

ROBINSON SEAGULL CRUISERS

"More People Than Ever Buying Boats", *POWER BOATING*, (December '35), 41.
"New Models", *RUDDER*, (February '36), 106.
"Robinson Mail Boat", *POWER BOATING*, (August '36), 63.
"Robinson Marine Construction Busy", *POWER BOATING*, (July '36), 61.
"Robinson Specifications 1935", *POWER BOATING*, (June '35), 32.
"Robinson to Specialize in Custom Built Craft", *MOTORBOATING*, (January '33), 245.

SEA-LYON BOATS

"Letter", from B. Stevanovic, (March '78).
"1931 Sea-Lyon Runabouts", *MOTORBOATING*, (January '31), 110-111.

TARONI OF ITALY

"Taroni 1961 Catalog", catalog, 1961 issue.

VENTNOR BOATS

"High Speed", *POWER BOATING*, (March '36), 63.
"New 235 Class Racer Shown", *MOTOR BOATING*, (January '49), 192.
"New Ventnors", *MOTOR BOAT*, (November '47), 63.
"Ventnor Appoints", *MOTOR BOAT*, (November '47), 63.
"Ventnor Boats Market on Delivery", *MOTOR BOAT*, (June '47), 68.
"Ventnor Specifications for 1935", *POWER BOATING*, (January '35).
"Ventnor Specifications for 1949", *MOTOR BOAT*, (January '49), 88.
"Ventnor Specifications for 1950", *MOTOR BOAT*, (January '50), 12.
"Ventnor Speed Merchants", *MOTOR BOATING*, (October '47), 98-99.
"What's New?" *MOTOR BOATING*, (April '48), 70.

Well, that's about it for *THE REAL RUNABOUTS, Volume II*. I hope that you enjoyed it very much. It was fun for me also, especially meeting all the great people who so graciously loaned material that appeared on these pages. We shall now move on to the conclusion where we shall look into the future and forecast the growth of our great hobby, Antique Boating. I think we shall see tremendous growth in our hobby in the next few years.

CONCLUSION

It has again been my distinct privilege to guide you through another series of articles on more of the inboard speedboat builders of the past. We must not just look back to the "good old days", but move on into the late 1970's with the aim of making Antique Boating and antique boats a hobby that both young and old alike can enjoy. Let's not become as some of our other collecting groups have, a bunch of small associations continually fighting with each other and doing no one any good at all.

Some of the exciting things that have happened just since *Volume I* was published would have to include the following events: The first Annual Chris-Craft Antique & Classic Boat Jamboree was staged successfully at the Thousand Islands Shipyard Museum in Clayton, New York. The four-day event was held in the last week of August, 1978 and was a huge success. Some of the features of the get-together included displays of boats, engines, piloted boat cruises, "how to" sessions, as well as picnics, dinners and other fun events. Nearly 100 antique as well as classic Chris-Craft cruisers and runabouts were in attendance at the show. Also, the Chris-Craft Antique Boat Club is enjoying phenomenal growth with membership now over 500 members. Two squadrons have been set up, one in Michigan and one in Connecticut. Not far behind, the Antique & Classic Boat Society, Inc. headquartered in New York state now boasts of six regional Chapters. They are located in the following areas: Finger Lakes of New York; Adirondack area of New York; Lake Hopatcong, New Jersey; Land-O-Lakes Chapter covering Minnesota and surrounding states, as well as Michigan and New England Chapters; and finally, Niagara, New York area Chapter. Memberships are increasing nicely for that group too. There are a number of other areas who are in the process of forming chapters. All in all, the vast majority of all antique boat clubs, societies, etc. are gaining new "converts" every day.

I think the one single area where the greatest amount of growth appears has to be in antique boat shows. Every year more and more new ones are "launched". Shows are being held for the first time in 1978 at Hessel, Michigan; Seneca Falls, New York; Alexandria Bay, New York; Buckeye Lake, Ohio; and Cayuga Lake Classic Boat Show in New York. This last show will prove quite interesting as all boats entered have to be built *after* 1945. This is a novel approach as most shows have numerous old craft but the later models are more or less relegated to lower importance.

Right here in Minnesota we have staged three shows to date and each year the number and quality of entries has increased from about thirty the first year to over 100 in 1978. This condition is prevalent all over the nation wherever antique boat shows are being staged. I have information that antique boat shows are beginning to appear all over Europe too. A friend advised me that he thought England would be staging a show similar to American versions this coming summer. Another sign of growth in our hobby is that the major boating magazines—such as *MOTOR BOATING*, *SEA*, *MOTORBOAT* and others—are beginning to, on occasion, run well-written articles with full-color photos illustrating various antique and classic boats, etc. You know when they begin to allocate space to such things there must be readers out there who want it.

Another sign of growth in our hobby is very visible in this book. For example, the number of firms offering refinishing, restorations, etc. is more than twice the number shown in *Volume I*. Of course, I have no way of knowing the quality of work offered by all these firms, but I feel that to be in such a specialized field you must turn out excellent work.

In conclusion, I want to thank all of my readers who invested in this *Volume II* as well as *Volume I*; all you who wrote me the kind letters, sent in old photos, comments, facts, etc. about firms we discussed in this book and the first one. It made all the hundreds of hours of research, writing, etc. well worthwhile. If I can be of any help to you concerning antique or classic speedboats, call or write me as I enjoy hearing from those with similar interests and I always answer my mail. Until *Volume III*, do have a good year and "Smooth Sailing" to you and yours!

ACKNOWLEDGEMENTS

Thanks to everyone who provided material for me to use in this book. Without your sharing of your material with me and the readers, there would not have been a second book. May God bless you for all your kindness.

Anspach, Dr. Denny—Sacramento, California
Arenz, Gean—Oconomowoc, Wisconsin
Bennett, Edward H., Jr.—Chicago, Illinois
Boesch Boats—Zurich, Switzerland
Brown, Tony—Mound, Minnesota
Bryan, B. B.—Evanston, Illinois
Calvin, Timothy—Akron, Ohio
Carey, Pete—Carnelian Bay, California
Clarke, Dick—Carnelian Bay, California
Comstock, Ted—Blue Mountain, New York
Desmond, Kevin—London, England
Dittericks, Jack—Detroit Lakes, Minnesota
Duke, A. H.—Port Carling, Ontario, Canada
Eckfield, K. C.—Berwyn, Pennsylvania
Edgewater Yacht Sales—Sausalito, California
Ellis, William C.—Lake Forest, Illinois
Firstbrook, John T.—Toronto, Ontario, Canada
Flood, Leo and Tom—Mt. Clemens, Michigan
Gage, Bill—Williams Bay, Wisconsin
Gervasoni, Gino—Sarnico, Italy
Gockel, Paul W.—Port Carling, Ontario, Canada
Hady, Mrs. Juanita—Clear Lake, Iowa
Hanson, Victor—Albert Lea, Minnesota
Henkle, Pete—Harsens Island, Michigan
Hermanson, Ms. Lynn—Albert Lea, Minnesota
Humphrey, Jim—Lake Geneva, Wisconsin
Irwin, Jim—Lakeport, New Hampshire
Jandra, Don—Cedar Rapids, Iowa
Jarrett, Dr. Tom—Chicago, Illinois
Katcher, Jeri and Keith—Mound, Minnesota
Kelly, Ardie L.—Newport News, Virginia
Kinn, Jack—Oconomowoc, Wisconsin
Kraywinkle, Glen—Little Falls, Minnesota
Langell, Bob—Mecosta, Michigan
Larson, Paul—Little Falls, Minnesota

Leather, John—Isle of Wight, England
Mathews, Dean—New Baltimore, Michigan
McBride, Bob, Jr.—Campbell, California
Meloon, Ralph C., Sr.—Orlando, Florida
Miller, Charles M.—New Baltimore, Michigan
Mitchey, Jack—Port of Lowestoft Research Society, Eng.
Mocksfield, Wayne—Lake Hopatcong, New Jersey
Mullenhagen, Herman—Algonac, Michigan
Murtaugh, Jim—Hessel, Michigan
Nelson, Jean and Ray—Cleverdale, New York
Nichols, Charles—New Baltimore, Michigan
Nollenberger, Bill—Piru, California
Paske, Jon and Tim—Minneapolis, Minnesota
Philbrick Boats—Oakland, California
Price, Don—Clayton, New York
Putz, George—Toledo, Ohio
Retiman, Marine—Jacksonville, Florida
Rudy, Don—Glendale, California
Sayres, Bud—Buckeye Lake, Ohio
Smith, William C.—Morristown, New Jersey
Stahovec, Joseph—New Baltimore, Michigan
Steinkamp, Gene—Cincinnati, Ohio
Stroud, Jack—Athens, Georgia
Teeter, Jackson—Orchard Lake, Michigan
Tennant, Les—Bracebridge, Ontario, Canada
The Mariners Museum—Newport News, Virginia
Underwood, Ken—Sausalito, California
Vander Syde, Paul—Albert Lea, Minnesota
Warner, F. Todd—Excelsior, Minnesota
Wells, Admiral E. R.—Manset, Maine
Weschoke, Ernest—Prescott, Wisconsin
Whiting, Dr. C. H., Jr.—Oneida, New York
Willock, Col. Roger (retired)—Cumberland-Foreside, Maine
Wright, Dave R.—Delafield, Wisconsin